ADO.NET:
From Novice to Pro,
Visual Basic .NET Edition

PETER WRIGHT

ADO.NET: From Novice to Pro, Visual Basic .NET Edition
Copyright © 2002 by Peter Wright

ISBN (pbk): 1-59059-060-0

Printed and bound in the United States of America 12345678910

Trademarked names may appear in this book. Rather than use a trademark symbol with every occurrence of a trademarked name, we use the names only in an editorial fashion and to the benefit of the trademark owner, with no intention of infringement of the trademark.

Technical Reviewer: Ildiko Blackburn

Editorial Directors: Dan Appleman, Gary Cornell, Jason Gilmore, Simon Hayes, Karen Watterson, John Zukowski

Managing Editor: Grace Wong

Project Manager: Tracy Brown Collins

Copy Editor: Nicole LeClerc

Production Manager: Kari Brooks

Compositor: Susan Glinert

Artist and Cover Designer: Kurt Krames

Proofreaders: Beth Christmas and Brendan Sanchez

Indexer: Carol Burbo

Manufacturing Manager: Tom Debolski

Marketing Manager: Stephanie Rodriguez

Distributed to the book trade in the United States by Springer-Verlag New York, Inc., 175 Fifth Avenue, New York, NY, 10010 and outside the United States by Springer-Verlag GmbH & Co. KG, Tiergartenstr. 17, 69112 Heidelberg, Germany.

In the United States, phone 1-800-SPRINGER, email orders@springer-ny.com, or visit http://www.springer-ny.com.

Outside the United States, fax +49 6221 345229, email orders@springer.de, or visit http://www.springer.de.

For information on translations, please contact Apress directly at 2560 9th Street, Suite 219, Berkeley, CA 94710. Phone 510-549-5930, fax: 510-549-5939, email info@apress.com, or visit http://www.apress.com.

The source code for this book is available to readers at http://www.apress.com in the Downloads section.

*This book is dedicated to all my former colleagues
at Enron Europe (none of whom had executive positions
in the company, all of whom were innocent pawns).
Don't let "them" get you down!*

Contents at a Glance

Contents

Foreword

IT IS A PLEASURE to be asked to say a few words about this book. Its timing couldn't be better, considering the increasing usage of Microsoft's .NET technology to enable organizations to examine enterprise business problems.

The business and technology landscapes have evolved considerably over the past few years, resulting in more demands from existing technology implementations that now focus on accelerating the time to market, reducing the development life cycle, and managing the investment in software projects. Having relevant intelligence structured and accessible in a timely manner from the masses of data that organizations have is key to their ongoing success. Microsoft's .NET technology enables companies to meet some of the changing needs in projects in which managing data is integral to running the business. The ability to understand and work with the technologies that enable access to this intelligence is an increasingly valued skill set. *ADO.NET: From Novice to Pro* facilitates the building of that skill set.

As a seasoned professional working in a consultancy across many industries, I have seen and continue to see firsthand how organizations struggle with technology and its potential. The "big picture" is important and completing the journey paramount, but it is also important to focus on the building blocks. In his book, Peter provides these building blocks in a simple and easily digestible form. His approach is to spell out the basics in a structured manner, providing tutorials and code samples throughout the book that enable you to bring the concepts to life. What is fresh about Peter's approach is that he explores ADO.NET as a pet subject of his, with a passion to communicate every nook and cranny of the technology.

If you have a passion for technology and wish to understand ADO.NET, then this book is a must-have on your desk and in your technology library. I am confident that this book will serve as a useful reference for you, as it provides valuable general information about and practical steps for the development of ADO.NET. Also, I expect you will take away more than a little insight into the impact .NET could have on development in your business.

I applaud Peter for writing such an essential tome of valuable information.

Ajit Ahloowalia
Avanade Inc.

About the Foreword Writer

AJIT AHLOOWALIA has over 12 years of professional experience with client/server and e-business solutions. He has been with Avanade since 2000, contributing his knowledge and expertise to help build and shape the company within the United Kingdom. Ajit's responsibilities at Avanade UK include managing and growing the business to enable it to deliver complex enterprise solutions that utilize Microsoft .NET technologies, integrating with and leveraging existing technology to solve business problems for clients.

Prior to joining Avanade, Ajit worked for Accenture, where he worked with clients focusing on developing strategy, program management, and defining architecture for large-scale, complex programs.

About Avanade

Avanade is the world's premier technology integrator for Microsoft solutions in the enterprise. With a significant presence in Europe, Asia-Pacific, and the Americas, Avanade delivers secure, reliable, scalable Microsoft-based solutions to help Global 2000 companies optimize their technology investments across the connected enterprise and accelerate the development and deployment of cross-industry eBusiness Solutions.

Founded in April 2000 as a joint venture between Microsoft Corp. and Accenture, Avanade offers customers unique value based on a heritage of commitment to superior service, paired with unmatched insight into cutting-edge Microsoft technologies.

About the Author

PETER WRIGHT is a principal consultant with Avanade Inc., based in London, England. He has over 10 years' experience designing, developing, and architecting applications using Microsoft technologies. At Avanade, Peter specializes in the architecture and development of .NET-enabled e-business solutions and mobile applications.

A regular contributor to the global technology press and an occasional speaker at industry events, Peter is also the author of ten books covering subjects as diverse as Visual Basic, object-oriented applications development, Delphi programming, and Linux GUI development.

When he's not tied to a keyboard, Pete juggles his spare time between spending time with his family (Heather and Ethan), flying, playing video games, and developing his unhealthy fascination with cryptography, network intrusion detection, and *Dexter's Laboratory.* Visit his Web site at http://www.codemonkey.demon.co.uk.

About the
Technical Reviewer

ILDIKO BLACKBURN is an English housewife—or that's what she might have you believe. Indeed, she may well fill the housewife role, but that description conceals the truth, which is a little more involved given that she was born and educated in Hungary as a computer scientist. So much for the English bit.

Also in common with many housewives these days, Ildiko runs and operates a number of IT consultancy companies in England, most notably Boost Data Limited (http://www.boost.net). In her role as consultant, she has been responsible for designing, developing, implementing, and project managing large client/server projects including multicurrency billing systems for UUNET and major system migrations into SAP and Siebel for WorldCom. Over the past 10 years, she has worked with Oracle, Sybase, and Microsoft SQL Server on the Windows NT/2000 and Unix platforms. More recently, Ildiko has been actively involved in developing and testing .NET applications. You can contact Ildiko at ib@boost.net.

Acknowledgments

THIS BOOK IS SOMETHING ridiculous like the eleventh book I have ever written. According to the saying, most people only have one book in them, and some of my critics would probably have been quite happy to see me stop there as well. However, after a break of about 2 years, here it is. New title, new technology, and new publisher—the best publisher in the world, in fact—what a comeback.

It's hard writing a book, and it helps to have a team supporting you, helping shape grunts into sentences, pushing when you don't want to do anything at all, and generally making sure you're the best you can be. I have to thank, first and foremost, above anyone else, three extremely talented ladies at Apress: Tracy Brown Collins, my project manager; Nicole LeClerc, my copy editor; and the formidable Ildiko Blackburn, my tech editor and reviewer. Aside from all having names that could have been plucked straight out of a 1920s detective movie, they are all exceptionally talented, dedicated, and extraordinarily professional people. This book would not exist without them. Also, thanks go to Gary Cornell, the single most charismatic publisher the world has ever known. Gary trusted me and respected my judgment when most would have assigned 15 other authors to the book to get it done in a hurry.

Also at Apress, Doris Wong and Grace Wong did fabulous jobs of just bringing everything together and wrapping it up, while Stephanie Rodriguez just scared me (just kidding).

Away from the world of publishing, I have to thank my employers at Avanade Inc. I am surrounded at work by the smartest IT people in the world and by a set of core values that really drive home that "good enough" is far from the way things should be. To everyone at Avanade London who has had to put up with endless "buy my book" plugs, thanks for your patience. I won't name names since someone will inevitably feel left out—you know who you are.

To "the parent crew," Lew, Sara, and my dad, John. Thank you for your wonderful support and help, especially when I was just too darn tired to do anything for myself.

Finally, to my wife, Heather, and my son, Ethan (not that he has a clue what I'm writing—at 3 months old, he'd rather eat this book than read it). "Thank you" is not a phrase with enough definition to tell you just how much you both mean to me.

Introduction

". . . but I'm more of a language guy."

—Gary Cornell (Apress), Barcelona, 2002

GARY MADE THAT COMMENT to me over lunch one steamy day at Tech-Ed in Barcelona, and it immediately struck a chord. I can "do" the server stuff in an application, and I like to think that I'm pretty darn hot when it comes to the design, development process, and architecture of a system. But, deep down, sitting with a notebook in the late night summer breeze with a glass of Chianti at my side, I'm more of a language guy. I love to explore new programming frameworks, but I dote on the languages used to implement them.

That would probably explain the trepidation with which I approached the development of this book. Like Gary, I'm a language guy, so the thought of spending months of my life writing about a database access technology really didn't fill me with too much eagerness.

As I started to map out ADO.NET, though, I experienced something of an epiphany (don't panic—I know this is a book on programming). .NET (the banner applied to a bunch of technologies from Microsoft) is not about programming languages, though the freedom to work with the language of your choice is a big bonus. .NET is not about having my server refusing to deal with your server in a well-defined way that doesn't hurt too many feelings. .NET is about the flow of data. .NET is about empowering one application to communicate and pool resources with another application developed in another part of the world by a completely different set of developers. .NET is about your data accessed anywhere, on any device, no matter what the format of that data. So, if data is the lifeblood of .NET, ADO.NET is the heart of it all, the organ that pumps the data seamlessly around the whole .NET physiology, the system that you should, if you treat it right, be able to rely on to do pretty much whatever you ask of it.

ADO.NET is a fantastic technology. It really does realize the dream of data anywhere, in any format, on any device. Compared to most other data access technologies (in fact, compared to *all* other data access technologies), ADO.NET has one massive selling point that beats them all: It just makes sense. Working with ADO.NET doesn't mean that you have to rethink your data access habits. In fact, where those habits are bad, ADO.NET provides you with the tools you need to implement great habits and throw the old ones in the trash.

I had a great time writing this book, and I truly hope the enthusiasm I developed in myself for ADO.NET comes across and rubs off on you.

Target Audience

I hate to label my readers—they usually respond by labeling me back on the Amazon.com reviews. With that said, I would probably have to concede that the primary audience for this book is people such as Gary and me—the language guys. You know Visual Basic .NET or C# (this edition focuses squarely on the former) pretty well, and you're familiar with the .NET Framework, what it means, and how to make use of it. You probably know that ADO.NET exists and you have a pretty good idea of what it does (you've heard the word "DataSet" bandied about with some gusto in the staff canteen). However, you don't actually have any hands-on, deep-and-dirty experience with ADO.NET. If you joined my team and I asked you to define a set of relationships between tables in a DataSet that directly map the hierarchical structure of a certain XML file, you'd probably start to feel that perhaps this isn't the job for you.

That's not to say there isn't a sideline audience that will benefit from reading this book. Perhaps you're a VB 6.0 developer who's just been unleashed on Visual Studio .NET. You need to get up to speed fast on everything you already know how to do (such as hit a database) and how to do it in the .NET way. With that in mind, you're a little shaky on the VB .NET syntax in places and would rather not have to explain to me the difference between a delegate and an event. Again, this book is ideal for you.

The final audience group holds the technically-minded director, project manager, or team lead—people that should know what the technology offers, but who don't really need to know it in fantastic detail. The introductions to each chapter and each section within a chapter should prove up to the task for you, and maybe even drag you down into the details full of hope and excitement when you realize just how wonderfully straightforward ADO.NET can be.

This book is not for newcomers to the world of computing, nor is it for programmers who've never touched a Microsoft technology before. You guys should probably hit the QuickStart .NET tutorials before you go anywhere else. Absorb them, understand them, and get comfortable with them, and then come back here and learn how to really apply your newfound knowledge.

Source Code and Support

There are plenty of code examples in this book, and they should all compile and run on your own machines. (Providing you have configured those machines correctly, of course. You may also need to tweak the database connection strings, since such things are always highly personal for security reasons.) If you are not up to typing the code in, you can download it from the Downloads section of the Apress Web site (http://www.apress.com).

How to Contact Me

Now the usual waiver. I have tried to ensure that there are no bugs in the code, and I'm fairly confident I've achieved that goal. However, you should bear in mind that the examples in the book demonstrate ADO.NET concepts. They are not best-of-breed architectural examples, nor are they there to indicate to you just how a good program should look or behave. They exist within the context of the chapter text that describes them, and no more. If you do have any problems with them, though, feel free to drop me a line at pete@codemonkey.demon.co.uk. I do try to answer everyone who e-mails me, but I can be notoriously slow due to a complex prioritized threading system I've installed in my head (wife and family are priority 1; Avanade Inc., my employer, is priority 2; writing new books is priority 3; and everything else comes somewhere after that).

I should warn you, I do tend to completely ignore those people who ask me to do their computer science homework (I'm tempted to publish a list of names here, but I'll resist) and those people who want me to either completely debug their enterprise-scale application or, worse yet, write it in my spare time.

CHAPTER 1

Welcome to ADO.NET

"It was a dark and stormy night."

Edward George Bulwer-Lytton, *Paul Clifford*, 1830

EVERY TIME I SIT DOWN to write a new book on Microsoft's latest technology, I, like most other authors, usually begin by expounding its virtues, singing its praises, and generally saying how things couldn't possibly ever get any better than this. Inevitably, though, we all grow far too familiar than is perhaps healthy with the technology in question and 2 to 3 months down the line start ranting about why on earth someone couldn't have found a simpler way to do XYZ. Database access is one such area.

In the beginning there was nothing to help out. If you wanted to do database access as a Visual Basic developer, you either needed to buy some proprietary library from a company destined to go out of business next Tuesday or switch over to dBASE, Clipper, or perhaps even the early FoxPro. If you were a C developer the situation was similar, but with far more choice in terms of which third-party library to buy.

Microsoft remedied the situation fairly quickly by adding in support for their Jet desktop engine and Data Access Objects (DAO). The first time I used them, I truly thought they were the future of all things database related.

Enter stage left, Remote Data Objects (RDO)—the absolute best thing to ever happen to data storage ever (well, that week at least). At last we had the technology we needed to deliver true client/server systems that fully utilized the power of a SQL Server back end. Wow.

OLE DB and ADO came next, and boy oh boy was I blown away. Finally there was a way of accessing any data from any data source in a uniform way. The birds sang, the sun shone, and my head began to ache with all the possibilities ADO offered.

When Archimedes discovered that eating too many Greek gyros caused the bath to overflow when he got in, the story goes that he jumped out of that bath and ran naked down the street whooping and cheering. The discovery of the principles behind volume and displacement was at once incredible and so stunningly simple that he couldn't believe he hadn't though of it before. Eureka!

I had heard a lot of noise about ADO.NET but didn't pay too much attention to it. I was too absorbed in learning C#, Visual Basic .NET (VB .NET) and all the wonderful other tools that Visual Studio .NET offered. Besides, history had taught me that although each new data access technology brought with it neat benefits and discoveries, they all inevitably ended up shoved in front of me in some consultancy role where for the umpteenth time I would be asked to write yet another database login module, or yet another data caching module, or fight my way through yet another data concurrency problem. Blah.

When I finally did sit down at a keyboard and start banging in some code from MSDN to try out ADO.NET I was stunned. I was blown away. I was completely, all-out, push-me-out-the-door-naked-and-call-me-Archimedes bowled over. The simplicity, the possibilities! *Eureka,* Bill! And this time, at last, Microsoft has really answered every single need and question in the book. The age of painless database development has arrived, and its name is ADO.NET (and the possibility that any enhancements from Microsoft could only make it better is simply astounding).

As with all great technologies, it's no use trying to run before you can walk. In this chapter you'll explore the suite of tools that Visual Studio .NET provides to help you on your way in your database development exploits. You'll look at the Server Explorer and how to use it to build a database. You'll also take a look at the Microsoft Data Engine (MSDE), Microsoft's fantastic SQL Server–compatible desktop database engine and your new best friend. You'll also take a brief look at just what ADO.NET actually consists of. By the end of the chapter you'll be well placed to start writing code in the next chapter, knowing exactly how Visual Studio .NET can help you produce great database applications.

What's Great About ADO.NET

This book is designed to teach you all you need to know to develop great data-managing applications using ADO.NET. There's a strong likelihood that many of you out there have dabbled with ADO in Visual Studio 6.0 to some degree. Many of you will also have some experience working with DAO and RDO. So, a good place to start then would be to take a look at ADO.NET to see just what it brings to the party that those other technologies don't.

First of all, let's get the misconceptions out the way. Despite its name, ADO.NET is not a natural evolution of good old-fashioned ADO. In fact, the two technologies couldn't be more different. ADO is designed as a tightly coupled solution for those developing client/server applications. Although you can tweak traditional ADO to pick up and work with data from a multitude of data sources, it is far better suited to connecting to a remote database and issuing queries against it than it is to trying to impose some order on an arbitrary set of files located on a collection of remote database and Web servers.

ADO.NET, on the other hand, is designed as *the* data access solution for .NET. That statement means a lot. Microsoft's .NET Framework is more than just a neat way to develop applications with any programming language. It is in fact an architecture that Microsoft fully expects to take us into the next age of computing. Microsoft sees that period of time as one being defined by freedom. Users will have the freedom to access their data and their applications anywhere, and on any device. At the end of the day, that sweeping statement means just one thing: the Internet.

Of course, you've probably already discovered that the .NET Framework is every bit as happy developing Windows desktop (and pocket desktop)–based applications as it is developing Web services and Web forms. ADO.NET is a complete object model that provides objects and methods tailored to both desktop and Web scenarios. If you want to produce an application that quickly hits a database and populates a Web page with the results, ADO.NET has the necessary objects to support you in that. If you want to perform some complex interrogation of data from multiple sources (XML files, spreadsheets, databases, text files, and even user input) as if they all came from the same source, ADO.NET can leap to your rescue there too.

In short, whereas traditional ADO forced you to bend the way you develop to fit in with its way of doing things, ADO.NET was designed to be completely flexible, extensible, and perfect for all types of data access development.

ADO.NET in 5 Minutes or Less

The structure of ADO.NET is very simple. So simple in fact that it can be summarized and understood in 5 minutes or less. If you are working with databases, then you rely on a collection of objects known as a *data provider* to get at your databases, retrieve data from them, run queries against them and, of course, post data back. Your application talks to a data provider directly through a DataReader or indirectly courtesy of a DataSet.

It's important to remember, though, that we are talking about a collection of objects. If, down the line, someone comes out with a data provider specifically designed to access object-oriented holographic databases at NASA, you know that person is talking about a set of objects, which you'll look at in a little more detail in a second.

Out of the box, as it were, the .NET Framework provides you with two data providers: one for OLE DB databases (Access, for example) and one specifically designed for SQL Server (and family). There's also an Open Database Connectivity (ODBC) data provider available for download from MSDN that is actually faster and better to use for any data source that has a viable ODBC driver; the OLE DB provider relies on marshalling .NET calls to COM calls, whereas the ODBC provider uses platform invoke to hit the underlying application programming interface (API) directly. However, since it isn't included with Visual Studio .NET, I won't focus on the ODBC provider at all in this edition of the book.

That's all there is to it. If you want to work with a SQL Server data provider, then you include a reference to the System.Data.SqlClient namespace in your project. If you want to work with the objects in the OLE DB data provider, you include a reference to the System.Data.OleDB namespace in your project. You can, of course, include both and work with data from a multitude of different sources.

Now that you've got the basics down, let's go into a touch more detail (not too much, though—that's where the rest of the book comes in).

The Connection Object

ADO.NET is perfectly able to work with data from any source, thanks to the awesome DataSet object, which you'll look at in detail throughout this book. However, when you're working with databases, everything starts and ends with a Connection object in your data provider. It's a simple enough beast: You create one of these, set its properties up, and call methods to connect to and disconnect from a database. Since it's a member of the data provider namespace, it makes sense that the Connection object you use is tailored to a specific data source.

The Command Object

Once you've got your Connection object set up and a connection established to a database, you could issue commands to the database through the data provider's Command object. Using this object you can fire off SQL queries to the database, call stored procedures, insert and update records in the database, and so on and so forth. However, the big benefit that comes from using ADO.NET over and above any other data access solution is simplicity; more often than not you won't work with a Command object directly, but you'll rely on the services of other objects in the data provider to work with them for you.

The DataReader Object

The DataReader object is a highly optimized, read-only, forward-only view of data from a database. It's about as close as you are ever going to get to a more traditional Recordset in ADO.NET.

The DataReader object is designed for those applications where you need to quickly grab a bunch of data out of a database and then drop your connection to it. Because it's forward-only and read-only, it's quite a lightweight object, ideal for use in ASP.NET applications, for example, where you may want to rapidly grab some

data to fill in a Web page. It's not the ideal choice for manipulating data, though—
that's where a DataSet comes in, but to use one of those you need to first set up a
DataAdapter.

The DataAdapter Object

This innocuous little beast is the key to developers experienced with Visual Basic 6.0
and earlier getting over their fear of bound controls. The DataAdapter, once again
a part of the data provider namespace, can be thought of as a semi-intelligent conduit
for everything to do with one specific set of data. Let me explain.

Armed with a connection, you can set up a DataAdapter to use that connection, in
that way telling the DataAdapter where its data comes from and where it goes.
(You can even switch the connection on the fly if you want to grab from one source
and write to another.) You then set up four data commands inside the DataAdapter.
These Command objects specify the queries or stored procedures that should be
used to get data, update it, create new rows, and of course delete rows. Now, the
DataAdapter knows that you are going to throw at it something known as a DataTable,
which as you might expect contains a set of columns and rows defining your data's
structure and contents. The Command objects then are able to reference columns
as parameters for their queries.

For example, if you had a query in the Select Command object of a DataAdapter
that returns three fields (A, B, and C), you can reference those fields in the Update
command (i.e., update all rows where A is the same as the new row's A data and set
fields B and C to those from the new row just passed to it).

The DataAdapter is designed to hit a database, use a DataReader to grab the
data, and then convert it to XML to build up a DataTable. For updates, it expects a
DataTable to work with, decodes the XML representation of it, and uses that to fill
in the blanks in the Update, Delete, and Add commands to fire information back to
the database. It sounds complex but it really isn't.

A typical way of working with a DataAdapter would be to build one in the usual
way, setting its connection and the four Command objects. You then ask the
DataAdapter to fill a DataSet (it's coming, more on that in a minute). The DataSet
could then be bound to controls on a Windows form or worked with program-
matically. When the user has finished his or her changes, a new DataSet is built
and passed back to the DataAdapter, which is able to automatically figure out
which rows were created, which were deleted, and which were changed, all
without any further intervention from you. You'll examine the DataAdapter in
some considerable detail throughout the rest of the book, so for now just trust me
when I tell you that the DataAdapter object, more than any other, is absolutely
awesome in its simplicity and power.

The DataSet and Friends

The true "wow" factor of ADO.NET comes when you leave the data provider's objects and start working with a DataSet. Many people mistakenly think that a DataSet is just the new name for a Recordset. It isn't. It's completely different.

A DataSet holds a collection of DataTables and DataRelations. A DataTable holds a collection of columns and rows, just like a table in a database. The DataRelations are used to relate the DataTables to each other.

A DataSet then is effectively a completely disconnected, in-memory database. You can build it by hand (through code, completely defining every single object yourself) or use one or more DataAdapters to build it for you, but the end result is a set of fully relational data stored in memory alongside the object using it (front end, middle tier—makes no difference), which can be navigated just like a full database.

That sounds dumb the first five or so times you read it, but then it clicks. Since you can build a DataSet through code as well as connect it to DataAdapters, there is nothing stopping you from grabbing data into a single dataset from a few spreadsheets here, a couple of XML documents over there, a text file on that guy's machine over there, and of course the big powerful SQL Server database farm you've got in the back office. You can then relate all that data from all those different data sources together and let the user navigate through it intelligently and even update it. When the user is finished, you can choose to handle the updates yourself (the DataSet is able to automatically build a new dataset of only the data that has been changed) or pass the modified dataset to a DataAdapter to automatically update a database.

The real kicker though is that a DataSet, like all the other components of ADO.NET, represents itself internally as XML. This means that you at last have an object in your data access arsenal that can pass entire clumps of relational data around without any restrictions. Need to grab a DataSet from a business object halfway across the world over HTTP? That's exactly what the DataSet is designed for. Need to pass a DataSet from one process to another? Marshalling is not an issue since you are effectively able to just pass text across the processes, which is a real no-brainer in .NET. The combination of DataSet and DataAdapter can also go a long way toward solving all those annoying concurrency issues that have been plaguing database application developers for years, and which were only set to get worse now that the age of online application development is well and truly on top of us.

The DataSet is the single most powerful and stunning object in the entire ADO.NET data framework—it's going to knock your socks off.

So, Let's Get Started!

Hold your horses, cowboy! This book is big, meaning that there's a lot more ground to cover than the simplified stuff you just read. First off, you need to know that Visual Studio .NET provides you with a whole set of tools outside of the .NET Framework itself to help you work with data, and in particular database servers. Before you go any further, it's worthwhile spending some time getting familiar with them. In the next chapter you'll start coding, but for now, let's get stuck into the integrated development environment (IDE), but from a database point of view.

MSDE

When ADO came along, one benefit it brought with it was the ability to access any database in almost the same way as any other. The idea was that you could design your application to connect to an Access database, for example, and then easily move the code over to talk to a SQL Server database when the time to deploy came along. In practice it was rarely that simple; there are many differences between the way that Access does things and the way SQL Server does things. In addition, actually migrating the database structure was rarely simple.

With ADO.NET you have the choice of either connecting to OLE DB–based data sources (such as Access) or making use of a highly optimized SQL Server data provider. The latter is, of course, infinitely more desirable. With a SQL Server database you can create powerful stored procedures, views of your data, triggers, and much more. In an ideal world, Microsoft would have us all develop our database applications using SQL Server.

With that in mind, around the time that Office 2000 came out, Microsoft released something known as the Microsoft Data Engine, or MSDE. It was actually included on the Office 2000 installation CD, but it was never installed by default. If you explore the CD, though, it's not too hard to find.

MSDE is also included with Visual Studio .NET. In a nutshell, MSDE is a cut-down version of SQL Server. It doesn't support triggers, but it does support pretty much everything else that SQL Server does, including views, stored procedures, and custom functions. More important, though, the file format of an MSDE database is identical to that of a SQL Server database, so you can indeed design and develop a database solution on your desktop now, and when the time is right you can simply copy the MSDE database files over to an installation of SQL Server and you have instantly scaled your solution.

MSDE offers more than just a neat migration path, however. It is itself a full-featured database, meaning that there is nothing stopping you from developing small-scale database applications with most of the goodies of SQL Server but without the cost (MSDE restricts your database sizes to 2GB). You can deploy MSDE with your finished applications with no runtime fees.

In addition, MSDE is fully integrated with Visual Studio .NET. You can configure your databases within Visual Studio and even remotely administer other MSDE databases from within the IDE. You can even use MSDE with SQL Server. In that case, SQL Server can act as a data replicator for your MSDE databases.

You'll be using MSDE for many of the examples in the book, and since MSDE is such a great resource for developing ADO.NET solutions, it makes sense to spend some time exploring it now. (If you have SQL Server, though, continue using it—everything you're about to do works just as well on SQL Server. After all, MSDE and SQL Server are, as far as Visual Studio .NET is concerned, the same.)

Setting It Up and Checking That It's Working

I hate books that walk the reader through installing software; it seems so pointless. You bought the book because you want to learn how to use the software, so it makes sense to assume that you've already installed it. In the case of MSDE, that's not quite true. It's really easy to not install MSDE when you install Visual Studio .NET, especially since a surprisingly small number of developers actually know what MSDE is.

Rather than waste your time, though, here's a simple way to check whether or not MSDE is installed. If after following these steps you find it isn't, then you can continue reading to find out what you need to do to get it installed. For those of you that did manage to get it installed first time through, give yourselves a pat on the back and skip to the next section.

Assuming you are using Windows 2000 or Windows XP, you can take a look at the running services on your computer and see if MSDE is in there. Go to the Control Panel, select Administrative Tools, and then select Services. Scroll down the list of services to see if you can find MSSQL$VSTE in the list and, if you can, check that it's running (see Figure 1-1).

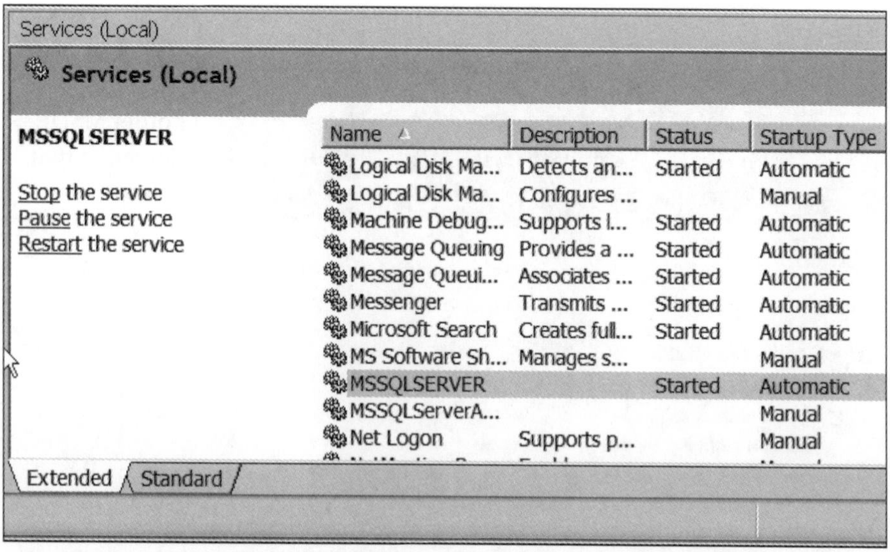

Figure 1-1. Using the Services browser in Windows XP and 2000, you can easily check that MSDE or SQL Server is installed and running.

In the screen in Figure 1-1 you can see that I'm running SQL Server; the highlighted line says MSSQLSERVER, which is fine. If you don't have access to SQL Server and are running MSDE, check for an entry that reads MSSQL$VSTE.

Alternatively, if you installed Visual Studio .NET into the default location on your computer, take a look in C:\Program Files\Microsoft SQL Server. If that directory exists and contains files, then it's quite likely that you've installed either MSDE or SQL Server itself. Both are suitable for the examples in this book and for working with the integrated database and server browser in Visual Studio .NET.

If, on the other hand, you don't have MSDE or SQL Server installed, then it's time to fire up the Visual Studio .NET installer once again. When the installer asks which items you wish to install, make sure the SQL Server Desktop Engine option is selected, as shown in Figure 1-2.

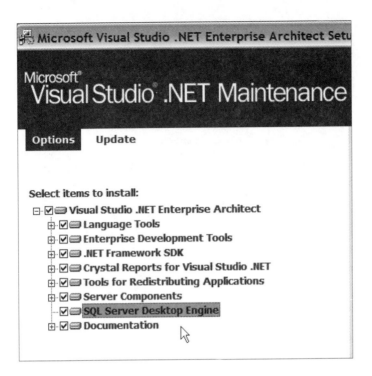

Figure 1-2. Checking the SQL Server Desktop Engine item at install time makes sure that MSDE is installed along with the rest of Visual Studio .NET.

Building the Sample Databases

Right out of the box, MSDE is pretty useless. It doesn't come with any sample data installed, there is no built-in tutorial to show you how to use it, and there are no helpful wizards when you first drop into Visual Studio to lead you through the process of getting a database set up. It just sits quietly behind the scenes, patiently waiting for you to ask it to do something.

Let's give it something to do then. Throughout the rest of the book you'll be working with a couple of sample databases, most notably the traditional Northwind and Pubs databases. When you install MSDE onto your computer, the installer does actually drop the necessary Transact SQL scripts into your system to build those databases, complete with some rough data to play with. In this section you'll look at how to actually run the scripts and build the databases.

TIP For those of you coming to the Microsoft database world from the likes of Oracle, Informix, or any of the other alternate database solutions, Transact SQL is the name given to the variant of SQL used in SQL Server and, of course, MSDE. It's similar to the SQL you are probably used to from those other platforms, and it just adds in some Microsoft-specific extensions such as standard variables and support for custom functions that can be called within a stored procedure. There's plenty of help in the online help documentation that comes with Visual Studio .NET on its idiosyncrasies and features, so I'll let you explore them at your leisure if you are new to Transact SQL.

Just in case you ever need to rebuild the sample databases again, the best way to do this is to build up a database solution in Visual Studio containing the scripts that will be used to construct the databases in the first place.

Fire up Visual Studio .NET and choose to create a new project. When then the New Project dialog box appears, select Other Projects, then Database Projects from the Project Types tree, and choose Database Project as the template to use, just like in Figure 1-3. Give your project a decent name (such as SampleDatabases) and click OK to get your project going.

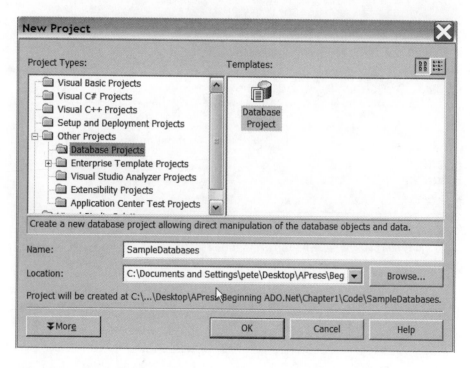

Figure 1-3. Database projects are a great place to hold all the scripts you need to rebuild a database from scratch.

The Database Link Properties dialog box will appear next (see Figure 1-4). All database projects in Visual Studio .NET need to be set up to connect to a specific database server at the very least, and ideally a database within that server. You don't have a database yet, so just select your machine from the server combo box, select "Use Windows NT Integrated security" as the security method to use, and then click the OK button at the bottom of the dialog box.

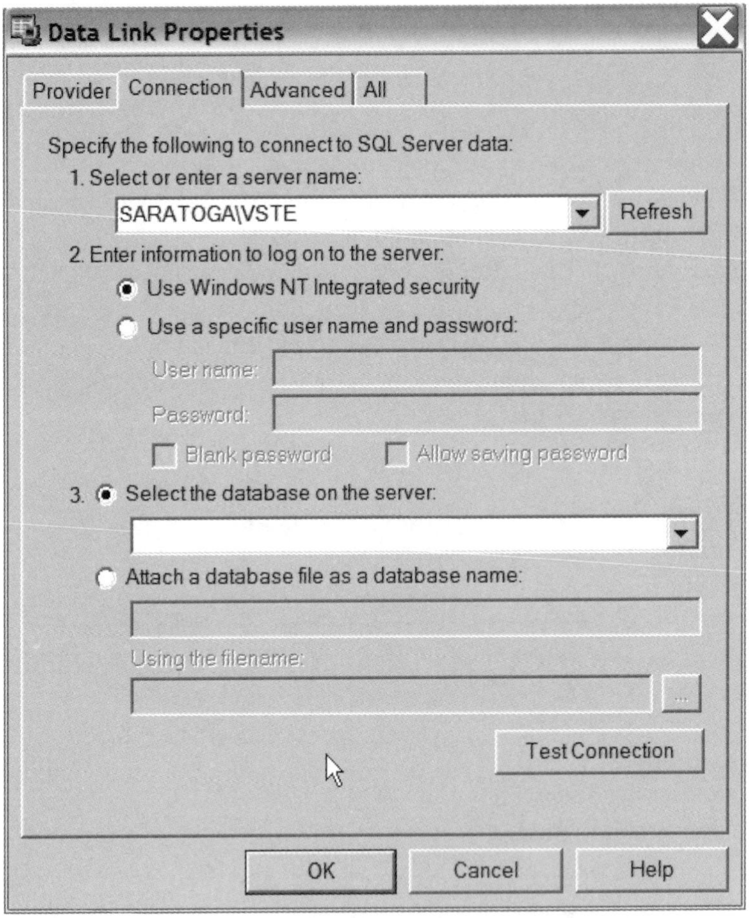

Figure 1-4. The Database Link Properties dialog box provides a handy way to set up a link between your project and a specific database server.

Your project will now be ready to go. There's nothing in it just yet, so the welcome page in Visual Studio won't change, but the Solution Explorer (usually displayed on the right within the IDE) will change to show you your database project's structure. More important, if you pop out the Server Explorer from the left-hand side of the IDE, you should see a connection to your local MSDE database has already been established and is ready for you to start running SQL scripts against it (see Figure 1-5).

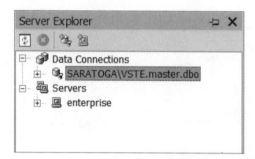

Figure 1-5. A reference to the appropriate database server is always stored inside a database project and is browseable from the Server Explorer slide-out panel.

Now you can go ahead and add in the scripts that will build up your sample databases.

Right-click the Change Scripts category of your new database project and choose Add Existing Item from the pop-up menu that appears. A traditional file dialog box will appear. Assuming you installed Visual Studio into the default locations, navigate to the C:\Program Files\Microsoft Visual Studio.Net\FrameworkSDK\Samples\Setup directory. In there you'll find two SQL scripts: instnwnd.sql and instpubs.sql. Add them both to your project.

With both the files in your project, try double-clicking one. You'll see the SQL within the file appear in the Visual Studio .NET editor, and just as if you were editing C# or VB .NET code, the editor recognizes the format of the code and applies syntax highlighting (see Figure 1-6). You'll also notice that the editor automatically draws a handy outline around every major SQL block—this is useful when you debug your own stored procedures, as you'll see later.

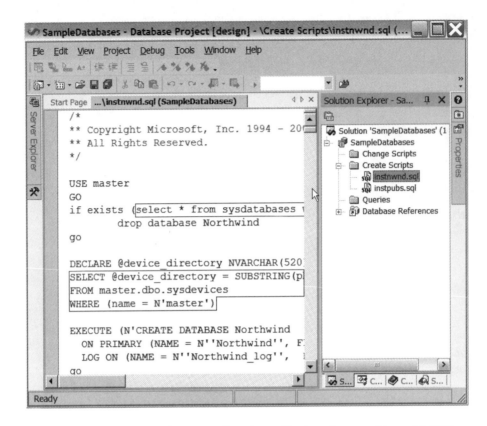

Figure 1-6. The Visual Studio .NET editor is as effective when working with SQL code as it is with any other .NET-enabled language.

All that remains for you to do now is to run the two scripts to build the sample databases. Since your project is already connected to a database server, running the scripts will cause the scripts to automatically work with that server.

To run them, right-click a script in the Solution Explorer and select Run from the pop-up menu. The databases are quite large, so it can take a while for the scripts to execute.

When the scripts are complete, your databases will be ready to use. You'll look at just how to explore them and work with them in a little while.

More Information on MSDE

Of course, there are many more behind-the-scenes features of MSDE than I have space to cover here. You can find plenty of information on MSDE, how to redistribute it with your applications, and how to upsize an application to SQL Server (hint: Just install SQL Server on top of MSDE) in the integrated help of Visual

Studio .NET. To access the integrated help, just click the help search button in the IDE and type in **MSDE**.

Visual Studio's Server Explorer

If you've worked with Visual Basic before, you should at this stage be thinking to yourself how wonderful it is that the days of Access-based databases for desktop applications are over. You may also be wondering just how you go about getting at all those neat MSDE features for yourself.

The answer lies in the Visual Studio .NET IDE, in a small slide-out panel usually found on the left side of the application known as the Server Explorer (see Figure 1-7).

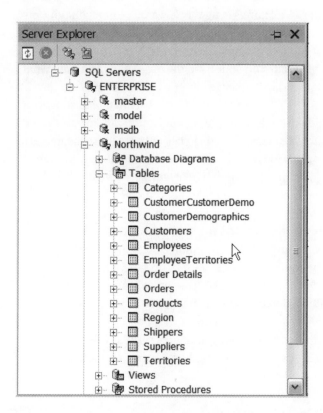

Figure 1-7. The Server Explorer provides you with all the functionality you need to build, manage, and configure your MSDE and SQL Server databases.

The Server Explorer gives you complete power over all your data sources, both local and remote. You can create tables, indexes, stored procedures, and custom functions, and you can even draw up database schema diagrams using it—all without having to leave the comfort of Visual Studio .NET. Mastering the Server Explorer is key if you intend to go anywhere with your ADO.NET development work in Visual Studio .NET.

Exploring Your Databases

Forgive me for stating the obvious, but the simplest and most common thing you'll want to do with your database servers is find out what's in them. What are the databases called, what are the tables within them, and are there any views set up?

Now that you have a couple databases set up in your MSDE installation, you can explore them with the Server Explorer.

Just click Servers, then click the name of your machine, and the list will grow to show you categories that you can explore. Using the Server Explorer, you not only have access to your databases underneath the SQL Servers category, but you can also look at any performance counters you may have set up with Microsoft Windows Instrumentation, the message queues on your host, the event logs, and even what Crystal is getting up to. Visual Studio's Server Explorer wraps it all up.

Double-click the SQL Servers entry and you'll see the list change to show you all the databases running under MSDE on your machine. Among them you should now see the Northwind and Pubs databases. Double-click either of those databases and you'll see yet more categories for you to explore, such as database diagrams, tables, stored procedures, views, and functions. Great stuff.

Have a play. Try exploring each subcategory and double-click to your heart's content on a number of the tables or stored procedures and see what happens. As long as you don't go randomly hitting keys on the keyboard after you open up a table or stored procedure, you shouldn't do any damage. In fact, even if you do double-click a table, leave the room, and come back to find the office monkeys have been banging away in the hope of producing the great American novel, all is not lost; that's why you created a database project in the first place. At any point in time you can rerun the installation scripts and they will rebuild your sample databases from the ground up (both the Northwind and Pubs scripts will overwrite your existing Northwind and Pubs databases in the process of rebuilding them).

Diagramming Database Schemas

By now you should be quite at home with exploring your databases within the Server Explorer. It's time now to look at some of the more powerful features of the Server Explorer. First up, database diagramming.

Open up the Northwind database in your Server Explorer and right-click the Database Diagrams heading, as shown in Figure 1-8.

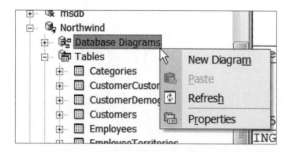

Figure 1-8. As with all the entries in the Server Explorer, the real power behind the scenes is unleashed with a click of the right mouse button.

At this point in time, there are no diagrams in the database, so go ahead and choose New Diagram from the menu. A new dialog box will appear asking you which tables you wish to see. Just to prove a point, click the top entry in the list and then Shift-click the bottom entry. You should have all the tables selected, so go ahead and click the Add button.

Visual Studio .NET will then build a full database schema diagram for the selected tables (complete with their relationships), insert that diagram into the database, and then display the diagram for you, as shown in Figure 1-9.

If you can't see the whole diagram on your screen (Visual Studio does tend to eat up a lot of screen real estate), just use the percentage drop-down on the Visual Studio toolbar to scale the image, just as if you were using Word or Visio and wanted a larger/smaller image.

This diagram is a far cry from the static images that you might produce in a Word document or with Visio. The diagram provides a way to affect a whole host of changes to the database structure and the table relationships.

The simplest way to work with table relationships is to click and drag; just click a field in one table and drag a link across to a field in another table. A relationship editor dialog box will pop up asking for more information on the relationship (such as should cascading updates be applied), and you're done.

You can also right-click any table in the diagram to bring up a comprehensive menu that allows you to do everything from viewing the data in a table, to adding and deleting fields, to adding and editing relationships and even setting up the indexes on the tables.

If you right-click in an empty area of the diagram, another pop-up menu appears that allows you to add in complete new tables and elect whether or not you want to view relationship names on the diagrams.

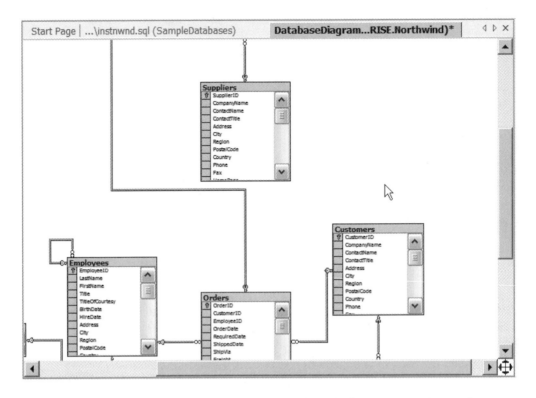

Figure 1-9. Bearing in mind that you are using Visual Studio here, not SQL Server, the amount of power available to database developers is astounding.

Adding Tables

As you just saw, you can add tables to the database by simply right-clicking in an empty area of the database diagram. Alternatively, you can right-click the Tables heading underneath the database concerned and choose New Table. The main document area of Visual Studio will change to show the table editor, a familiar sight I'm sure to all those of you who've ever created tables with Access or SQL Server before.

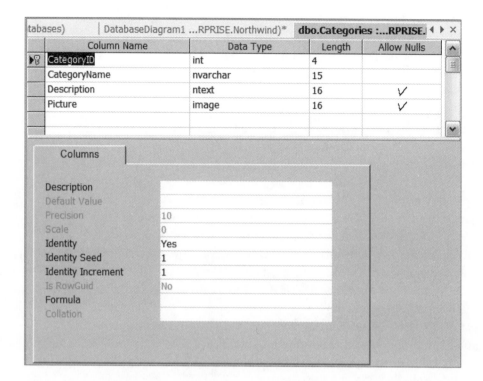

Figure 1-10. Visual Studio .NET's database table editor

In the top part of the panel, you enter the names for your table's columns, select their data type, specify the column's length in bytes (some types, such as BigInt, come with a preordained length), and finally specify whether or not the column can ever be left empty when a new record is inserted.

The tabbed panel at the bottom allows you to define further information about the selected column. For example, if the column is to be an autoincrementing ID number, you can specify what value should be applied to the first record in the table and how much the ID should increment by each time a new record is added. You can also assign a description to the column to make maintenance a little easier and even specify default values for columns. On the autoincrementing front it's worth pointing out that by using a combination of database functions and stored procedures, it's possible to come up with a far more sophisticated way of assigning a unique ID to a record—you'll look at what's involved with creating stored procedures and functions in a little while.

You should also notice the small toolbar at the top of the table editor.

The key icon at the left of the toolbar allows you to specify the primary key of a table. Just select one of more columns from the table editor grid and then click the key icon. A small key will then appear next to the columns that have been set as the primary key of the table.

The next icon, a hierarchical tree, allows you to edit relationships the table has with other tables in the database; it's actually a lot easier to define and work with relationships from the database diagram where you can just drag and drop links between tables instead of working through a complex dialog box.

You can define additional indexes for your table with the third icon on the toolbar. The final icon allows you to check and manage the constraints on your database. In English, this allows you to set conditions that must be met when new rows are added to or removed from your table. For example, you might not want orders to be entered into an order tracking system without a valid customer number attached to the orders in question.

This has been a somewhat whirlwind tour of the features of the table editor since I'm assuming that most of you have come across something very similar before. As always, though, the built-in MSDN help in Visual Studio .NET is an abundant source of further information should you need to drill down in a lot more detail on any aspect of the table editor.

Adding Views

Views are read-only subsets of one or more table's data. They provide a great way to set up "views" of the data in your database without having to write a bunch of custom stored procedures to do the same and without having to embed complex logic in your application to realize the relationships between the data in the database. A typical use for views is when your users will need to analyze data outside of your application. For example, there are quite a few users out there who like to have their databases provide views of the data they contain in a format that can be read into Excel. Some more advanced users like to drill down into data with a custom data analysis tool or custom reporting tool such as Crystal Reports. Views are the solution in this case.

Since views are read-only, you don't run the risk of your users accidentally editing the data they retrieve, and views also allow you to expose data on a user-by-user or group-by-group basis. Accounting department users can see a view of orders tailored to them, for example, while the sales team has a more limited view showing just summary information on each customer and the orders that customer has placed.

The sample Northwind database provides just such a set of views. Just expand the Views tab in the Server Explorer to see them, and then double-click a view to see the data that it exposes. Try it now.

Creating a view is simplicity itself. Just right-click the Views heading in the Server Explorer and select New View from the pop-up menu that appears. Visual Studio .NET will instantly present you with a table select dialog box similar to the one you saw when you built the database diagram earlier. Select the tables that you want to pull data from in your view and the IDE will change to show those tables, with their relationships drawn in.

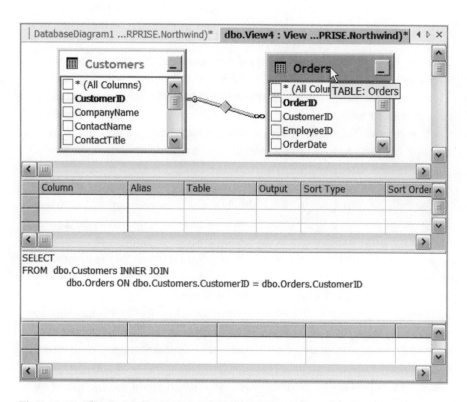

Figure 1-11. The view editor in Visual Studio .NET is both powerful and simple to use.

Notice how each column in the selected tables has a check box to the left of its name. To add the column to the view, just select the check box. As you do so, you'll see the columns added to the column grid and the stored procedure that will be used to build up your view being built for you automatically. At any point you can click and drag the columns in the column grid to change their order, or you can even just click in the SQL Editor and write some SQL code by hand.

When you are done, just click the Save icon on the main Visual Studio .NET toolbar to save and name your view, or right-click in the SQL code pane to check the SQL or even run it to see what the results of your view will look like.

It's worth pointing out the Sort Type and Sort Order columns in the column grid. Using these you can not only choose to sort the output by a column in either ascending or descending order, but you can also specify the order of the sorted columns. For example, you could choose to see a list of customers sorted first by their name, then by their city. The Name column's sort order would be 1; the City column's sort order would be 2.

Adding Stored Procedures

Adding stored procedures to your database adds an essential level of power to your database. Rather than having SQL code embedded throughout your application, you can write stored procedures to carry out anything from adding records and deleting records to automatically updating whole bunches of records or just selecting records. Using Stored procedures in this way (as opposed to handling the logic in your code) decouples your application from the database to a certain extent. It's possible after deploying the database and application to completely change how new records are added to a table without having to modify, recompile, and redistribute the application. Since almost every full development language known to humankind can access a database and run stored procedures, you also ensure that the same logic is applied to database access regardless of whether it's your application working with the database, a script on some ASP.NET page, or some as yet unimagined application developed in the future. You know all this stuff already, I know, but I just wanted to make sure.

Actually adding a stored procedure to the database works in a similar fashion to building up a view. Just right-click the Stored Procedures heading and select New Stored Procedure from the pop-up menu. The SQL Editor appears, as shown in Figure 1-12.

Okay, I admit that at first glance this looks nothing like the configuration of panels that appear when you choose to add a new view into the system. The reason behind that is that whereas a view is designed to do nothing more than grab a bunch of data and return from the database, a stored procedure can be considerably more complex, returning data as well as updating it, and in some instances perhaps not even touching the database contents at all, so it makes no sense to instantly fire up the SQL Designer to start building a Select statement. The Designer is there, though.

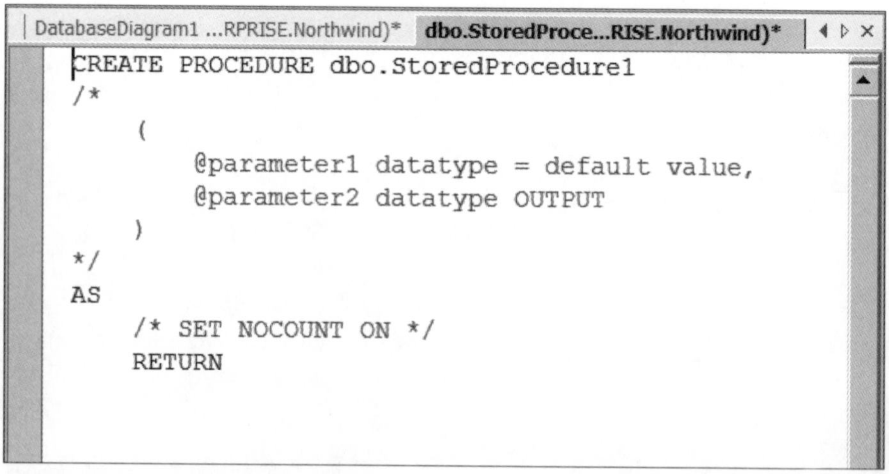

```
DatabaseDiagram1 ...RPRISE.Northwind)*   dbo.StoredProce...RISE.Northwind)*    ◀ ▷ ✕

CREATE PROCEDURE dbo.StoredProcedure1
/*
    (
        @parameter1 datatype = default value,
        @parameter2 datatype OUTPUT
    )
*/
AS
    /* SET NOCOUNT ON */
    RETURN
```

Figure 1-12. The SQL Editor appears by default when you choose to add a new stored procedure to your database.

Despite the rather bland appearance of the SQL Editor, it wraps up a considerable amount of functionality and power. If you intend to do a lot of work with either SQL Server or the MSDE, then you're soon going to think of Visual Studio's SQL Designer as your new best friend.

The default view the SQL Editor presents is the code pane. Just like the VB .NET Code Editor in Visual Studio, this is a syntax highlighting editor that you can use to just key in the Transact SQL code for your stored procedure. The editor will automatically draw a frame around distinct blocks within your Transact SQL statement, allowing you to easily see the separate chunks of functionality in your stored procedure. The real power comes when you right-click in those highlighted blocks.

Be careful just where you do right-click, though. The context menu in Figure 1-13 is the one that holds all the power, providing a set of options for working with the SQL block itself. If you click outside of a highlighted block, a very different menu appears.

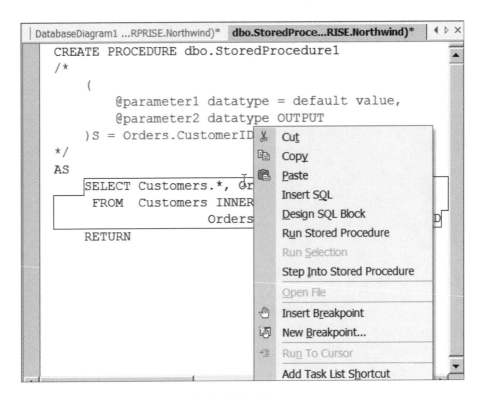

Figure 1-13. The context menu for the SQL Editor pane

The language that's used to write stored procedures in SQL Server and MSDE is Microsoft's own flavor of SQL, known as Transact SQL (T-SQL). Exploring everything that Transact SQL can do and all the nuances of its syntax is a whole book in itself and thus a bigger subject than I can cover in full here. If you have never worked with a SQL Server database and want to learn everything that you can do with T-SQL, go into the online help and do a search on "Transact SQL"—you'll find a whole bunch of information in there to help you get started. Alternatively, take a look at the sample stored procedures included with the Northwind and Pubs databases. To take a look at the source behind one of them, just double-click it. The SQL Editor pane will open and show the stored procedure, replacing the CREATE NEW line at the top of the stored procedure with ALTER PROCEDURE to enable you to make changes if you wish to.

The pop-up menu, as you can see in Figure 1-13, lets you add items to the Visual Studio Task List so that you can effectively add notes on further work that you need to do on your stored procedures. You can also insert breakpoints and debug your T-SQL code.

The two most interesting options on the menu are the Design SQL Block and Insert SQL items. The Design SQL Block menu item will take you through to the

SQL Designer that you saw when you looked at creating views. Using the Designer, you can select the tables to be used in the SQL block, the fields, select order, and so on. Clicking Insert SQL also takes you into the Designer but allows you to build new SQL blocks within the stored procedure. You can also right-click in the SQL Designer and choose Change Type to switch from designing a Select statement to working with an Insert, Update, or Delete statement.

The key to all the functionality in the SQL Editor is that magic right-click button. Have a go at it yourself and take a look at some of the options available to you.

Adding Functions

Think of a database as a car. Tables are the fuel, stored procedures are the engine, and functions are the difference between producing a top-of-the-line Ford and a Rolls Royce. That's an oversimplification, but it should drive a point home to those out there who haven't done much hands-on database (as opposed to data-based application) development. Functions are much like stored procedures. They are made up of Transact SQL code that just like a stored procedure can be used to update your data in any number of ways. Unlike stored procedures, though, a function call can be embedded in another Transact SQL statement. For example:

```
INSERT INTO Customers ( customername, datecreated)
     Values ( 'Peter', ::DateOfFirstOrder('Peter') )
```

In the preceding example, DateOfFirstOrder is a hypothetical function that searches the database for the date the new customer actually placed their tentative order and returns that value ready for inserting into a new regular customer table.

Functions can be used to calculate a value in the middle of a stored procedure or simplify the stored procedure by abstracting all those ugly SQL joins out to a self-contained entity or two that can do the grunt work for you. They are incredibly useful, versatile, and powerful.

SQL Server allows you to create three types of functions, which despite their names are not all that intimidating: inline functions, table-valued functions, and scalar functions. You can create all three by right-clicking the Functions heading in the Server Explorer and then selecting the type that most suits your needs.

In a nutshell, an *inline function* is just like a select stored procedure—it returns a table-style set of data from the database. A *table-valued function*, on the other hand, returns a table variable, a table that you effectively define within the function, specifying the column names and data types as part of the function. A *scalar function* just returns a scalar value, such as an integer, a string, or another "simple" data type. The hypothetical DateOfFirstOrder() function shown previously would be a scalar function.

Once again, there's far more to this than I could possibly cover here. Take a look at the online help for more information on functions and how to write them.

Summary

I hope by now that you have a pretty good overview of just what makes ADO.NET so great, as well as hands-on experience with the tools that Visual Studio .NET provides to make your database much more productive and, more important, easier than in previous versions. You should also by now have built the sample MSDE databases that you'll be using throughout the rest of the book.

In the next chapter, you'll depart from the theoretical and move to the practical, and you'll experience firsthand the power ADO.NET brings to developers.

CHAPTER 2

Fundamental ADO.NET Code

"I sell here, Sir, what all the world desires to have—POWER."

—Matthew Boulton, 1776

IN THE LAST CHAPTER I touched on the fundamental technologies that make up ADO.NET. I also led a quick tour of the facilities in Visual Studio, paying special attention to those parts designed to make your life easier as a developer of database applications. It was all great stuff, and very valuable, but hardly something that's going to impress the eager client paying your hourly bills. In this chapter you start coding.

This chapter is not an exhaustive tour of everything you ever wanted to know about working with ADO.NET; if it were, the book would remain the same, but with two very long chapters and nothing else. In this chapter you're going to take a look at the fundamentals. How do I connect to a database? How do I extract data? How do I manipulate that data or explore the structure of my databases? Consider this chapter to be a detailed introduction to the fundamentals. A year from now when you've been doing nothing but coding Web services and you've completely forgotten the very basics of just grabbing a bunch of data from a database, this is the chapter you'll refer to. Since this chapter covers the very fundamentals of working with ADO.NET, you should also consider this chapter the very foundation of the rest of the book. You can use it to kick you off, and then explore the other chapters as you see fit to "drill down" (love that phrase) in more detail into the areas of your choice.

Let me get one thing out of the way real quick, though. This book is about database application development, not the finer points of building a stunning user interface. There are chapters in the rest of the book that touch on the essentials of building Web and desktop graphical user interfaces (GUIs), but in this chapter you're going to stick with the console. The code required to output data to the console is minimal and it allows you to focus on the core of database development without getting unduly sidetracked. Feel free to update the example code in this chapter on your own as an exercise at a later date when you're happier with the Windows Forms controls.

So, let's get started.

The Most Basic Basics

I'm ashamed to say it, but I recently went on an interview and couldn't for the life of me find the right answer to one of the interviewer's questions. The question was simple: "If you have the perfect team, a sound design and project plan, the very best tools, and a fabulous time line for your project, what's the first problem that you need to address, the most important hurdle to leap to ensure your project stays on target?" I sat, dumbfounded. "Estimation of time," I answered.

"Already done and sorted out," the interviewer replied, grinning.

I then started wildly hitting everything but the right answer—gold plating, team management, client management, source control, coding standards. I considered answering "My obvious stupidity" at one point but thought better of it. The smirks continued from the other side of the interview desk. In the end I gave up and told him so.

"Development environment," he responded. He was right!

No matter how fabulous the development tools, how wonderfully loose the time lines of the project, or how incredibly talented the team, if the development environment isn't set up, you're going to get royally whacked at every major juncture. I'm not going to talk you through setting up source control, backup servers, team infrastructure management software, and so on here, but the development environment you give yourself in Visual Studio for even the simplest ADO.NET project is as important as the huge technical infrastructure around the mythical project the interviewer was asking me about.

I'll assume that you've already walked through Chapter 1, so you know that the MSDE engine at the very least is installed, and you've set up the sample databases inside it (Northwind and Pubs). If you haven't, then scurry on back there and sort it out. I'll wait here.

Back? Okay—the next step is your Visual Studio project itself. I'm going to assume you're using Visual Basic .NET (VB .NET) from this point in; if you're a C# developer, or even a Managed C++ one, the chances are good that you'll be able to pick your way confidently through some rudimentary VB .NET examples.

Setting Up Your Project

This is the only time in this book that I'm going to talk you through setting up an ADO.NET console project for VB .NET. Refer back here when you start projects later on if it slips your mind just how to do it.

First, fire up Visual Studio .NET and choose to create a new VS .NET solution. Make sure you choose from the list of Visual Basic .NET project templates and select the Console Application as the one you want (see Figure 2-1).

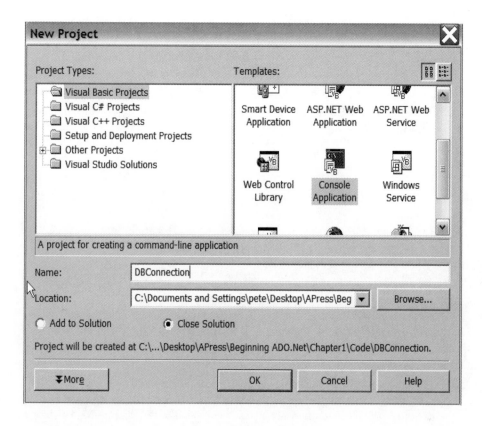

Figure 2-1. Most of the projects that you'll create in this chapter will be VB .NET–based console ones.

Give the project a name, such as DBConnection. As soon as you click the OK button, Visual Studio .NET creates your blank project and presents you with the code window ready to go. The project also has a reference automatically set to the System.Data namespace, the namespace that you'll need to use to work with ADO.NET. Expand the References branch of your solution within the Solution Explorer and you should see the System.Data reference there.

Setting up a reference in your project to System.Data is essential if you're going to be doing any database work in your application. You still need to explicitly import the data provider that you're going to use. In your case, you're going to work with the SQL Server data provider, so all that's required is to add an Import statement to the top of your code module:

```
Imports System.Data.SqlClient
```

If you were going to connect to an OLE DB data source, you'd need to import System.Data.OleDb.

Importing the data provider namespace in this way makes the various objects that comprise the data provider available to you. For example, by importing System.Data.SqlClient you have access to the SQL Server client's DataReader, DataCommand, and Connection objects—objects specifically designed to work with a SQL Server–compliant data source. Import System.Data.OleDb and you'd get access to DataReader, DataCommand, and OleDbConnection objects designed to work with more "traditional" data sources.

 New to .NET

There's something else you need to add to your VB .NET code's Imports line, and that is the statement Option Strict On. You'll see this in the next example and in every single code example in this book.

Setting Option Strict On forces VB to use strict type checking, which forces you the developer to make sure that when you assign one type to another, the two are compatible. For example, you can easily assign a byte to an integer without any loss of data, but you can't necessarily go the other way around. With Option Strict Off, VB will check all assignments and try to accommodate your needs. This obviously takes time and results in far slower VB .NET code than you should expect.

Setting Option Strict On will make the compiler check all your assignments at compile time and force you to make explicit type casts when there is a question as to what should happen. The result is much leaner, faster compiled code. Using Option Strict On should be considered essential for all VB programmers, not only because of the runtime speed implications, but also because it's just good programming practice to make explicit casts instead of relying on a compiler to guess what you meant.

Connecting to a Database

With your project set up, the next step is to actually connect to the database. This involves creating a SqlConnection object, initializing it, and then calling Open(). Let's take a look at some code to see how it actually all works; feel free to key this into your project after you have read the walk-through.

```
Option Strict On
Imports System.Data.SqlClient
Imports System.Console

Module Module1
```

```
Sub Main()
    Dim dbConnection As SqlConnection
    Dim dataSource As String = "SARATOGA\VSTE"
    Dim database As String = "Northwind"

    ' Let's set up the connection ready to go
    dbConnection = New SqlConnection("Data Source=" & dataSource + _
                ";Integrated Security=sspi;" + _
                "Initial Catalog=" + database)
    Try
        ' Go ahead and open up the connection
        dbConnection.Open()

        WriteLine("Database connection established.")
        WriteLine("Database is version " + dbConnection.ServerVersion.ToString)
        WriteLine("Your workstation is " + dbConnection.WorkstationId.ToString)

        ' Finally, close the connection down
        dbConnection.Close()

    Catch ex As Exception
        ' An exception occurred, so let's elegantly present it
        WriteLine("An error occurred connecting to the database")
        WriteLine(ex.ToString)
    End Try

    ' To stop the console window vanishing when the app finishes,
    ' prompt the user to press a key
    WriteLine("Press Enter to continue")
    ReadLine()
    End Sub
End Module
```

The first thing that should strike you, especially if you have done any work at all with the ADO of old, is just how much code there is to achieve something so simple. Don't be misled; much of the code here just sends text out to the console window to let you know what's going on. If you were to strip out all the unnecessary stuff and just focus on the database connectivity, the program would look like this:

```
Option Strict On
Imports System.Data.SqlClient


Module Module1
```

```
Sub Main()
    Dim dbConnection As SqlConnection = _
    New SqlConnection("Data Source=SARATOGA\VSTE" + _
        ";Integrated Security=sspi;" + _
        "Initial Catalog=Northwind")
    Try
        dbConnection.Open()

        ' Your database code goes here

        dbConnection.Close()

    Catch ex As Exception
        ' Your exception handler goes here
    End Try

End Sub
End Module
```

In fact, if you took out the exception handler, you could get the real meat of the code down to just three lines: one to create the SqlConnection object, another to open the connection, and another to close the connection. Looking at the code in that light, you should be able to see that it's really not that much different from the old way of doing things. The new stuff lies in the connection string's new format. You'll look at that more in a moment. Right now, let's explore the example in full.

```
Imports System.Data.SqlClient
Imports System.Console
```

The two Import lines at the top of the module bring in the namespaces that you're going to work with; without them, the code would be much larger, as you'd need to fully qualify each and every object you use with its namespace. For example, instead of just calling WriteLine() to output some text to the console, you'd have to call System.Console.WriteLine(). That soon gets tedious, hence the Imports.

The meat of the code lies in the main() subroutine, starting with three variable declarations:

```
Dim dbConnection As SqlConnection
Dim dataSource As String = "SARATOGA\VSTE"
Dim database As String = "Northwind"
```

The first declaration is the most important—it declares an object variable to hold the Connection object you need to connect to your SQL Server or MSDE database. As I mentioned before, this object is part of the data provider, and since you're using the SQL Server data provider, the Connection object you need is of type SqlConnection. If you were working with the OLE DB data provider, then that line would have created an OleDbConnection.

The second two variables are just for convenience and specify the server that you're going to connect to, and the database within that server. In ADO.NET terms, these are known as the *data source* and *catalog.* For the code to run on your machine, you'll need to change the dataSource variable to match the name of the machine that your database is on. In my writing cave (really, it has no windows and only a single lightbulb), the machine is called Saratoga and since I'm using MSDE as the database server, I need to suffix the machine name with "\VSTE". If your machine name is MyServer and you're also using the MSDE server, then you would change the dataSource to "MyServer\VSTE". You can pick up the correct name to use from a quick glance over at the name of the database server in Visual Studio's Server Explorer.

With that out of the way, you can actually create a Connection object:

```
dbConnection = New SqlConnection("Data Source=" & dataSource + _
                ";Integrated Security=sspi;" + _
                "Initial Catalog=" + database)
```

Be careful not to get confused here—creating a Connection object is not the same as connecting to a database. Actually establishing the database connection requires a second operation. You create a Connection object first to specify the database and security model you intend to use, and then you call Open() on that connection.

Those of you who have worked with ADO/RDO/DAO will already know that the string being used here is called a *connection string;* it defines the machine, the database, and the security settings you want to use to connect to the database. Data Source is used for the machine; Initial Catalog is used for the database on that machine. The Integrated Security setting tells the SQL Server data provider whether or not the application has a secure connection to the database. If there is a secure connection, then the identity of the user account running the code is used to connect to the database. If there isn't a secure connection, then the username and password need to be specified in the connection string. This is achieved using the "User ID" (note the space between "User" and "ID") and "Password" modifiers, similar to the way it worked back with ADO.

The Integrated Security modifier can actually take one of three values. True and False are the main ones used to indicate whether the connection is secure or not. SSPI means exactly the same as passing in True in the current release of ADO.NET.

With the Connection object set up, the next step is obviously to use it. The Open() method of the SqlConnection object takes no parameters at all and doesn't return a value to you. If the connection is opened, then your code will continue quite happily. If the connection is not opened, an exception will be thrown.

 New to .NET

The use of exceptions and exception handlers when working with ADO.NET (and indeed the rest of the .NET Framework) is a major style change to the way that we should all work. C and C++ developers in particular had it hard before .NET. Since the Windows API was never intended to work with exception-aware languages (such as C++), all functions would return a value to the caller, known commonly as an HRESULT. It was the duty of the diligent programmer to check every single return value to make sure that an error had not occurred before continuing. This added untold bloat to the code and a degree of programming overhead that only a rare few were willing to put up with (judging by the amount of crash-happy code out there).

An exception will stop a program in its tracks, so the addition of exception handlers to catch unwanted conditions in code is no longer an optional extra; it's a requirement. Exceptions in Visual Basic .NET are trapped in Try…Catch…End Try blocks and can wrap up huge chunks of code if necessary, making their addition to code a relative no-brainer. In the case of ADO.NET, exceptions can be raised for something as trivial as an invalid username and password combination, or for something as serious as a severed connection to the database. Since all exceptions are equal in the power they have to stop your application dead, ignore exception handlers at your peril.

```
Try

        ' Go ahead and open up the connection
        dbConnection.Open()

        WriteLine("Database connection established.")
        WriteLine("Database is version " + dbConnection.ServerVersion.ToString)
        WriteLine("Your workstation is " + dbConnection.WorkstationId.ToString)
```

```
    ' Finally, close the connection down
    dbConnection.Close()

Catch ex As Exception
    ' An exception occurred, so let's elegantly present it
    WriteLine("An error occurred connecting to the database")
    WriteLine(ex.ToString)
End Try
```

Assuming the connection opens without any surprises, WriteLine() is used to output information about the Connection object; the sample code here writes out the server version and workstation ID, as well as a reassurance that the connection did indeed open.

Finally, the connection is closed, just as you would expect. But hang on for a second. Much publicity has been given to the garbage collection system built into .NET. Using it, developers are not under such pressure to clean up the states and instances of their objects since the .NET Framework can do it all for them. Database connections are an exception. Though it might seem perfectly reasonable to expect the code inside the SqlConnection object to automatically close the connection when the object is destroyed, that doesn't happen at all.

ADO.NET provides extensive support for connection pooling behind the scenes. More often than not, you'll never have to spend too much time worrying about how the connections are pooled. However, you do need to control when connections are drawn from and returned to the pool. That's where the Open() and Close() methods come in. Open(), just as its name indicates, gives you an open connection to a database, but it could be either a brand-new connection or one from the pool. Conversely, Close() returns a connection to the connection pool. ADO.NET leaves it to you to control precisely how resources in the connection pool are used. Failing to explicitly Close() a connection when you're done with it can result in the connection pool not updating properly and connections within it can be left "hanging." With a system managing thousands of connections to a resource as finite as a database, hanging connections can soon cause you untold problems. Always close your connections when you're done using them.

New to .NET

This whole "explicit" Close() requirement of ADO.NET is not as cumbersome as it may first appear. The object-oriented (OO) nature of the .NET Framework (something that may still be a little unfamiliar to you if you come from a Visual Basic background) means that it's trivial to create your own Connection object that subclasses the SqlConnection object. In that object you could override the class destruction event handlers and explicitly close the connection when the object goes out of scope.

There's no such thing as a free lunch, though, and while that approach is perfectly legal in a true OO application, the other programmers on your team may not be so happy. Explicitly calling Close() in your own code makes it obvious to those reading the code where and how you control the lifetime of a connection. A much more "team-friendly" approach to the problem would be to have all your database access held in small business classes (classes that focus on business needs). These objects could be designed to have extremely short life cycles and explicitly close the database connections they use when they are destroyed. That way, you know the connection is always destroyed when your business code is done using it, and your fellow programmers can see that with a cursory glance over your classes.

While an OO approach to programming provides you with unparalleled freedom and flexibility in your implementation, the OO approach to development also brings in the old adage "enough rope to hang yourself." Fire up your word processor; choose a 48-point bold, italicized, underlined font; and in the center of the page, type **CODE FRIENDLY!**. Then print it out and stick it to the wall above your monitor. Your code should always strive to be explicit and self-documenting.

The final few lines of code are quite straightforward, so I won't dwell on them. Just output more information to the console on the state of the application and wait for the user to press a key before terminating the program and closing the console. When you work with console applications, it's important to do something at the end of the program to stop the console from instantly vanishing from view when the program terminates.

```
' To stop the console window vanishing when the app finishes,
' prompt the user to press a key
WriteLine("Press Enter to continue")
ReadLine()
    End Sub
End Module
```

Exploring the Connection

I've covered connecting to a database using the SQL Server data provider in some length now. For something so seemingly trivial to accomplish, you may wonder why I went to all the effort. The reason is that the Connection object is more than just a handy object to create when you need to hook into a database. It can also be used to completely control connection lifetime and, more important, connection pooling.

The SQL Server data provider in .NET automatically handles pooling and garbage collection of connections in a very simple and powerful way. When you create a new connection, the data provider searches its internal connection pool to see if other connections have previously been requested with the exact same connection string as your own. If they have, then a pooled object can be used. On the other hand, if the data provider has never seen the connection string you used before, it will create a new connection pool from which to allocate and manage database resources. This all happens behind the scenes, normally, but you do have some control over it.

My explanation is actually simplified. The data provider manages pools of connections primarily based on the connection string, allocating a new pool to each new connection string it sees. Those pools are in turn subdivided based on the "transaction context." A set of connections is assigned to the pool to be used by threads with no transaction context, and a set of connections is assigned to the pool for each and every transaction context that subsequently requests a connection. You'll find out a lot more about transaction contexts later on in the book (Chapter 11 if you're in a hurry).

At first, this may seem a pretty dumb way to work. After all, if all your applications connect to the same database the same way, then the chances are that all those applications will share the same connection pool. That's hardly useful when one of the applications is a Web application serving 3 million users for short connections, while another serves 10 users, each using multiple connections with long lifetimes. The devil, as they say, is in the details.

Since a connection pool is allocated based on the connection string used, ADO.NET allows you to specify an application name in the connection string (using the Application Name modifier). The connection string can also specify the minimum and maximum number of connections to the pool, as well as control the length of those connections' lives. Suddenly, ADO.NET's connection pooling becomes quite useful. You can have completely different pools set up for completely different applications and even for completely separate portions of a single application. If you store the connection strings outside the compiled assembly, then you can even fine-tune the connection pooling properties of the data provider without having to recompile, at last handing off that odious task to system administrators who live for such tedium. Whether you do it yourself or have a sysadmin do it for you, the .NET performance monitor can be used to track the status of your data providers at runtime with no additional code needed on your part.

Your connection pools can be managed using the Connection Lifetime, Connection Reset, Pooling, Max Pool Size, and Min Pool Size connection string modifiers.

Connection Lifetime controls how long before a connection should be automatically destroyed and is useful in clustering and load balancing.

Pooling can be set to either True or False, and of course it specifies whether connection pooling should be used in your application. It follows that Max Pool Size and Min Pool Size control just how many connections should be automatically created in a new pool and how many connections that pool can hold.

There are a great many connection string modifiers available to you to use and you'll explore them all when you look at transactions, concurrency, and pooling in Chapter 11.

Working with Data

Once you've connected to the database, the next thing you'll most likely want to do is get at the data inside that database. ADO.NET provides you with two approaches: the DataReader and the DataSet.

The DataReader

Those of you coming to ADO.NET from standard ADO, RDO, or even DAO will instantly recognize some of the functionality of the DataReader, and in some respects a close family resemblance to the Recordset. The reason for this is that a DataReader provides a way for you to access a set of rows from a database, in a forward-only fashion, similar to a forward-only Recordset.

The SqlDataReader (as always, there's an alternate reader for accessing data from an OLE DB data source) provides you with a connection-based approach to reading data. You need to have a connection open to work with the data in a SqlDataReader, and you need to close the connection (and SqlDataReader) when you're done accessing data. In that respect, a DataReader is a very traditional way of working with data. You open a connection, issue a command over that connection to get at your data, and navigate the results with a DataReader. When you're done, the DataReader is discarded and the connection is closed. ADO.NET also provides a "disconnected" view of data, through the DataSet object. I cover that in more detail in the next section.

The key part of that previous statement is "issue a command over that connection." In order to access data using ADO.NET, you first need to create a

SQLCommand object. As its name implies, the SQLCommand object is used to issue a command to the remote database, whether that command is straight SQL code or a call to a stored procedure. With a SQLCommand set up to retrieve data, you then call the SQLCommand object's ExecuteReader() method. This executes the command and returns a reader to you. Although a Connection object is required in order to navigate through the rows in a DataReader, the DataReader itself is not aware of that connection. Instead, the DataReader is linked to a SQLCommand, and the SQLCommand is linked to a connection (see Figure 2-2).

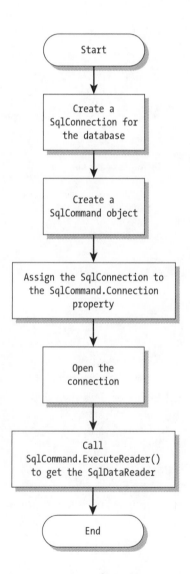

Figure 2-2. The sequence of events to go through to get hold of a DataReader

This is all best illustrated through code, so go ahead and start up a new project and call it DataReaders. As before, this project should be a VB .NET console project. Here's the code for the main module:

```
Option Strict On
Imports System.Data.SqlClient
Imports System.Console

Module Module1
    Sub Main()
        ' Set up the connection object ready to hit the database
        Dim dbConnection As SqlConnection = _
            New SqlConnection("Data Source=SARATOGA\VSTE;" + _
                    "Integrated Security=sspi;" + _
                    "Initial Catalog=Northwind")

        ' Set up a command object to go and run our query
        Dim employeeCommand As SqlCommand = New _
            SqlCommand("SELECT EmployeeID, LastName, FirstName  FROM Employees", _
                dbConnection)
        Try
            ' Open the connection to the database and the command
            ' against it to give us a reader.
            dbConnection.Open()
            Dim reader As SqlDataReader = employeeCommand.ExecuteReader()

            ' Make sure that we have more records to read,
            ' and then start looping through them
            Dim bMoreRecords As Boolean = reader.Read()

            Do While bMoreRecords
                WriteLine("Employee ID " + reader.GetValue(0).ToString() + _
                    ", First name " + reader.GetValue(1).ToString() + _
                    ", Last name " + reader.GetValue(2).ToString())
                bMoreRecords = reader.Read()
            Loop
            reader.Close()

            'Finally, close the connection down.
            dbConnection.Close()
```

```
        Catch ex As Exception
            WriteLine("A problem occurred...")
            WriteLine(ex.ToString())
        End Try

        ' Ask the user to press a key so the console window doesn't just vanish
        WriteLine("Press Enter to continue")
        ReadLine()
    End Sub
End Module
```

The first few lines of code should be familiar by now; they import the namespaces that you're going to work with and then set up the Connection object ready to hit the database. This is exactly the same as the first example I covered in this chapter, with the difference being that in this case, the data source and database names are not predeclared in strings. Remember, when you key this code into your own project, you'll need to change the name of the data source to match the name of the computer you have MSDE installed on (just as you did with the connections example back at the start of the chapter).

With the Connection object set up, the code then moves on to setting up a Command object:

```
    ' Set up a command object to go and run our query
    Dim employeeCommand As SqlCommand = New _
        SqlCommand("SELECT EmployeeID, LastName, FirstName  FROM Employees",
            dbConnection)
```

The SqlCommand object's constructor is overloaded, meaning that there are many different sets of parameters that you can pass to a SqlCommand object when it is created. The syntax used here should be self-explanatory; I pass in a SQL statement as the first parameter and a Connection object to use as the second. This sets up the link between the SqlCommand object and a specific data connection. You could also set up the command with a string, connection and transaction, or even just a string. You'll look into those options in more detail later in the book.

 **New to .NET**

If you are new to .NET and come from a Visual Basic background, you may find "overloading" a difficult concept to grasp initially. It's actually very simple, though, and it's one of the cornerstones of object-oriented programming. Overloading allows a developer to create any number of methods or functions all with the same name, but each with a different set of parameters and different functionality.

Think of a car rental system for a second. In the bad old days, developers may have had to write any number of routines for renting a vehicle. These could have been named RentMPV, RentCar, RentTruck, RentAnyAvailable, and so on. In the case of RentMPV, the number of seats might be specified as a parameter, whereas for RentCar the user of the system may be expected to pass in a boolean specifying whether or not the car is a convertible. With overloading, the rental system could have just one method (RentVehicle()) declared many times. One instance of RentVehicle() takes a boolean parameter, another takes an integer parameter, another takes two integers specifying the tonnage and number of wheels (for renting a truck). The use of the rental system's classes doesn't have to remember a whole bunch of different method names now, but just one: RentVehicle(). The compiler decides which implementation of that method to use based on the parameters passed in.

Overloading is used to great effect throughout the .NET libraries, and of course within ADO.NET. It makes your life simpler by forcing you to remember just key method names instead of a bunch of method names, each suited to a subtly different task.

Now that the connection and command have been set up, the next step is to open that connection and grab your DataReader. Opening the connection is simple enough; as before, a call to the SqlConnection object's Open() method is all it takes. If an error doesn't occur, the connection was successfully opened.

Grabbing the SqlDataReader, the object that you'll use to navigate through data on the server, is achieved by asking the command to execute and return a Reader.

Try

```
' Open the connection to the database and the command
' against it to give us a reader.
dbConnection.Open()
Dim reader As SqlDataReader = employeeCommand.ExecuteReader()
```

ExecuteReader() is used when executing a stored procedure or SQL query that will return rows of data. It executes the query on the database and creates a DataReader (in this case a SqlDataReader, since you're using the SQL Server data provider) for you to navigate the data. Of course, not all commands return rows of data, so ExecuteReader() is not the only way of running a command.

There are actually four execute methods attached to a Command object. ExecuteScalar() is used for those queries and stored procedures that return a single result code, much like a typical function in any programming language. Since all results from a database can be treated as rows of data, ExecuteScalar() returns the first column of the first row of the result of the query as a generic object.

ExecuteNonQuery(), as its name suggests, is used to execute code on the server that is not a query. Typically, this would be an Update, Insert, or Delete call, or a stored procedure that actually affects data. ExecuteNonQuery() returns an integer value, which for Update, Insert, and Delete calls is the number of rows affected. For any other type of call, the value returned is –1.

The final execute method is ExecuteXMLReader(). SQL Server 2000 can return the result of a query as an XML document. Calling ExecuteXMLReader() with this type of query will hit the database as usual and produce an XMLReader for you to navigate the resulting XML results.

I cover all these different Execute functions later, but for now let's concentrate on ExecuteReader and the DataReader it returns.

DataReaders are very easy to use. Since they are forward-only, you can only navigate through the rows of data sequentially, from the first row and through each subsequent row until the last. When the DataReader is first returned to you, the cursor (the pointer to the current row) is positioned ahead of the first row of data. So, the first thing you need to do with a DataReader is tell the DataReader to "read" the next row:

```
Dim bMoreRecords As Boolean = reader.Read()
```

The Read() function returns a Boolean value. If Read() is able to move on to the next row, it returns True. If, on the other hand, your DataReader was empty, or the cursor was pointed at the last row of data, Read() would return False. So, in the example program, you call Read to check that your DataReader actually has rows of data to read, before entering a loop to display key fields of that data and move through the returned rows.

```
Do While bMoreRecords
    WriteLine("Employee ID " + reader.GetValue(0).ToString() + _
        ", First name " + reader.GetValue(1).ToString() + _
        ", Last name " + reader.GetValue(2).ToString())
    bMoreRecords = reader.Read()
Loop
reader.Close()
```

When there are no more rows of data to read, the loop exits and the DataReader is closed.

As with SqlConnection objects, closing the DataReader when you are done is vital. While the DataReader is open, the connection associated with it is kept very busy and cannot be used for anything else. That's one of the downsides to DataReaders—they need a connection for as long as you are working with them, and in many of today's application environments, connection resources are a precious commodity. The connection will only be freed for use by other aspects of your code once you have explicitly closed down the DataReader. The same applies to closing the connection down—you can only do this once the associated DataReader has finished using the connection and been closed down itself.

Closing a DataReader is not a trivial activity, though, at least behind the scenes. When you close a DataReader, the ADO.NET framework will move through all remaining rows in the Reader in order to update the DataReader's RecordsAffected property. This property can only be read once a DataReader is closed down. In addition, the Command object that returned the data is updated when the Reader is closed. If the command makes use of any output parameters, then these will be automatically filled in when the DataReader is closed. On the surface, this set of operations doesn't appear too nasty. However, if your query was particularly complex or returned a large number of rows, calling Close() on a DataReader can potentially take a long time to run. That's a long period of time in which your code is doing nothing, and the precious connection resource that you were working toward freeing up is still busy and in use.

There is a way around this, and from that point of view the preceding example program is quite badly written. If you don't intend to make use of any output parameters in your command, and you have no intention of working with the DataReader's RecordsAffected property, you should call the Cancel() method on the Command object *before* calling Close() on the DataReader. Doing these two things (Cancel() on the command, then Close() on the Reader) will allow the Reader to close down instantly, without any hit on your execution time at all.

I've talked about getting the DataReader, navigating through it, and closing it, but what about reading the data in the rows the code navigates through? Take another look at the code inside the loop:

```
WriteLine("Employee ID " + reader.GetValue(0).ToString() + _
                ", First name " + reader.GetValue(1).ToString() + _
                ", Last name " + reader.GetValue(2).ToString())
```

Reading values from columns can be a tricky process. The common type system (CTS) defines a set of standard data types that all .NET-aware languages can make use of in order to interoperate. In addition, the .NET Framework classes (including ADO.NET) make use of these types in order to be useable by all .NET languages. As those of you who have ever struggled to convert an Oracle Timestamp into a VB Date value know, though, databases can have their own set of types, and these can differ quite dramatically from the types available in your programming language of choice.

ADO.NET provides three solutions to this dilemma for you. First up, you can call GetValue on a DataReader to return any column as a generic object, just as I do in the example program. Since all first-class objects in .NET implement the ToString() method, this is a great way for the example program to grab a field, any field, regardless of type, and output its value as a string.

The DataReader also provides a full set of Getxxx methods where "xxx" can be replaced by the name of any standard .NET type—for example, GetInt64, GetString, GetDateTime, and so on. Just as with GetValue, these methods all expect to be passed an integer in order to identify the specific column you are after (the first column in a row is always column number 0).

Finally, every DataProvider should provide a set of Get routines to return objects matching the database column's actual data type. In the case of the SQL Server data provider, these are known as the GetSqlxxx methods. For example, GetSqlString, GetSqlMoney, GetSqlGuid, and so on. There's a full listing of all the routines in the SqlDataReader's online help.

These types are known as the SqlDbTypes. Although you cannot declare variables of these types in your own code, they are used a great deal with stored procedures to specify the types of data required for stored procedure parameters. SqlDbType defines an enum that you can use in your code to refer to SQL Server data types by name.

The DataSet

DataReaders are a wonderfully quick way to obtain a set of results from a single data connection. ADO.NET DataReaders offer little new functionality compared to good old-fashioned ADO Recordsets. The real power of ADO.NET actually lies in something known as the DataSet.

Despite the similarities in their names, DataSets have absolutely nothing in common with the Recordsets of old. A Recordset in standard ADO allows you to navigate through rows of data returned from a database. You can also navigate through more than one set of rows sequentially; when you reach the end of one set of rows, you can pull in the next and navigate that. DataReaders can do that too.

A DataSet, on the other hand, is best thought of as a disconnected, in-memory, relational data-store. Sure, you can treat it just like a disconnected Recordset, but to do so would be to waste the power that the DataSet has to offer. A DataSet holds tables of data and relationships between them. Using a DataSet, you could easily pull a complete table from one database, a subset of a table from another, and an XML document from a Web site, and then link them all together internally to allow you to navigate between them just as if you were using an incredibly powerful database. All this is done "disconnected." Connections are established to grab the data, obviously, but once it's been grabbed the connection is dropped. Where a DataReader is ideal for simply reading through a bunch of records from a database, a DataSet can also be used to modify those records and even create new ones. When you've finished making the changes you require, the DataSet can spawn a new dataset of only modified data that can then be passed back to the server for updating en masse. DataSets are an incredibly powerful addition to your database development arsenal.

In addition to all that, DataSets are able to output all their data as an XML document. This at last gives developers an easy way to pass what are actually very complex objects from one method to another, across machine and network boundaries. As you'll see later in the book, this includes the Internet, making use of the HTTP protocol to pass the XML representation of the DataSet between machines that could potentially be on different continents.

Let's see a simple DataSet in action. Fire up a new VB .NET console project and call it DatasetsExample. You need to be careful when naming your projects because if you named this project DataSet, the name of the project would conflict with the name of the DataSet class itself and cause all sorts of problems. Key the following code into the project to get a feel for how DataSets work (don't forget to change the server name in the connection string to match your own server name, as usual):

```
Option Strict On
Imports System.Data.SqlClient
Imports System.Console

Module Module1

    Sub Main()

        ' Just as always, set up the connection first.
        Dim dbConnection As SqlConnection = _
            New SqlConnection("Data Source=SARATOGA\VSTE;" + _
                "Integrated Security=sspi;" + _
                "Initial Catalog=Northwind")

        ' Similar to using a data reader, we need to build a
        ' command using our connection
        ' to grab the data we're interested in.
        Dim employeeCommand As SqlCommand = _
            New SqlCommand("SELECT * from Employees", _
                dbConnection)
```

```vb
' Now we can go ahead and create a data-adapter - this will
' be used to automatically
' populate our dataset.
Dim nwDataAdapter As SqlDataAdapter = _
    New SqlDataAdapter(employeeCommand)

Try
    WriteLine("Opening the database connection.")
    dbConnection.Open()

    Dim nwDataSet As DataSet = New DataSet()
    WriteLine("Filling the dataset.")
    nwDataAdapter.Fill(nwDataSet)
        dbConnection.Close()

    ' Even though the connection has been closed, we can
    ' still interrogate our
    ' dataset, and even navigate through it if necessary.
    WriteLine("The dataset contains " + _
        nwDataSet.Tables.Count.ToString() + " table(s).")
    WriteLine("The first datatable consists of " + _
        nwDataSet.Tables(0).Rows.Count.ToString() + _
        " rows, each holding " + _
        nwDataSet.Tables(0).Columns.Count.ToString() _
        + " columns of data:")

    ' Let's walk through the columns collection and find out a little more
    ' about them.
    Dim employeeColumn As DataColumn
    For Each employeeColumn In nwDataSet.Tables(0).Columns
        Write("    " + employeeColumn.ColumnName)
        WriteLine(" (" + employeeColumn.DataType.ToString() + ")")
    Next

    ' We can also walk through the rows collection and the
    ' columns collection
    ' together to print the value of every field in the table
    Dim employeeRow As DataRow
    For Each employeeRow In nwDataSet.Tables(0).Rows
        For Each employeeColumn In nwDataSet.Tables(0).Columns
            Write(employeeRow.Item(employeeColumn.Ordinal))
        Next
        WriteLine(" ")
    Next
```

```
        Catch ex As Exception
            WriteLine("An exception occurred...")
            WriteLine(ex.ToString)
        End Try

        WriteLine("Press Enter to continue")
        ReadLine()

    End Sub
End Module
```

The code starts off much the same as the DataReader example. It establishes a Connection object and then sets up a Command object to retrieve the data that you are interested in. It then goes on to create a DataAdapter, the key to using DataSets with actual databases (remember, DataSets can be created manually without the aid of a database of any kind).

```
' Now we can go ahead and create a data-adapter - this will be used
' to automatically
        ' populate our dataset.
        Dim nwDataAdapter As SqlDataAdapter = _
            New SqlDataAdapter(employeeCommand)
```

If a DataSet is a disconnected view of one or more tables, a DataAdapter is the conduit between the DataSet and the database. It provides data to the DataSet on demand and can also be used to manage every aspect of amending data, adding new records, and deleting records. This is particularly useful when you work with DataSets to build up a list of changes to data offline. The modified DataSet is fired back to the DataAdapter, which then decides whether the changes made constitute new records, deletions, or amendments, and runs an appropriate stored procedure or block of SQL code.

Just as with the other objects in ADO.NET, the constructor of the DataAdapter is overloaded. In the example here, when the DataAdapter is created it is passed a prebuilt Command object used to select data. Since the Command object not only contains the query to run, but also a link to the database connection to run the query against, the DataAdapter is now completely configured to hit a specific database and grab data from it.

When a single command is passed to a DataAdapter constructor, that Command object is assumed to return a set of rows and will be used for selecting data. However, you can also create a DataAdapter and send the constructor the string of a SQL query and a Connection object; you don't actually need to create a Command object if you really don't want to (I do in the example for completeness).

In fact, you can even just send two strings to the DataAdapter's constructor: The first is the SQL query to use, and the second is the connection string. The DataAdapter will then be responsible for setting up the Connection object and the Command object internally.

Back to the example code. Having created the connection, command, and DataAdapter, the next step is to actually go ahead and build the DataSet.

```
Try
        WriteLine("Opening the database connection.")
        dbConnection.Open()

        Dim nwDataSet As DataSet = New DataSet()
        WriteLine("Filling the dataset.")
        nwDataAdapter.Fill(nwDataSet)
            dbConnection.Close()
```

Since I created the connection in the first place (instead of deferring to the Adapter to do it for me), I'm also responsible for manually opening and closing the connection, as you can see at the beginning and end of the preceding code block. I shouldn't just throw that past you in a blasé way, though—one of the most wonderful features of a DataSet is the fact that it lets you work with data in a disconnected way, so that dbConnection.Close() call at the end of the block really is a big deal. You open the connection, tell the Adapter to Fill() your DataSet, and then close the connection down. It's no longer needed. All the data you need now lives in your DataSet object completely separate from the connection, so you're free to return that connection to the connection pool for another user to make use of.

The call to Fill() is all that's required to completely build your DataSet. When the routine returns, the DataSet will come back with a single DataTable (another ADO.NET object that you'll look at shortly) populated with the results of the select query. It's worth noting, though, that Fill()'s use is not limited to building a brand-new DataSet. It's a wonderful method that can be used to refresh a DataSet as well. If the DataSet passed to the Fill() method already has data inside, the DataAdapter will run the Select query and then check the DataSet's existing data to see if any of it needs to be refreshed as a result of changes to the database since you last grabbed it.

Fill() is also overloaded. You can pass in a DataSet and a DataReader to the method if you so choose, and the DataAdapter will then quite happily use the DataReader to populate or refresh the DataSet. You can even specify specific tables inside the DataSet to populate with the data. For example, you may want to grab a list of employees from three or four different databases. By passing in the name of a table along with the DataSet, you can ensure that a bunch of DataAdapters all feed their data into the one table inside the DataSet.

There are a great many options open to you when working with DataAdapters, and you'll cover them all in full as you work through the next chapter.

So, you've got your populated DataSet now. What does it contain and how do you examine it? That's where the next block of code comes in.

```
Dim employeeColumn As DataColumn
        For Each employeeColumn In nwDataSet.Tables(0).Columns
            Write("     " + employeeColumn.ColumnName)
            WriteLine(" (" + employeeColumn.DataType.ToString() + ")")
        Next
```

A DataSet consists of DataTables, usually one for each different query you run. You can, of course, also create your own and populate them manually with code. Given how object oriented .NET as a whole is, DataTables are a dream to work with. Each DataTable consists of a collection of DataColumns and a collection of DataRows. You can use the DataColumn collection to find out more about the structure (aka schema) of a DataTable, and you can use the DataRows to get at the actual data in the table.

In the preceding block of code, a simple For-Each loop iterates through the Columns collection of the first table in the DataSet. In the example here, there is only one table in the DataSet, so it's safe to simply refer to the table as table number 0. You can also find the specific DataTable you need by referring to it by name.

For each column in the DataTable, the code just writes out the name of the column and then calls the column's DataType object to write out the data type used for that column.

Navigating through rows in a DataTable is very similar.

```
Dim employeeRow As DataRow
        For Each employeeRow In nwDataSet.Tables(0).Rows
            For Each employeeColumn In nwDataSet.Tables(0).Columns
                Write(employeeRow.Item(employeeColumn.Ordinal))
            Next
            WriteLine(" ")
        Next
```

Here you just iterate through the rows, and for each row write out each column. Notice how the columns all have an Ordinal property to get their ordinal position in the table. This is used in the example to tell each row exactly which item of data on that row you are interested in.

The big thing to note when working with DataSets is just how object oriented everything is. You work with rows as first-class .NET objects. This, of course, means that you can change their data, just as if you were changing properties of any other object. In the next chapter you'll explore the further capabilities of the

DataAdapter and the DataSet to see how to manage XML data, as well as handle updates, additions, and deletions to rows of data.

You should have the very basics of DataSets down now, but there is still much to learn. Remember, DataSets can represent themselves as XML documents, and they can even build themselves from an XML document. There's also the small matter of setting up relational links between different DataTables in a DataSet, as well as the opportunities afforded to you by being able to create tables, rows, and columns in code to build a DataSet without a database in sight. These are just some of the topics you'll dive into in the next chapter.

Summary

As the title promised, this chapter explored the fundamentals of working with ADO.NET. You've seen how to establish a connection to your database, set up a database project, and obtain data through both a DataReader and a DataSet. You've also touched on DataTables and DataAdapters.

You've only scratched the surface, though. You should have enough information now to connect to any SQL Server–compliant database and run rudimentary queries on the data, but in the next chapter you'll take things to the next level. In Chapter 3, I'll cover the GUI components available to those of you working on the Windows desktop with ADO.NET applications, and I'll also delve into much greater detail with DataTables, DataAdapters, DataRelations, and the all-powerful DataSet.

CHAPTER 3

Data Commands
and DataReaders

"Computers are anti-Faraday machines. He said he couldn't understand anything until he could count it, while computers count everything and understand nothing."

—Ralph Cornes, 1991

I FIRMLY BELIEVE that dealing with the data-access part of an application is as complex a task as any other field of software engineering. You often see on writers' bios and at the bottom of resumes the statement that so-and-so is "a data-access specialist" in addition to his or her many other talents in the field of software production. I'm one for advocating a whole new title for those that specialize in data access. They shouldn't be called programmers, but should instead call themselves "shapers of data," or "grand magi of the information ether."

My reasoning for this is quite simple. It's dead easy for anyone to connect to a database with any modern development tool, grab some data, and then present it on screen for the user to play with. However, diving beneath the surface and exploring every nuance of working with data-access architectures, database schemas, and the sheer wealth of possibilities offered by even the most modern data access API is something normally left to the programming deities.

In the last chapter you did that with which most developers would be content. I showed you how to connect to a database, run a query or two, and then work with the results, all at a very high level. In this chapter and the next I'll start you on journey to deity status as you dive into extreme detail on every aspect of working with Data Commands and DataReaders. In the next chapter you'll dive even deeper and explore the fantastic world of the mighty DataSet and friends.

Why Use Data Commands and DataReaders?

Regardless of whether you choose to use DataSets or DataReaders in ADO.NET, the fundamental approach to obtaining data from a database remains the same. You establish a connection, do something over that connection, and then close the connection. The difference between the two approaches really comes down to just how long you want to have that connection open.

The DataReader approach requires that the connection be held open for as long as you need to work with the data exposed by the DataReader. It figures that if your application has to undertake a considerable amount of processing on each record in the Reader, then the connection will also be held open for a considerable amount of time. In addition, the Command object used to fill the DataReader will only get to complete its processing when the Reader is closed down. At that point, the Command will update the **RecordsAffected** property of the Reader and also fill in any output parameters in the command. This process alone can take some time if the query being used is large or complex.

So, if the downside to using Readers is the length of time they can hold a connection open, why use them at all? More important, when is the right time to use them?

It's all a question of balance. The alternative to using a DataReader is to rely on the all-powerful DataSet to give you a view of data that can be manipulated, inter-rogated, and navigated while disconnected from the data source. However, creating a DataSet can be a lengthy process in itself, and since the very nature of a DataSet is to provide you with an "in-memory" representation of one or more tables of data, it can also be quite system-resource intensive. A DataReader, on the other hand, is fast to create, can be extremely fast to run (you can cancel the command to prevent it doing its normal cleanup when the Reader closes), and is very light in terms of the amount of memory and system resources it needs.

So, the choice of DataReader over DataSet is initially one of preference. Additionally, DataReaders are ideally suited to certain types of applications. A Web service, for example, is created when a method is called and destroyed when the method returns. If only a small amount of processing is needed per row of data, then a DataReader is ideal for this type of solution; in the worst case, the connection to the data source will only be held open for as long as the Web service method is running. The same applies to ASP.NET and Web Forms solutions. They too are created and destroyed on demand, but additionally they could have a vast number of clients using them. So, resources are in scarce supply and runtimes are necessarily small—ideal ground for the DataReader, I think you'll agree.

Finally, if you have come to ADO.NET from an ADO background, then DataReaders can be an ideal way into the world of ADO.NET; the way they work bears a close resemblance to the Recordsets of old.

To summarize, you use a DataReader if

- Resources on the machine executing the code are scarce (many clients, for example).

- The time spent processing the rows of data will be short.

- You only want to grab a single "table" of information.

- You don't want the overhead that comes with a multitable, in-memory database alongside your application.

Command objects, on the other hand, are not optional. Regardless of whether you choose to go with a DataReader or a DataSet, you are going to have to use Command objects. There is a closer link between a Command object and a DataReader than there is between a Command object and a DataSet, hence the reason this chapter covers DataReaders and Commands together.

Data Commands

There are a number of core objects in ADO.NET—objects that you simply can't do without if you intend to do any data-access development. **Connection** would be one, since without a connection you can't access a database in the first place. Data Command is another. A Data Command is an object representing a query or stored procedure. I use the word "query" here since it's easier to write over and over than "SQL statement," but what I mean is, of course, a block of text in your code that comprises a valid SQL statement.

Data providers in ADO.NET are required to implement a Data Command in order to run queries and stored procedures against a database. To do so, the author of a data provider implements the IDbCommand interface in one of its own objects, as shown in Figure 3-1.

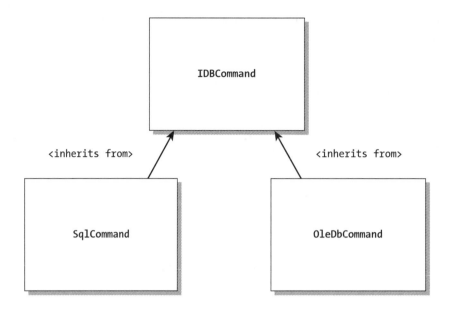

Figure 3-1. All data providers must provide a Data Command object that implements IDbCommand.

With the two data providers that come with VS .NET, you have two Data Commands: SqlCommand and OleDbCommand. Both inherit from IDbCommand, and thus both function the same way (allowing, of course, for the differences in the syntax of a query on the various different OLE DB–compliant databases out there). As before, I'll focus on the SQL Server data provider here (all you OLE DB fans out there, don't panic—Chapter 10 covers the differences between the two providers).

Why Is a Command an Object?

It may seem strange at first that we have a command as an object. In fact, that's a feeling one gets initially looking throughout ADO.NET: Everything is an object. After all, why not just open a connection and provide us all with a method on the connection to issue queries and run stored procedures?

The object approach actually makes a lot of sense. You can set up a whole bunch of Command objects in code to run a set of recurring stored procedures and prepared (compiled) queries, and use them as and when needed, without repeatedly incurring the cost of setting up each call separately.

The properties of the Command object also make it a snap to easily change the way that a command runs and very simply get at the return results for nonqueries and scalar queries. You can set up a parameterized query and then repeatedly fire it at the database, just changing a parameter property on the fly. After a while, it seems strange to even think of running queries against a database without using an object to represent the query.

Of course, if you're fresh from the world of ADO, then you already know what I'm talking about; queries are objects in ADO as well.

Running Nonqueries

In the examples so far, I've used Command objects to issue pure queries to the database, SQL statements that select rows of data and then expose those rows of data through DataReaders and DataSets. There will be times when you'll want to issue queries against the database that don't actually return rows of data, though—queries that may delete, update, or even insert new rows. In ADO.NET-speak, these are known as *nonqueries,* and they are executed by calling **ExecuteNonQuery()** on the Command object in question.

Start up a new VB console project (call it NonQueries), and key in the following code. Don't forget to change the server name to match your own database server's name.

```
Option Strict On
Imports System.Data.SqlClient
Imports System.Console

Module Module1

    Sub Main()

        Dim con As SqlConnection = New SqlConnection( _
            "Data Source=SARATOGA\VSTE;Initial Catalog=Northwind;" + _
            "Integrated Security=SSPI")

        Dim command As SqlCommand = New SqlCommand( _
            "UPDATE Customers SET Country='United Kingdom' WHERE Country='UK'", _
            con)

        Try
            con.Open()

            WriteLine("Rows affects = " + command.ExecuteNonQuery().ToString())
```

```
        command.CommandText = "UPDATE Customers SET Country='UK' " + _
            "WHERE Country='United Kingdom'"
        WriteLine("Resetting data - rows affected = " + _
            command.ExecuteNonQuery().ToString())

        con.Close()
    Catch ex As Exception
        WriteLine("An error occurred... " + ex.ToString())
    End Try

    WriteLine("Press Enter to exit.")
    ReadLine()
End Sub

End Module
```

I'm not going to walk through the whole source, since by now you should be familiar with how to establish a database connection and open it, and why you need to close it when you're done. I've highlighted the most important lines of code in bold. Let's take a closer look.

First up, a SqlCommand object is created, using the Connection object previously defined and the text of the nonquery in the constructor:

```
Dim command As SqlCommand = New SqlCommand( _
            "UPDATE Customers SET Country='United Kingdom' WHERE Country='UK'", _
            con)
```

This is obviously a nonquery. It simply changes the country of any customer in the Northwind database from UK to United Kingdom. You wouldn't expect this SQL statement to return any rows of data to you.

As you can see from the first call to **ExecuteNonQuery()**, a result is returned, and in this case it's written out to the console as text.

```
WriteLine("Rows affects = " + command.ExecuteNonQuery().ToString())
```

When working with SQL statements that Update, Insert, or Delete, SQL Server and MSDE both return a count of the number of rows affected by the query. In the case of any other query (such as a nonquery stored procedure) the result is –1. So, running the command the first time through should cause an integer to return specifying just how many customers got updated.

I could have ended the program there, but it's always a good thing when working with the sample databases to put them back the way you found them. Doing so in this case also provides me with a great opportunity to show you a little more about the workings of the SqlCommand object.

Typically, you'd specify the SQL statement you want to run as part of the call to the SqlCommand's constructor. However, you can change and set up the SQL text after the SqlCommand has been created by modifying the **CommandText** property:

```
command.CommandText = "UPDATE Customers SET Country='UK' " + _
                "WHERE Country='United Kingdom'"
WriteLine("Resetting data - rows affected = " + _
                command.ExecuteNonQuery().ToString())
```

Here, even though the command has already been run, it's quite valid to just fire in some new SQL into the Command Text property and then tell the command to run again. In this case, the new SQL statement puts the data back just the way it was when you started and again outputs the number of rows affected to the console. Just as you would expect, if everything's fine, you should see the same row count appear for each call, as you can see in Figure 3-2.

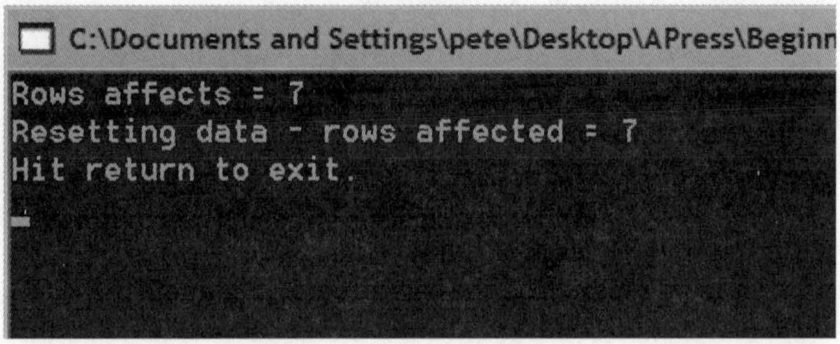

Figure 3-2. Two different nonqueries running through the same SqlCommand object

Running Scalar Queries

ADO.NET's Command objects also support execution of *scalar queries*. These are similar to nonqueries, in that they don't return a set of rows that needs navigating. They differ from nonqueries in that they do return a value that needs to be interrogated. You may have a stored procedure that outputs a single value, for example, to give you a unique key for a new record. A more common example, though, is the Count aggregate function, which is used in SQL queries to return a count of the number of records meeting a specific criterion:

```
SELECT Count(*) FROM Customers WHERE Country='UK'
```

Scalar queries can be run by calling **ExecuteScalar()** on the SqlCommand object. What actually happens is that the function returns the value of the first column of the first row of data returned. This means that if you wanted to, you could execute a standard selection query as a scalar one without any side effects (other than the hugely inefficient use of bandwidth). ExecuteScalar() actually returns an object, so it's up to you to cast it to the appropriate type if the scalar query returns anything more intricate than a simple integer.

Start up a new project (call this one ScalarQueries) and type this lot in (once again, don't forget to change the name of the server to match your own):

```vbnet
Option Strict On
Imports System.Data.SqlClient
Imports System.Console

Module Module1

    Sub Main()

        Dim con As SqlConnection = New SqlConnection( _
            "Data Source=SARATOGA\VSTE;Initial Catalog=Northwind;" + _
            "Integrated Security=SSPI")

        Dim command As SqlCommand = New SqlCommand( _
            "SELECT Count(*) FROM Customers WHERE Country='UK'", _
            con)

        Try
            con.Open()

            WriteLine("There are " + _
                command.ExecuteScalar().ToString() + _
                " customers in the UK in the database.")

            con.Close()
        Catch ex As Exception
            WriteLine("An error occurred... " + ex.ToString())
        End Try

        WriteLine("Press Enter to exit.")
        ReadLine()
    End Sub
End Module
```

Once again, I've highlighted the most interesting lines in the code in bold.

Working with Parameters

Parameterized queries are a staple of most data-access development; rare is the live database stored procedure that doesn't require parameters. Additionally, while it is possible to do some tedious string tweaking to build up a SQL statement including all the parameters to the query in the actual SQL statement, it's much more elegant to use parameter objects.

For those that haven't used them before, a parameterized query looks like this:

```
SELECT CompanyName, City FROM Customers WHERE Country = @CountryCode
```

In this statement, @CountryCode is a placeholder. It allows you to show SQL Server the format of the query and tell it that there will be an additional value passed in, called @CountryCode, that should be substituted for the text @CountryCode in the query.

In ADO.NET, parameters are objects. Within the SQL Server data provider, they are SqlParameter objects. ADO.NET takes a straightforward, commonsense approach to working with the parameters to a command. Since you always issue commands to SQL Server through a SqlCommand object, parameters belonging to the command are held in a collection called, appropriately enough, Parameters. This collection consists of a set of SqlParameter objects—one for each parameter in the command. Despite the commonsense approach adopted by ADO.NET, the current version does not automatically add objects to the Parameters collection based on the contents of the SQL statement in the Command object; you need to add parameters to the collection manually.

You can achieve this in two ways. The first, and perhaps more traditional, approach is to create the SqlParameter objects themselves and then add them to the collection. This is easy enough since the constructor of a SqlParameter object is overloaded in a variety of useful ways.

```
Dim myParameter as SqlParameter = New SqlParameter( "param1", SqlDbType.VarChar)
Dim myParameter as SqlParameter = New SqlParameter("param1", SqlDbType.VarChar, 15)
Dim myParameter as SqlParameter = New SqlParameter("param1",  myObject)
```

There are actually five ways to use the SqlParameter constructor, but I've only listed three here; the other two refer to **RowVersions**, something you'll cover in the next chapter when you dive into DataSets in more detail.

The various constructor formats are actually pretty easy to use and somewhat self-explanatory. The first one creates a SqlParameter object and assigns it a name, and specifies the data type of the parameter. Notice that the types are chosen from the SqlDbType enumeration.

The second constructor call does the same as the first, but it uses an integer as a final parameter to specify the maximum size of the parameter. This is extremely handy and gets around the problem of having code cause SQL Server errors by passing in too much data for a parameter. By defining the type and size of the SqlParameter when it's created, ADO.NET is able to truncate the data before passing it over the wire to SQL Server.

The final constructor is actually the most commonly used format. It gives the parameter object a name and a reference to another object. This object is used as the value of the parameter and is the value passed to SQL Server at runtime. With the other two constructors, you are forced to manually set the **Value** property of the SqlParameter to the object you wish to pass to the database.

Having created your parameter, the next step is to add it into the Parameters collection of your SqlCommand object, a simple enough exercise:

```
myCommand.Parameters.Add( myParameter )
```

What could be easier? Well, just calling Add() and doing away with all that object creation malarkey would be a heck of a lot easier.

The Parameters member of a SqlCommand object is a collection, but not a standard one. It is actually an object of type SqlParameterCollection. SqlParameterCollection implements the IList and ICollection interfaces from the .NET Framework in order to work just like any other collection you might use in your .NET programming, but it also overloads the Add method.

 **New to .NET**

IList and ICollection are two interfaces. *Interfaces* are nothing scary—they are simply empty classes that exist for no other reason than to be implemented by other classes. In the case of IList and ICollection, the interfaces define all the methods and properties that another class would need to contain in order to be considered a list or collection. SqlParameterCollection implements both these interfaces and so can be treated as either a list of parameters or a collection of parameters in your code—the choice of which interface to rely on is up to you. Take a look in the online help in Visual Studio .NET for more information on these powerful interfaces and how to work with classes that implement them.

Instead of just Add()ing an object to the collection, Add() is overloaded to accept the same parameters as the SqlParameter's constructor. The overloaded Add() methods will create the SqlParameter object for you and return it in order for you to work with the Parameter's other properties. For example:

```
Dim myParameter as SqlParameter
MyParameter = myCommand.Parameters.Add( "paramname", objectToPass )
System.Console.WriteLine( myParameter.Value.ToString() )
```

In summary, then, once you have a parameterized SqlCommand set up, it's trivial to add in the SqlParameter objects to the command's Parameters collection.

Time now to see this all in action. Fire up a new VB console project (call this one QueryParameters). The code for the module looks like this (you haven't forgotten that you need to change the server name to run on your machine, have you?):

```
Option Strict On
Imports System.Data.SqlClient
Imports System.Console

Module Module1
    Sub Main()

        ' First up, set up the connection and command
        dim connection as SqlConnection = _
            New SqlConnection("Data Source=SARATOGA\VSTE;" + _
            "Initial Catalog=Northwind;Integrated Security=SSPI")
        Dim command As SqlCommand = New SqlCommand( _
            "SELECT COUNT(*) FROM Customers WHERE Country = @Country", _
            connection)

    Try
        ' Open our connection ready to go
        connection.Open()

        Dim customerCount As Integer

        ' Add the @Country parameter to the parameter list,
        ' with a value of "UK"
        command.Parameters.Add("@Country", "UK")

        'Run the query and grab the result
        customerCount = CType(command.ExecuteScalar(), Integer)
        WriteLine("There are " + customerCount.ToString() + _
            " customers in the UK")
```

```
            ' Now change that @Country parameter's value - you can refer
            ' to a SqlParameter in the Parameters collection by name
            command.Parameters("@Country").Value = "Germany"
            customerCount = CType(command.ExecuteScalar(), Integer)
            WriteLine("and there are " + _
              customerCount.ToString() + _
              " customers in Germany")

            ' Finally, don't forget to close down that connection
            connection.Close()

        Catch ex As Exception
            WriteLine("There was a problem with the code..." + _
                ex.ToString())
        End Try

        Console.ReadLine()

    End Sub

End Module
```

Take a look through the code, and pay special attention to the bold lines; it's all commented and so shouldn't be too difficult to decipher.

The first thing to notice is the SQL statement itself:

```
SELECT COUNT(*) FROM Customers WHERE Country = @Country
```

It's a simple scalar query that counts the number of customers in a given country, the name of the country being supplied as a parameter. The important thing to note is that even though the at (@) symbol is used in the SQL Server data provider to specify where a parameter lives, it's also included as part of the parameter's name. Take a look at the code that adds the parameter to the Command to see what I mean:

```
command.Parameters.Add("@Country", "UK")
```

As you can see, the name of the parameter is @Country, not simply Country. This is important because the name is used to match the parameter not only in the query, but also for you to refer to the parameter from the Parameters collection by name. You can see this in the code. After the parameter has been added and the query run, the parameter is changed. More specifically, its value is changed, and the query is run again:

```
command.Parameters("@Country").Value = "Germany"
```

 New to .NET

There's an important thing to note about how this code works, if you are new to .NET. The Value property of the SqlParameter class is actually defined as a generic object. The code shown here, though, sets a string into the property. In .NET everything, without exception, is an object. By setting the value property to "Germany," I'm actually creating a string object and assigning it to the property. This is, of course, different from the old VB way of doing things, where a string is an integral data type and not a complex object.

The same would apply if I had set the Value property to 12. An integer object would have been created whose value would be 12, and it would be assigned to the Value property.

By default, parameters that you create are input parameters; they feed values "into" a stored procedure or query. Some queries use parameters as both input and output values, and others use parameters simply to return data to the caller. The "direction" of a parameter can be controlled using the SqlParameter's **Direction** property. It can be set to **ParameterDirection.Input**, **ParameterDirection.Ouptut**, **ParameterDirection.InputOutput** or **ParameterDirection.Return.**

Output, InputOutput, and Return parameters are all set when the Reader is closed, or immediately upon the SqlCommand finishing its ExecuteScalar or ExecuteNonQuery calls. You can get at the values of these parameters using the Value property you saw earlier.

Other Parameter Properties

There are other properties attached to a SqlParameter object that may come in handy from time to time, especially if you want your code to make use of the extensive data-checking facilities that ADO.NET automatically provides when setting up the specific type and attributes of parameters.

You've already seen how to specify the data type of a parameter at creation time. This can also be controlled through the **DbType** and **SqlDbType** properties.

Both are actually linked. Setting a value into DbType specifies the .NET data type to be used for a parameter. Setting a value into SqlDbType sets up the data type that SQL Server expects a parameter to hold. They are linked in that if you set one up, the other is automatically set up for you. Not only does setting these properties help in terms of checking the data that you set into a parameter, but ADO.NET will also more easily be able to convert a value entered into a parameter into the type of value that the database expects. If, on the other hand, you don't set one of these properties up, ADO.NET will imply the data type to use based on the type of the value set into the parameter at runtime. Obviously, this can cause problems if you inadvertently set a value of an illegal type into a SqlParameter object.

You can find a complete list of valid values that can be set into these properties in the Visual Studio online help under "DbType Enumeration," "SqlDbType Enumeration," and "OleDbType Enumeration" (for those of you with a hankering to work with the OLE DB data provider).

Aside from specifying the data type of a parameter, the SqlParameter class also provides properties to control the exact size and scope of the data.

When you work with numeric parameters, the **Scale** and **Precision** properties control the resolution and size of numeric values passed through the parameter. Scale is used to set up the number of decimal places to use, and Precision specifies the number of digits to the left of the decimal point, as a maximum.

For non-numeric data, **Offset** and **Size** come in handy. Offset returns the actual size of the parameter's value in bytes for nontext parameters or characters for textual parameters. Size is used to set up the maximum allowable size of the value (again in bytes for nontextual parameters and characters for textual ones).

Stored Procedures

Stored procedures are a fantastic way of separating business rules out from the application. As I'm sure most of you know, a *stored procedure* is a SQL statement (query, nonquery) precompiled and stored on the database server. Since the code is precompiled, it is processed faster than issuing a query direct from a command. Additionally, using stored procedures means that the code in your application need only know the stored procedure's name in order to run it. The actual SQL code behind it is safely tucked away in the database where it can be upgraded and maintained without forcing all the users to endure an upgrade of the application every time a simple bit of SQL needs changing.

Using stored procedures in ADO.NET is stunningly simple. You create a Sql-Command object, just the same as always, but instead of dropping a bunch of SQL into the command when it's constructed (or through its CommandText property), you simply specify the name of the stored procedure that needs to run on the server. If the stored procedure makes use of parameters, those parameters need to be added to the SqlCommand's Parameters collection just as before. The only difference that you need to be aware of when working with stored procedures is that you'll need to tell the command that you are about to run a stored procedure. This is handled by the **CommandType** property.

Let's take a look.

```vb
Option Strict On
Imports System.Data.SqlClient
Imports System.Console

Module Module1

    Sub Main()
        Dim connection As SqlConnection = New SqlConnection( _
            "Data Source=SARATOGA\VSTE;" + _
            "Initial Catalog=Northwind;Integrated Security=SSPI")
        Dim command As SqlCommand = _
            New SqlCommand("Employee Sales By Country", _
            connection)
        command.CommandType = CommandType.StoredProcedure

        Try
            command.Parameters.Add("@Beginning_Date", #7/1/1996#)
            command.Parameters.Add("@Ending_Date", #8/1/1996#)

            connection.Open()

            Dim reader As SqlDataReader = command.ExecuteReader()

            Dim nIndex As Integer

            Do While reader.Read()
                For nIndex = 0 To reader.FieldCount - 1
                    Write(reader.GetValue(nIndex).ToString + " ")
                Next
                WriteLine("")
            Loop

            reader.Close()
            connection.Close()
```

```
        Catch ex As Exception
            WriteLine("There was a problem with the code..." + _
                ex.ToString())
        End Try

        WriteLine("All done - press Enter to exit")
        ReadLine()

    End Sub

End Module
```

The code is simple enough; it sets up a SqlCommand object, opens the connection to the database, and runs a stored procedure called "Employee Sales By Country." That stored procedure also takes two parameters (which I'm sure you are sick to death of now) and needs to set them up before it runs. A SqlDataReader is returned, and this is used to print out every field of the resulting records on the console.

The key to this whole program is just one line of code:

```
command.CommandType = CommandType.StoredProcedure
```

This line tells the SqlCommand that you are going to run a stored procedure. By default, a SqlCommand expects to contain a SQL statement. So, if that line of code were missing, the program would bomb with an error, since "Employee Sales By Country" is not a valid SQL statement. Telling the command that you are calling a stored procedure ensures that the code is not checked for errors until it hits the database.

For those of you wondering just how on earth I figured out what the names of the parameters to the stored procedure were, just double-click the stored procedure's name in the Server Explorer and the code behind the stored procedure will be shown in all its glory.

Incidentally, while I'm on the subject, there is a halfway house (in terms of performance) between a SQL statement embedded in a command and a stored procedure. It's called a *prepared statement.*

When you embed SQL inside a SQL command, that SQL code is checked and compiled each and every time the command is executed. Obviously, if you intend to rerun a command over and over, the hit in performance could be substantial. A stored procedure gets around that problem by having the code stored in and precompiled on the database. You can, however, precompile a standard SQL statement. All that's required is a call to the SqlCommand's **Prepare**() method. This will compile the SQL statement and flag the command as being "prepared." The SQL code will no longer be compiled each and every time the command is executed, but will instead just run.

More on DataReaders

You took a brief look at the SqlDataReader back in the last chapter and saw how easy it is to get data out of a database and navigate it. There's a lot more that the DataReader can do, though, so this section will fill in the holes.

It's easy to think of the SqlDataReader as a single object that provides a convenient mechanism to navigate through rows of data (the Read() method). That's only half the story. SqlDataReader actually implements three very useful interfaces, as you can see in Figure 3-3.

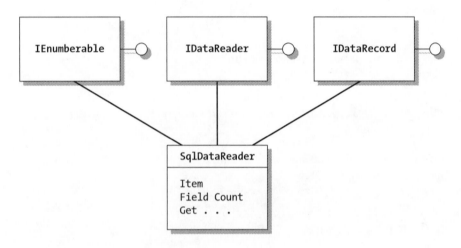

Figure 3-3. The key interfaces exposed by the SqlDataReader

The ability to navigate from row to row, as well as from result set to result set, is provided by the IDataReader interface. As you move to a new row of information, the values of the columns in that row can be examined through the properties exposed by the IDataRecord interface. In addition to all that, though, the fact that the SqlDataReader object exposes the IEnumerable interface means that you are not limited to navigating through records in a nasty, old-fashioned Do-While Read() loop. You can iterate through the records with a nice, new For-Each loop, with each element in the loop being returned as a DbDataRecord object (an generic database object that also implements IDataRecord), as shown in Figure 3-4.

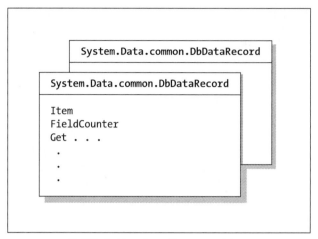

SqlDataReader Enumeration

Figure 3-4. Running For-Each over a SqlDataReader lets you walk through the DbDataRecord objects that together form a result set exposed by the Reader.

You can see the effect this has on code with a simple example (the results are shown in Figure 3-5):

```
Option Strict On
Imports System.Data.SqlClient
Imports System.Console

Module Module1
    Sub Main()

        Dim connection As SqlConnection = New SqlConnection( _
            "Data Source=SARATOGA\VSTE;" + _
             "Initial Catalog=Northwind;" + _
             "Integrated Security=SSPI")

        Dim command As SqlCommand = New SqlCommand( _
            "SELECT * FROM Employees", connection)

        Try
            connection.Open()
            Dim reader As SqlDataReader = command.ExecuteReader()

            WriteLine("Iterating through the Employee records")
```

```vbnet
        ' Declare a DBDataRecord object so that we can easily iterate the rows
        ' in the SqlDataReader.
        Dim dataRecord As Common.DbDataRecord

        ' Isn't this so much nicer than that nasty
        ' old Do While reader.Read() loop
        For Each dataRecord In reader
            WriteLine(dataRecord.GetValue(1).ToString() + " " + _
        dataRecord.GetValue(2).ToString())
        Next

        reader.Close()
        connection.Close()

    Catch ex As Exception
        WriteLine("There was a problem with the code... " + ex.ToString())
    End Try
    WriteLine("All done. Press Enter to exit")
    ReadLine()

    End Sub
End Module
```

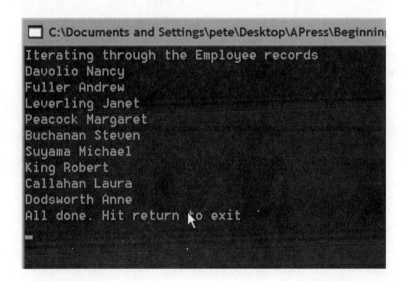

Figure 3-5. Iterating records by running For-Each over a SqlDataReader

Using this technique, you can do away with the Do-While loops of old, and instead iterate through the rows with a nice For-Each loop. The bold lines show how; just declare an object of type **System.Data.Common.DbDataRecord** and then use that to For-Each over the Reader. The result will be a loop that reads every single row of data exposed by the Reader.

Notice how the code to actually print out the field values hasn't really changed from the last chapter when you did use the Do-While approach. The DbDataRecord object implements the IDataRecord interface, just the same as the SqlDataReader. This is actually the interface that's used to give the DataReader its Get…() methods and the FieldCount property to find out how many fields are in a row.

When you use Read() on a Reader to move to the next row of data, the Reader updates an internal DbDataRecord object. When you call the Get…() methods on the Reader, these are simply passed down to the internal DbDataRecord object. Using a For-Each loop to iterate the DbDataRecords then is not only more elegant, it's also more efficient.

Data Types

Remember the discussion about data types back when you were looking at the SqlCommand object? If you do, you may recall that I said that ADO.NET will automatically convert data from a database into a valid .NET type for use in your code. The DataReader (or, more precisely, the IDataRecord interface it exposes) has a member called Item. This is really little more than an array of .NET CTS-compliant objects, one for each column of data. You can find out just how many columns are in the current row using the FieldCount property of either the DataReader or a DataRecord, and then simply pull items out of the Item array using the appropriate Index number. It's then quite easy to ask the object to tell you its type. Try out this block of code to see what I mean:

```
Option Strict On
Imports System.Data.SqlClient
Imports System.Console

Module Module1
    Sub Main()
        Dim connection As SqlConnection = New SqlConnection( _
            "Data Source=SARATOGA\VSTE;" + _
            "Initial Catalog=Northwind;" + _
            "Integrated Security=SSPI")
```

```
        Dim command As SqlCommand = New SqlCommand( _
            "SELECT * FROM Employees", connection)

    Try
        connection.Open()
        Dim reader As SqlDataReader = command.ExecuteReader()

        WriteLine("Data types in the Employee table")

        ' The reader needs to be positioned on a valid row in order to
        ' interrogate the columns in that row, so we need to do a Read()
        reader.Read()



        ' Loop through the items in the result set. FieldCount tells us how
        ' many items there are, but the items are referenced starting at item 0
        Dim itemIndex As Integer
        For itemIndex = 0 To reader.FieldCount - 1
            WriteLine(reader.Item(itemIndex).GetType().ToString)
        Next

        reader.Close()
        connection.Close()

    Catch ex As Exception
        WriteLine("There was a problem with the code... " + ex.ToString())
    End Try
    WriteLine("All done. Press Enterto exit")
    ReadLine()
    End Sub
End Module
```

As you can see if you run the code (see Figure 3-6), each column is actually
converted into a standard .NET type and exposed through the Item property. This
allows you to get at the data directly rather than having to go through the Get...()
method calls (GetInt(), GetString() and so on). Why would you want to do this?
Well, it all comes down knowing the data that you are working with. Most developers are fully aware of the data types a particular query is going to give them.
However, there are occasions when you don't. You may be developing a generic
data explorer and thus have no idea just what queries the user is going to run or
what format the results of those queries will take. Since the DataReader exposes
the columns of a row as standard CTS types, you can use standard .NET type

manipulation code to find out what types of data are in a row, and then deal with them accordingly.

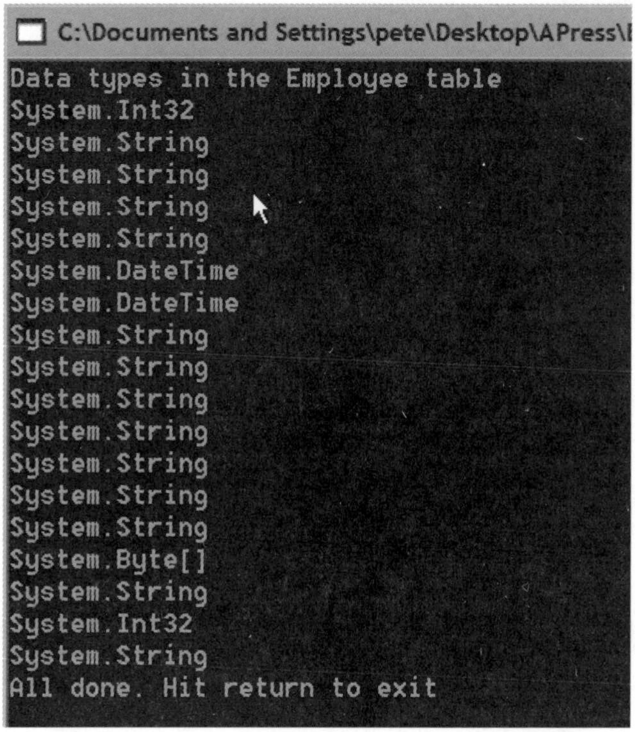

```
C:\Documents and Settings\pete\Desktop\APress\
Data types in the Employee table
System.Int32
System.String
System.String
System.String
System.String
System.DateTime
System.DateTime
System.String
System.String
System.String
System.String
System.String
System.String
System.String
System.Byte[]
System.String
System.Int32
System.String
All done. Hit return to exit
```

Figure 3-6. Using the Item property to get directly at the data in a row

Using the Get...() methods is more appropriate, though, in most applications. Making an explicit call to, for example, GetInt() shows the readers of your code that you're explicitly asking for an integer from a specific column. If the data isn't an integer and can't be converted, you'll get an exception; such an occurrence could, after all, constitute a serious bug in your code (expecting an int when actually your column is an array of bytes), and so an exception is the most appropriate course of action to take. Directly accessing columns through the Item property puts the onus on you to do the type conversion from generic object to specific CTS type and can overcomplicate the code.

Obviously, the Get...() methods and the Item property have another big limitation. They return to you column values, not column information. If you were writing a generic data-management tool, then you'd probably want to know more information about the actual schema that sits behind your rows of data. That's where a method called **GetSchemaTable**() comes in. GetSchemaTable returns a

DataTable object, a new ADO.NET object that provides you with highly detailed information about the actual definition of the columns in the database. You can find out the column names, sizes, whether they are part of a key, whether they are autoincrementing numbers, and much more besides. I'm not going to go into any detail on DataTables just yet, though—I cover them extensively in the next chapter.

Summary

As far as Commands and Readers go, you now pretty much know it all. As I mentioned earlier, there are some elements that I've glossed over here (notably the two other ways to construct a command and a description of what a DataTable object is), but by and large you're good to go. Among other things, you learned

- A new way to iterate through the rows of data in your Reader

- How to run parameterized queries

- How to run stored procedures

- How to work with every aspect of a parameter in a query

- How to run nonqueries

- How to work with scalar queries

In the next chapter you'll take all of this one step further as you dive deep into the mighty DataSet object. While the Reader is useful and certainly has its place, it's the DataSet object that really shows just what ADO.NET can do.

CHAPTER 4

DataSets Inside Out: Tables

"What is the use of a book," thought Alice, "without pictures or conversations?"

—Lewis Carroll, *Alice's Adventures in Wonderland*

I HAVE TO ADMIT IT: I'm in love with ADO.NET's DataSet. Coming from a background steeped in RDO and ADO, the .NET way of data access appears at once obvious, elegant, and commonsense. The DataSet embodies all those principles and then some. If there is one object within ADO.NET that typifies the radical new approach ADO.NET takes to things, and the inherent power of the framework, it is the DataSet.

I took you on a brief tour of the DataSet back in Chapter 2. You saw how it could be used as an alternative to the Reader, a means of holding a single table disconnected from the database for later interrogation without the use of a database connection. It's capable of a great deal more than that. I mentioned before that the DataSet is really an in-memory, disconnected database, a way of holding a set of tables, their relationships, and indexes in memory to be toyed with at your leisure. To be precise, though, a DataSet is really a conduit. A DataSet acts as a container for a group of table objects and a group of relationship objects to link the tables. Additionally, a table is a container of rows and columns, each row also referencing the set of fields that define it. You can add tables into a DataSet manually through code, from an XML document, or from one or more databases. In the latter case, a DataSet makes use of a DataAdapter to handle the low-level details of selecting the data and processing any updates to that data.

Over the course of the next two chapters, you'll dive into these subjects at great length. In this chapter, I'll focus on building a strong foundation and explain one of the key components of the DataSet: the DataTable.

The DataSet and Its Place in ADO.NET

Figure 4-1 shows, graphically, where the DataSet fits into the grand scheme of things.

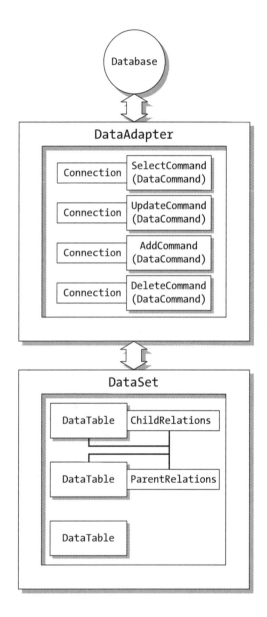

Figure 4-1. Where the DataSet fits in

Figure 4-1 shows the most common arrangement of objects in ADO.NET when working with DataSets. I say "most common" because you don't have to work in this framework at all. The tables contained in the DataSet in the diagram are all assumed to have come from a database via a DataAdapter, but there is nothing stopping you from writing code to manually build the tables and add them into the DataSet without the aid of a database or adapter. You can even build an entire DataSet (including tables and relations) from an XML document.

Take a look at the DataAdapter part of the diagram and you'll notice something interesting. When you worked with DataSets earlier in the book, you used a DataAdapter with a single select command in order to grab a single table of data from a database. As you can see in the diagram, the DataAdapter actually contains four commands; one is used to select data, another to update it, another to add new rows to the database, and a final one to delete rows. The thing to note here is that each has a Connection object attached (as you know from the description of Command objects in the last chapter). There is nothing stopping you from using different databases to handle the update, delete, select and add operations should you so desire.

The commands themselves need some attention as well. Those of you who have used SQL to any extent will already know that it's unusual to have an Update statement update more than one row in a live application; your users typically ask to make changes to a single row and the update command then locates and changes that specific row. The same normally applies to the add and delete commands. Since the DataSet maintains offline copies of entire result sets, how can these commands intelligently do their work?

DataTables maintain a value known as the RowVersion for each row of data they contain, and the DataSet is able to interrogate this value. When you make a change to the data contained in a DataTable (change the data, add a new row, or delete a row), the old row is held in the offline table and a new one is created with the RowVersion set to indicate just what change brought about the new row. When the time comes to save the data back to the database, the DataSet is able to produce a copy of itself containing only the changed data. This DataSet of changes can then be passed to the DataAdapter, which uses RowVersion to identify which command to run for each modified row of data. The commands themselves make use of the values of the rows of modified data as parameters to the actual SQL statements or stored procedures. If that all sounds terribly confusing, don't worry: When you actually use this in a short while you'll find that it's one of those wonderfully straightforward processes that makes you sit back and whisper, "Of course—that makes so much sense."

There is one other important feature of DataSets that I haven't explored. In the past, if you wanted to pass a bunch of data across boundaries you had a problem. For example, if objects on a remote server within the organization needed to pass a result set to another machine, all sorts of hoops had to be jumped through, usually involving nasty string arrays and other similar ill-fitting solutions. If that boundary happened to be between two machines in different countries, connected by the Internet, developers would inevitably have to resort to an expensive third-party library to help them out. DataSets are able to represent their entire contents and structure as XML, though. Since XML is really just a textual representation of any kind of data, it's dead easy to pass across any boundary, even the Internet. XML effectively eliminates the boundary problem of data passing. More on this little gem later.

DataTables

Although this is the first of two chapters exploring DataSets, this one actually focuses on DataTables. DataTables are the fundamental object you'll work with most of the time when you deal with DataSets; they contain everything that defines a set of data, including the rows, schema, constraints, and relationships to other tables. You simply cannot work with a DataSet unless you know how to work with DataTables.

Two of the most important properties of the DataTable object are the **Rows** and **Columns** properties. They are the meat on the bones, if you like; Rows define the contents of the table, and Columns define the format (schema) of those rows of data. You can see this graphically in Figure 4-2.

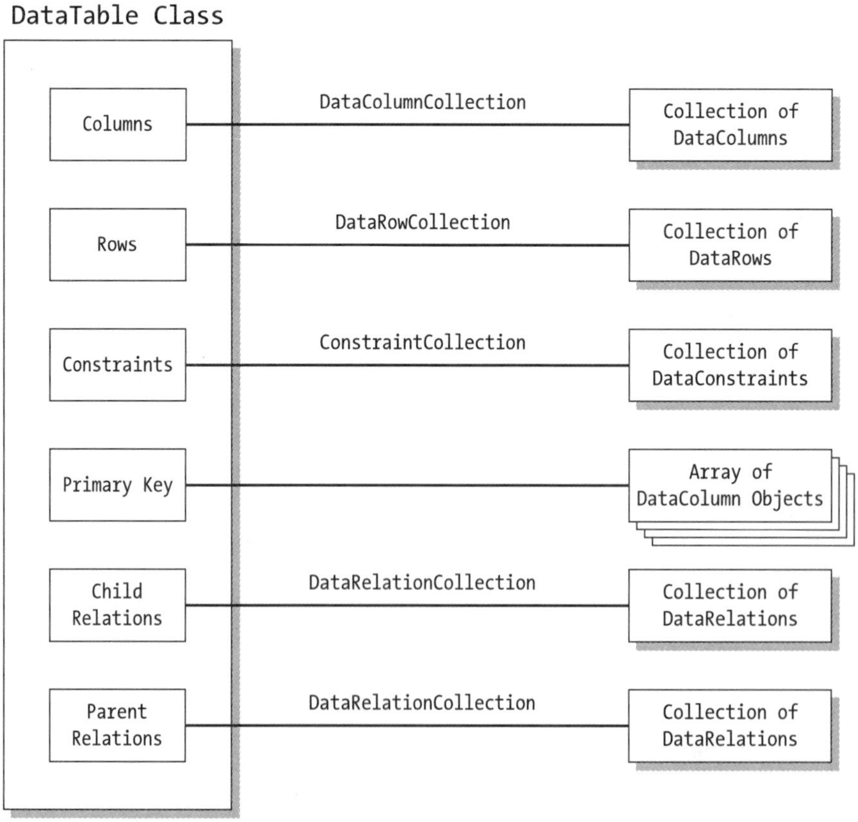

DataTable Class

Figure 4-2. The key elements of the DataTable class

The Rows property is actually an object of type **DataRowCollection**, which itself provides access to a collection of **DataRow** objects. Just as with the Parameters collection you saw when working with Commands in the last chapter, Microsoft chose to implement a new *type* to manage the collection, instead of just defining the property as a generic collection object, in order to override the Add() method and make life easier. You'll see this when you write code shortly to build up the rows in a table by hand. Similarly, the Columns property is a **DataColumnCollection** object that provides access to a collection of **DataColumn** objects.

When you add or in any way change the data held in the rows of the table, the **DataTable** object will keep track of the original version of the row (in the event of a change) and also mark the row's state to flag up just what happened. These changes can all be accepted in the offline table, and the originals discarded, with a call to AcceptChanges() on the table. This typically happens after a call to the DataAdapter, though. When a DataSet is passed to a DataAdapter, the Adapter can interrogate each row to find out exactly what changes, if any, took place to a row and then call the appropriate command to handle those changes.

Exploring DataTable Structure

Let's take a look at DataTables in action now. You're going to create a table to hold some details of pets, in memory. It's a simple table devoid of any relationships to other tables, and not containing any field constraints. It will illustrate the point, though.

Fire up Visual Studio .NET and start a new VB .NET console project (call this one DataTables), then key in this code into the main class.

```
Option Strict On
Imports System.Console

Module Module1

    Sub Main()

        WriteLine("Creating the 'Pets' table...")
        Dim petsTable As DataTable = New DataTable("Pets")

        WriteLine("Adding columns into the table")
        petsTable.Columns.Add("PetName", System.Type.GetType("System.String"))
        petsTable.Columns.Add("Breed", System.Type.GetType("System.String"))
        petsTable.Columns.Add("Age", System.Type.GetType("System.Int16"))
```

```vbnet
    ' Let's interrogate the columns now to find out more about them
    WriteLine("There are now " + petsTable.Columns.Count.ToString() + _
        " columns in the table")
    Dim currentColumn As DataColumn
    For Each currentColumn In petsTable.Columns
        WriteLine("Column Name : " + currentColumn.ColumnName + ", Type : " + _
            currentColumn.DataType.ToString() + _
            ", Ordinal : " + currentColumn.Ordinal.ToString())
    Next

    ' Let's add some values into the table now
    petsTable.Rows.Add(New Object() {"Frisky", "Tortoise", 112})
    petsTable.Rows.Add(New Object() {"Fluffy", "Grizzly Bear", 6})
    petsTable.Rows.Add(New Object() {"Spike", "Hamster", 1})

    WriteLine("There are now " + petsTable.Rows.Count.ToString() + _
        " rows in the table")
    Dim currentRow As DataRow
    For Each currentRow In petsTable.Rows
        WriteLine(currentRow.Item(0).ToString() + ", " + _
            currentRow.Item(1).ToString() + _
            ", " + currentRow.Item(2).ToString())
    Next

    WriteLine("All done. Press Enter to exit")
    ReadLine()
End Sub

End Module
```

Run the code and you'll see a console like the one in Figure 4-3.

The code creates the table and also outputs some simple information about its schema, adds some rows to the table, and then prints out their values. Let's take a wander through the code line by line.

The first thing you should notice is the Imports statement at the top of the code:

```vbnet
Imports System.Console
```

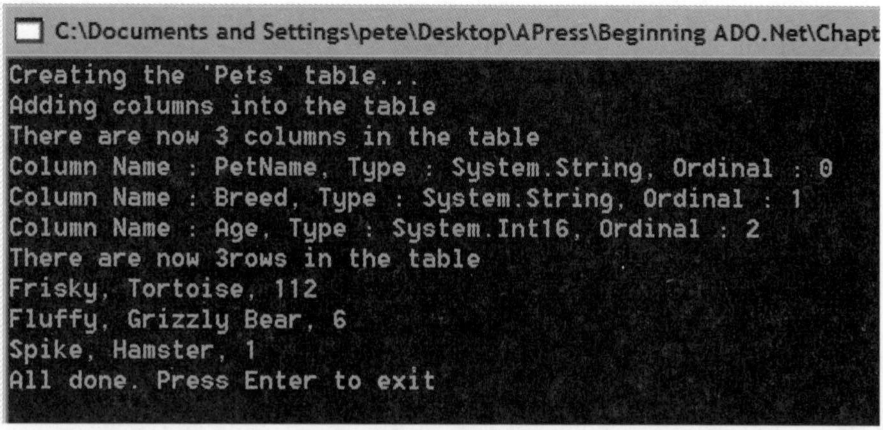

```
C:\Documents and Settings\pete\Desktop\APress\Beginning ADO.Net\Chapt
Creating the 'Pets' table...
Adding columns into the table
There are now 3 columns in the table
Column Name : PetName, Type : System.String, Ordinal : 0
Column Name : Breed, Type : System.String, Ordinal : 1
Column Name : Age, Type : System.Int16, Ordinal : 2
There are now 3rows in the table
Frisky, Tortoise, 112
Fluffy, Grizzly Bear, 6
Spike, Hamster, 1
All done. Press Enter to exit
```

Figure 4-3. Structure and contents of a DataTable

In all the other sample applications so far, you've imported the **System.Data.SqlClient** namespace in order to work with the SQL Server data provider. This example doesn't need to do that; you don't ever connect to a real database here, and you just need access to the generic ADO.NET DataTable, DataRow, and DataColumn objects. These are not part of a specific data provider, but instead belong to the **System.Data** namespace. Since a reference to System.Data is automatically added to the project, there's no need to explicitly add a line to Imports System.Data. However, that's not to say that adding a line that reads "Imports System.Data" is a bad idea; if you're developing a class that may be reused in other projects, you can't guarantee that those projects have an explicit reference to System.Data. Adding the Imports statement to the top of your own classes can actually be a good habit to get into since you are in effect declaring the namespaces your own code will use, making reuse of those classes a lot more clear-cut.

Within the Main() function, the first thing you need to do is create the DataTable object that the rest of the code works with:

```
Dim petsTable As DataTable = New DataTable("Pets")
```

There are two constructors available to you if you want to create a DataTable manually: You can create the table passing no values to the constructor at all, or you can pass a string in, just as the example does. The latter approach assigns a name to the table, since all DataTables should have names. If you don't pass in anything, then a default name will be supplied.

The next step is to go ahead and create some columns, adding some structure to your new table.

```
petsTable.Columns.Add("PetName", System.Type.GetType("System.String"))
petsTable.Columns.Add("Breed", System.Type.GetType("System.String"))
petsTable.Columns.Add("Age", System.Type.GetType("System.Int16"))
```

As always, there are a number of ways to achieve this. You could create the DataColumn objects manually and then set up the properties of each object before passing the column object to **DataTable.Columns.Add**(). Alternatively, the **Add**() method is overloaded to allow Add() to create the column for you. In the case of the example code, the parameters specify the name of the column and the data type. You could also pass in a third parameter, also a string, to specify an expression for the column. This allows you to define columns that use aggregate functions to automatically calculate their values or simple mathematical expressions to work out a result based on a calculation. You'll explore data column expressions a little later when you take a look at filtering and sorting rows of data.

With the columns created, the next step is to find out a little about them. As you might expect, the DataColumn object exposes a whole bunch of properties to find out exactly how the column is defined and what kind of data it will allow.

Exploring the DataColumn

Take a look at the code that walks through the DataColumns:

```
Dim currentColumn As DataColumn
For Each currentColumn In petsTable.Columns
    WriteLine("Column Name : " + currentColumn.ColumnName + ", Type : " + _
        currentColumn.DataType.ToString() + _
        ", Ordinal : " + currentColumn.Ordinal.ToString())
Next
```

Here, a For-Each loop is used to move through the columns and print out each column's name (the **ColumnName** property), data type (the **DataType** property), and the column's ordinal position (the **Ordinal** property). The DataType property is an interesting one since it returns a **System.Type** value, so in order to find out just what that is, you need to call **ToString**() on the returned type to see the textual name of it. The inverse was used to define the type earlier.

```
petsTable.Columns.Add("Breed", System.Type.GetType("System.String"))
```

Here **System.Type.GetType**() is used with the string name of the type to get the actual System.Type value to define the column's data type.

Of course, ColumnName, DataType, and Ordinal are not the only properties available to you. There are properties available to define every aspect of a column with as much control as you would get in a standard database field editor.

The **AllowDBNull** property, a Boolean property, specifies whether or not a column can contain a null value. Setting it to True on a DataColumn allows nulls in that column.

The **MaxLength** and **DefaultValue** properties provide more control over the contents of the column. It goes without saying, but I'll say it anyway: MaxLength defines the maximum length of string data in a column, and DefaultValue sets a default value to be assigned to columns in new rows. If you assign data to a column beyond the maximum length, the DataColumn will truncate that data.

Three properties on DataColumn allow the definition of autoincrementing fields. Setting the **AutoIncrement** property to True can set up a field as an auto-incrementing field. The start value for that field is set into the **AutoIncrementSeed** property and the amount to add to the seed for each subsequent row added is controlled through the **AutoIncrementStep** property. Just by way of an example:

```
Dim newColumn As DataColumn = DataTables.Columns.Add( _
        "AutoField", System.Type.GetType("System.Int32"))
newColumn.AutoIncrement = True
newColumn.AutoIncrementSeed = 1000
newColumn.AutoIncrementStep = 10
'First row will contain a value of 1000, second will hold 1010,
' third 1020 and so on.
```

You can also specify whether the values in a DataColumn should be unique, and whether or not they are read-only. Set the **Unique** property to True to force uniqueness checking on values in the column, and set the **ReadOnly** property to True to prevent the code or user from changing values in a column at runtime.

Expressions

Aside from setting up the data type and size of a column, ADO.NET also allows you to set expressions into a column. This is done using the **DataColumn.Expression** property. *Expressions* are simple strings that provide a column with a way to automatically calculate its value based on other values within the row, table, or even other tables related to the current one. For example, you may have a column that needs to automatically calculate the sales tax on an order or a bulk discounted price for a specific product your company offers for sale. To achieve this, you'd simply code something similar to this:

```
columnBulkPrice.Expression = "UnitPrice * 0.9"
```

When a new row is added, this column will automatically set its own value to be the value of the UnitPrice column (assuming there is one, of course), minus a 10% discount.

Using the Expression property you can enter any simple mathematical expression you like, or you can use the SQL aggregate expressions Count(), Sum(), Avg(), and so on.

You can even work with strings in an expression. Strings can be joined together using the + operator, or you can make use of Len and SubString to really interrogate the value of a string column in the expression. You may, for example, choose to split out the area code of a phone number by pulling out the first three digits of a phone number field, and then use that field later to link to the region table:

```
columnAreaCode.Expression = "SubString(Phone, 1, 3)"
```

Conditions are also allowed in expressions. For example, the AreaCode field is only really useful if there is a phone number entered into the Phone field greater than seven characters in length (123 456 7878, for example, shows 123 as the area code, whereas 456 7878 doesn't have an area code you can use).

```
columnAreaCode.Expression="IIF( Len(Phone)>7, SubString(Phone, 1, 3), '000'"
```

Here, if the phone field holds more than seven characters, you can set the AreaCode field to hold the first three; otherwise, the area code is set to "000" (which presumably in our live system will link to an Area record of "Unknown").

DataRows

DataColumns define the schema of the table, but it's the **DataRows** of a table that most people will be interested in; they define the values within the table, the actual table data. With your columns defined, the example program sets about adding rows into the table. It's surprisingly easy to achieve.

```
' Let's add some values into the table now
    petsTable.Rows.Add(New Object() {"Frisky", "Tortoise", 112})
    petsTable.Rows.Add(New Object() {"Fluffy", "Grizzly Bear", 6})
    petsTable.Rows.Add(New Object() {"Spike", "Hamster", 1})
```

Just as with the data columns and the Columns property, there are two ways to add rows into the table. You can either create a DataRow object and pass that to the Row's Add() method to add it into the Rows collection, or you just can call Add() and pass in an array of objects. In the latter case (the way things are done in the example program), the objects are assigned to the columns in the table in the order they are passed in. So, the first element of the array gets assigned to the first column, the second element of the array goes into the second column, and so on.

There will be many times when this approach doesn't cut it in the real world. It may be more trouble than it's worth, for example, copying data from entry areas in the GUI of an application into an array in order to pass the array through to the Add() method. In that case you'll need to create a DataRow object first, and then pass that new DataRow object across to the Add() method. Be careful, though—this isn't as simple as it seems.

You can't just create a DataRow object and drop some values into it in the usual way; the DataRow object needs to know just how many columns of data you are dealing with and what the format of those columns is. Instead, you need to ask the DataTable you're working with to give you a new, clean row matching the format of the table. This is achieved through the **NewRow()** method. Values are put into the columns of the new row returned through the row's Item property. So, if you were to rewrite the preceding code to add rows using this approach, you'd end up with a chunk of code like this:

```
Dim newPetRow As DataRow

newPetRow = petsTable.NewRow()
newPetRow.Item("PetName") = "Frisky"
newPetRow.Item("Breed") = "Tortoise"
newPetRow.Item("Age") = 112
petsTable.Rows.Add(newPetRow)

newPetRow = petsTable.NewRow()
newPetRow.Item(0) = "Fluffy"
newPetRow.Item(1) = "Grizzly Bear"
newPetRow.Item(2) = 6
petsTable.Rows.Add(newPetRow)

newPetRow = petsTable.NewRow()
newPetRow(0) = "Spike"
newPetRow("Breed") = "Hamster"
newPetRow(2) = 1.0
petsTable.Rows.Add(newPetRow)
```

There are a couple of important things to note about this approach to adding rows. First up, notice how you can reference columns through the row's Items property both by name and by ordinal position. Second, and much more important, notice that calling NewRow() does not automatically add a new row to the table. Calling NewRow() simply creates a new DataRow for you to work with, but you still need to call Add() to actually add it to the table's Rows collection.

New to .NET

Other than the format of the code, if you come to .NET from a Java background, the previous rewritten chunk of code should appear quite straightforward to you. However, if you are coming to .NET from a C, C++, or Visual Basic background and read the code closely, you may come up with a niggling question about how it does its work.

You'll notice that the chunk only creates a single object variable, newPetRow, to hold the new DataRows. This single object is then used in repeated calls to NewRow() and Add(). It's easy to think, wrongly, that the code won't work, since it appears to create an object, set its properties, add it, and then change it before adding it again. Many people see this and think automatically that they're working with just one object that changes dramatically through the course of the code and not three objects (one for each row).

What's actually happening here is that a reference to a DataRow is created—that reference being called newPetRow. When the reference is added to the Rows collection of the table, the object's reference count is effectively increased. This means that when a subsequent call to NewRow() is made, the object variable refers to a brand-new object, and the old one stays alive inside the Rows collection. If you were to remove that row from the Rows collection, the object would be destroyed since there are no more references to it held anywhere.

In .NET it is quite legal to repeatedly assign new objects to a single object variable—you aren't changing a single object, you're just creating new ones and assigning references to them to a variable. When they're no longer referred to by any other objects or collections, the new objects will be destroyed.

Once the new rows are added to the table, navigating them is as easy as iterating through a collection.

```vbnet
Dim currentRow As DataRow
For Each currentRow In petsTable.Rows
    WriteLine(currentRow.Item(0).ToString() + ", " + _
        currentRow.Item(1).ToString() + _
        ", " + currentRow.Item(2).ToString())
Next
```

A DataRow object variable is created and this is used in a simple For-Each loop to move through the rows of the table. As each row is retrieved, the Item property is used to pull the values of the columns in the row. The Item property can be passed either an ordinal column number or the name of a column.

Having shown you the laborious way to access values in columns here, I should also point out the shorthand approach so your colleagues don't laugh at you. Instead of writing DataRow.Item(columnname), you could just as easily write DataRow("columnname") to achieve the same results. The choice of which to use is up to you—I use them interchangeably based on whether or not I need to improve the clarity of the code (DataRow.Item is far more intuitive in some instances).

Working with Null Values

Before ADO.NET came along, working with database Null values was a tricky affair. You see, Null can be a valid value in a database. It's different from zero for an integer or an empty string. It symbolizes that there is absolutely no data available for a column, that nothing has been entered and there is no default in place for that column. I'm sure that most of you who have worked with previous incarnations of Microsoft's data-access strategies have come across Nulls and the problems they bring. The classic example is pulling text from a string column in a database using VB and displaying it on-screen; VB can't handle Null as a string, and so the resulting code invariably crashes when you try to print a Null string. The equally classic workaround in previous versions of VB was to always print "" plus the null value—an empty string plus Null in VB 6.0 and earlier always results in an empty string.

ADO.NET's DataRow class provides two handy methods to work with null values: **IsNull()** and **SetNull()**. They are quite straightforward to use.

IsNull() returns True if a specific column contains a Null value, providing you with a simple way to extend your code to cope with such fields. It's worth noting that it's a requirement of the data provider to make sure this method works, so regardless of the format the database you're working with uses for Nulls, you can be sure that IsNull() will always return an accurate True or False value to show an empty column.

```
If currentRow.IsNull("PetName") then
        ' Do something to cope with the Null value
EndIf

If not currentRow.IsNull(0) then
        ' Do something only if we don't have a Null value
EndIf
```

Bear in mind here that IsNull() works with the DataRow object, and not the object returned from the DataRow's Item property. Also, notice how IsNull() works with both column ordinal numbers and column names.

SetNull(), as its name implies, lets you force a column to a Null value.

```
If not currentRow.IsNull(0) then
    CurrentRow.SetNull(0)
EndIf
```

Again, SetNull() works with both ordinal column numbers and column names.

Editing Columns

So, you know now how to create a table from scratch, as well as how to add rows of data to the table. Let's move on to take a look at editing those rows and changing the data that they hold.

The process of handling the edits is quite straightforward. Put the Row that you want to change into Edit mode with a call to the row's **BeginEdit**() method, and when you're done call either **CancelEdit**() to abort the changes or **EndEdit**() to accept the changes. There is actually a little more to it than that, as you'll see when you get into the row versions and states in a little while. When you make changes to the data in a column, the table will actually preserve the original data, allowing you to accept or reject all changes made to a table en masse. More on that a little later. For now, let's just write a tiny application to add a row, and then change it to see how edits work—I've deliberately broken this one up into a function or two so that you can keep the Main() function focused on the task at hand, so don't panic too much at the size of the code. As usual, this is a VB .NET console project, and I've named it EditingRows.

```
Option Strict On
Imports System.Console

Module Module1

    Sub Main()

        Dim newTable As DataTable = CreateTable()
        AddRows(newTable)
```

```vbnet
        Dim thePet As DataRow = newTable.Rows(0)
        ' Print out the new row
        PrintRow(thePet)

        Write("What breed should Snuggles really be ? ")
        Dim newBreed As String = ReadLine()

        ' Ok, put the new row into edit mode
        thePet.BeginEdit()
        ' Change the breed of the pet to the value entered by the user.
        thePet.Item("Breed") = newBreed
        ' Finally, end edit mode, which stores the changes in the table.
        thePet.EndEdit()

        ' Now print out the new pet details
        PrintRow(thePet)

        WriteLine("All done. Press Enter to exit")
        ReadLine()

End Sub

' CreateTable()
' Creates our Pets table, holding PetNames, Breed and Age.
Private Function CreateTable() As DataTable
        Dim newTable As DataTable = New DataTable("Pets")
        ' Use a with clause to simplify the code when adding the
        ' columns into the table.
        With newTable.Columns
            .Add("PetName", System.Type.GetType("System.String"))
            .Add("Breed", System.Type.GetType("System.String"))
            .Add("Age", System.Type.GetType("System.Int16"))
        End With
        ' Now that we're done with the table, we can return it
        ' out of the function to the main() routine.
        Return newTable
End Function
```

```
' AddRows( DataTable )
' Adds a single row into the table to hold details of our
' sample pet, Snuggles - the Reticulated Python.
Private Sub AddRows(ByVal theTable As DataTable)
    Dim newRow As DataRow = theTable.NewRow()
    newRow.Item("PetName") = "Snuggles"
    newRow.Item("Breed") = "Reticulated Python"
    newRow.Item("Age") = 10
    theTable.Rows.Add(newRow)
End Sub


' PrintRow( DataRow )
' Prints out the pet name, breed and age from a DataRow passed into
' the method.
Private Sub PrintRow(ByVal theRow As DataRow)
    WriteLine(theRow.Item("PetName").ToString() + " is a " + _
        theRow.Item("Breed").ToString() + _
        " aged " + theRow.Item("Age").ToString())
End Sub



End Module
```

I'm not going to go into any detail explaining what the CreateTable(), AddRows(), and PrintRow() functions in this example do, since you should be able to figure them out for yourself by now. The interesting stuff lives in the main() function. When run, the program should look like that in Figure 4-4.

Figure 4-4. Changing data in an application is a pretty common requirement. The Pets database becomes far more valuable with the capability to accurately record the breeds of pets.

The code to edit the data in the table is simple enough.

```
' Ok, put the new row into edit mode
    thePet.BeginEdit()
    ' Change the breed of the pet to the value entered by the user.
    thePet.Item("Breed") = newBreed
    ' Finally, end edit mode, which stores the changes in the table.
    thePet.EndEdit()
```

After calling the functions to create the table and then add a single row to it, the Main() function asks the user to enter a new breed for the pet in the database and then makes the edit using the preceding three lines of code.

BeginEdit(), EndEdit(), and CancelEdit() provide you with some degree of control over committing the changes to the table. BeginEdit() puts the table into edit state, and EndEdit() stores the changes in the table. Similarly, CancelEdit() abandons any changes that may have been made. Actually changing a column of data is, as you can see, as simple as assigning a new value to the column through the DataRow's Item property.

Here's something to try. Comment out the BeginEdit() and EndEdit() lines and run the program yourself. The edits are still stored in the table, which begs the question, Why call BeginEdit() and EndEdit() at all?

The obvious answer is that, as I pointed out, these methods, along with CancelEdit(), provide you with some control over the edits and whether or not you want them committed to the table. BeginEdit(), EndEdit(), and CancelEdit() also do something else behind the scenes.

Columns can have constraints applied to them that force checks to be applied to any data added into a row. Using the Edit methods allows you to control just when those checks will be applied to the data. If you edit the data in a row by simply assigning data to the Item property, then the checks are applied as soon as the data is assigned. Using the Edit methods, the checks are applied to all changes made as soon as EndEdit() is called. BeginEdit(), EndEdit, and CancelEdit() also suspend events on the table and row. You'll look at events in a moment, but in a nutshell if you use the Edit methods, you can be sure that no event-handling code is going to fire while your code or users edit the data, which of course provides you with considerable control over the flow of your code and a helping hand when it comes time to debug it.

Deleting Rows

Strangely enough, there are two ways to delete a row from a table in ADO.NET. Though that might not sound too weird, consider this: One of the methods won't actually delete the row, but it is actually the preferred way of doing things, whereas the other method is rarely used and really does make sure the row is deleted. I'll explain.

The simplest way to get rid of a row from a DataTable is to call **RemoveAt()** on the Rows collection of the table; rows of data are stored in a pretty much standard collection within a DataTable, so standard collection methods such as RemoveAt() can be called to manipulate those rows. This is not the best way of doing things. Calling RemoveAt() will actually delete the row from the table permanently, and when you're working with databases, DataSets, and DataAdapters, that's rarely the result you want. You could also call the similarly named Remove() method—whereas RemoveAt() expects to be passed a row number to remove, Remove() expects to be passed a DataRow. This DataRow serves as a bookmark, allowing the Remove() method to immediately jump to the required row and delete it. Obviously, this is a very fast operation. This does of course assume that you have a reference to the DataRow to remove on hand in order to be able to pass it to the Remove() method.

I mentioned earlier how DataAdapters work and how they are used with DataSets to build up collections of DataTables. I don't really want to give too much away before you start to explore these things in detail in the next chapter, but there is one important concept I mentioned before that I want to touch on again. A DataAdapter can do all the grunt work for you; it can build your tables in a DataSet and also examine the resulting tables for changes in order to determine whether to run an add, edit, or delete query against the database to bring the database in line. For deletions, what the DataAdapter needs is a way of identifying which rows need to be deleted. If you simply go ahead and remove a row from the collection, the DataAdapter has no way of knowing that the row even existed.

The alternate method of deleting rows gets around this problem by flagging rows as needing deletion. All you need to do is find the DataRow object in question and call its **Delete()** method. This sets the deleted flag on the row, which enables the DataAdapter to easily identify which rows to delete. In addition, it provides you with a handy way of accepting or rejecting all changes made to a table in one go.

```
MyTable.Rows.RemoveAt(123) ' Remove the 124th row - bad way of doing things
MyTable.Rows(123).Delete() ' the preferred way of deleting a row
```

Ultimately, the approach you use depends on your own needs. The RemoveAt() method can be handy from time to time, but it performs the same functionality as calling Delete() followed by AcceptChanges(); if you're building up a DataSet with all changes in it tracked, using either of the Remove methods can cause you an annoying and hard-to-track-down bug. However, the Remove() method (where you pass in a reference to the DataRow you want removed) is a lot faster to use at runtime than either Delete() or RemoveAt(). For that reason, you may want to add additional code to your application to track deleted rows by hand and go with the much faster Remove() method if speed is an important requirement of your code.

Row States and Versions

I write books and articles using Microsoft Word. It has a bunch of features I never use, a bunch more features that I probably don't even know about, and a stack of features that scare the living daylights out of me. It also has some neat little tricks up its proverbial sleeve that I adore. One of them is found on the Tools menu and is called Track Changes. If I turn that particular feature on, what Word does is mark the sections of the document that I change. If I delete lumps of text, the new text is shown in a different font style and color, and the old text is shown with a line through it. If I change things around, the same thing happens. Word tracks my changes and allows me to see, in one document, both the old and the new.

If I suddenly have a brain futz, I can elect to abandon all my changes and start over from the original unchanged document. I can also review my changes and accept them, at which point the deleted text vanishes, the changes I made are made permanent (well, as permanent as text in a word processor can ever be), and I can start making changes that are tracked once again. Why would I even think you would care about this? Well, ADO.NET's DataTables work the same way.

Any change you make to the data inside a DataTable is tracked and flagged. Delete a row properly (using the row's Delete() method) and the row is flagged for deletion but not actually removed from the table. Make a change to some existing data in the table and the old data is stashed away and flagged as being original, while the new data is stored in the table and flagged as being modified. All these things let DataAdapters do their job painlessly and also allow you to easily write applications that allow users to add, edit, and delete data to their hearts' content but with a nice, handy safety net under any changes they make. At any point in time, you can allow your users to accept the changes they made, reject the changes, and of course you can write code very easily that lets your users review all their changes.

The key to this functionality lies within the DataRow class. The **RowState** property lets you find out whether the row in question is unchanged, modified, deleted, detached from a table, or recently added. The **HasVersion**() method lets you find out if a particular version of a row is available. In addition, the DataRow provides **AcceptChanges**() and **RejectChanges**() methods to accept or reject all changes to an individual row. The DataTable class also has those two methods, but they work on the entire table contents instead of just a single row of information.

The RowState property can hold any value from the **DataRowState** enumeration. Let's explore them all with a simple example. Start up a new VB .NET console project and call it RowStates.

```vb
Option Strict On
Imports System.Console


Module Module1

    Sub Main()

        ' First, create the table
        Dim newTable As DataTable = New DataTable("TestTable")
        newTable.Columns.Add("Name", System.Type.GetType("System.String"))

        ' Now add in a row
        Dim newRow As DataRow = newTable.NewRow
        newRow("Name") = "Peter"
        WriteLine("The row's state after creation is " + _
                newRow.RowState.ToString())

        newTable.Rows.Add(newRow)
        WriteLine("The row's state after adding to the table is " + _
            newRow.RowState.ToString())

        newTable.Rows.Remove(newRow)
        WriteLine("The row's state after removing it from the table is " + _
            newRow.RowState.ToString())

        newTable.Rows.Add(newRow)

        newTable.AcceptChanges()
        WriteLine("The row's state after accepting changes is " + _
            newRow.RowState.ToString())

        newRow("Name") = "Gary"
        WriteLine("After changing a column's value, the state is " + _
            newRow.RowState.ToString())

        newRow.Delete()
        WriteLine("Deleting a row changes the row state to " + _
            newRow.RowState.ToString())
```

```
        newTable.RejectChanges()
        WriteLine("After rejecting the changes, the row's state becomes " + _
            newRow.RowState.ToString())


        WriteLine("All done. Press Enter to exit")
        ReadLine()


    End Sub


End Module
```

The program is simple enough. It builds a small table, and at each stage of editing the data in the table, it prints out the row's RowStatus property to show you how it works. Figure 4-5 shows the application in action.

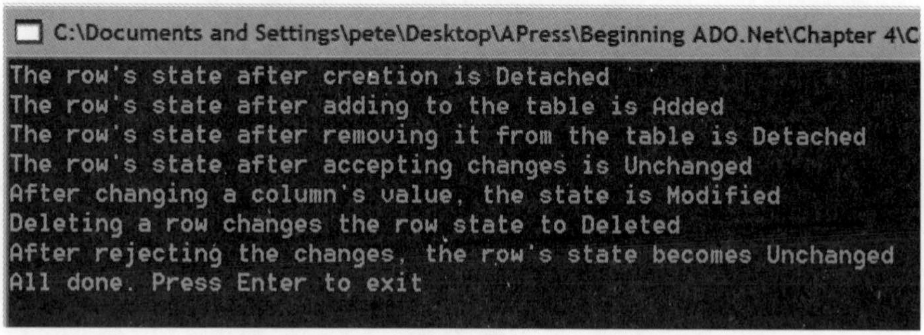

Figure 4-5. Notice the changing RowStatus at each stage of editing a row in a table.

```
        Dim newRow As DataRow = newTable.NewRow
        newRow("Name") = "Peter"
        WriteLine("The row's state after creation is " + _
                newRow.RowState.ToString())
```

Immediately after a row is created, the RowStatus property takes on a value of Detached. This means that the row is created, but not yet added to a table.

```
    newTable.Rows.Add(newRow)
        WriteLine("The row's state after adding to the table is " + _
                newRow.RowState.ToString())
```

Passing the new row to DataTable.Rows.Add() changes the status from Detached to Added. However,

```
newTable.Rows.Remove(newRow)
WriteLine("The row's state after removing it from the table is " + _
    newRow.RowState.ToString())

newTable.Rows.Add(newRow)
```

calling Remove() detaches the row once again—this is important to remember. A Remove()'d row is not flagged as removed in the table: It is physically removed.

```
newTable.AcceptChanges()
WriteLine("The row's state after accepting changes is " + _
        newRow.RowState.ToString())
```

Calling AcceptChanges() on the table changes the row's status once again. This time, the status is set to Unchanged. Because you've told the table to accept any changes you've made to it (in this case, adding a row back in after removing it), the status of each row in the table is set to Unchanged, just as if it were a row originally in the table when you first created it, or when you first pulled it out of a database.

```
newRow("Name") = "Gary"
WriteLine("After changing a column's value, the state is " + _
        newRow.RowState.ToString())
```

That last set of code is quite interesting. It changes the row's status to Modified, since you "modified" unchanged data. However, if there hadn't previously been a call to AcceptChanges, the row's status would remain as Added. If you modify an unchanged row, it becomes Modified, but if you modify an Added row, it remains set to Added. So, what happens when you Delete a newly modified row?

```
newRow.Delete()
WriteLine("Deleting a row changes the row state to " + _
        newRow.RowState.ToString())
```

The status is changed to Deleted. At each stage, the row keeps track of the most relevant status. It would make no sense to leave a Modified row at Modified after deleting it—you're most interested in the fact that it has been deleted.

```
newTable.RejectChanges()
WriteLine("After rejecting the changes, the row's state becomes " + _
    newRow.RowState.ToString())
```

Rejecting the changes made to a table reverts every row of data back to the original unchanged record. In this case, it is also quite interesting. Your sample row reverts back to the row that you had when you first called AcceptChanges earlier (the Name is set to "Peter"). The row does not revert back to the change you made before deleting it.

The RowState property provides you with an easy way to get at the Status of the current row. What about retrieving the other versions of a row, though? How do you find out if another version of a row even exists within a table? That's where the **HasVersion**() method comes into play.

HasVersion() expects to be passed a value from the DataRowVersion enumeration; this could be any of Current, Default, Original, or Proposed. Unlike the RowStates, these can get a bit confusing to work with, so let me explain what they mean.

Current is obvious enough. If HasVersion(DataRowVersion.Current) returns True, then you know that there is a current version of a row available to you. This does not apply to Deleted rows, though. Even though the Delete() method simply flags a row for deletion, the very concept behind deleting is that once it's happened, the row is no longer available. So, even though an original row may exist in a table after it's been deleted, there is never a current row available.

Default means a number of things, based on the row's state. If the row's state is Added, Modified, or Unchanged, the Default version of a row is the current one. If a row has been deleted, then the Default version of that row is Original, and if a row is detached, the default version of the row is Proposed. To be quite open with you, I have no idea why DataRowVersion.Default would ever be used—all rows regardless of their state will always have a Default version available.

The original version of a row, on the other hand, is straightforward enough. t is the version of the row that was in the DataTable since the last call to AcceptChanges(). If your table consists of rows of data loaded from a database, then the Original version of a row will be the one pulled out of the database. If changes have been made and AcceptChanges() called, then the original version of the row becomes the one that was in place when AcceptChanges was called. Obviously, there are times when no Original version is available, such as after adding a new row, before calling AcceptChanges(). HasVersion(DataRowVersion.Original) is thus a good way of finding out which rows in a table are new.

The last version, Proposed, is a neat one. A Proposed version of a row only exists when a row has not yet been added to the table's Rows collection and during an Edit operation (that is, after BeginEdit() and before EndEdit). Retrieving the Proposed version of a row and comparing it to the original version is a handy way of finding out just what the user changed and how. For those of you not using BeginEdit() and EndEdit() in your code, Proposed versions of rows are still available to you. When you change a column of data without calling BeginEdit(),

ADO.NET will call BeginEdit() for you behind the scenes. When you call AcceptChanges(), EndEdit() is implicitly called.

HasVersion() is undoubtedly useful, then, for finding out if certain versions of a row exist, but how do you actually get at the data in those other versions of the rows? Simply pass across the version you are interested in when retrieving a column of data. For example,

```
NewRow("Name", DataRowVersion.Original)
```

provides you with access to the Original version of the Name column in this row. Similarly,

```
NewRow("Name", DataRowVersion.Proposed)
```

lets you get at the proposed version after an edit. You can see these things in action with a simple modification to the preceding sample code. Simply replace all calls to WriteLine() with a call to a new routine called PrintRowDetails(). The complete code, with the PrintRowDetails() method, looks like this:

```
Option Strict On
Imports System.Console


Module Module1

    Sub Main()

        ' First, create the table
        Dim newTable As DataTable = New DataTable("TestTable")
        newTable.Columns.Add("Name", System.Type.GetType("System.String"))

        ' Now add in a row
        Dim newRow As DataRow = newTable.NewRow
        newRow("Name") = "Peter"
        PrintRowDetails(newRow)
```

```
        newTable.Rows.Add(newRow)
        PrintRowDetails(newRow)
        newTable.Rows.Remove(newRow)
        PrintRowDetails(newRow)
        newTable.Rows.Add(newRow)
        newTable.AcceptChanges()
        PrintRowDetails(newRow)

        newRow("Name") = "Gary"
        PrintRowDetails(newRow)

        newRow.Delete()
        PrintRowDetails(newRow)

        newTable.RejectChanges()
        PrintRowDetails(newRow)

        WriteLine("All done. Press Enter to exit")
        ReadLine()

    End Sub

    Private Sub PrintRowDetails(ByVal newRow As DataRow)

        WriteLine("------The row's current state is " + newRow.RowState.ToString())
        If newRow.HasVersion(DataRowVersion.Current) Then
            WriteLine("The current version of the row is " + _
                newRow("Name", DataRowVersion.Current).ToString())
        Else
            WriteLine("There is no 'current' version of the row available")
        End If

        If newRow.HasVersion(DataRowVersion.Default) Then
            WriteLine("The default version of the row is " + _
                newRow("Name", DataRowVersion.Default).ToString())
        Else
            WriteLine("There is no 'default' version of the row available")
        End If
```

```
If newRow.HasVersion(DataRowVersion.Original) Then
    WriteLine("The original version of the row is " + _
        newRow("Name", DataRowVersion.Original).ToString())
Else
    WriteLine("There is no 'original' version of the row available")
End If


If newRow.HasVersion(DataRowVersion.Proposed) Then
    WriteLine("The proposed version of the row is " + _
        newRow("Name", DataRowVersion.Proposed).ToString())
Else
    WriteLine("There is no proposed version of the row available")
End If


    End Sub

End Module
```

If you run this version of the application, you'll see much more information about the row's state and versions, as shown in Figure 4-6.

In the next chapter, you'll look at everything to do with navigating around DataSets and tables, and you'll see that you can even select all rows from a table that match a given version.

```
C:\Documents and Settings\pete\Desktop\APress\Beginning ADO.Net
------The row's current state is Detached
There is no 'current' version of the row available
The default version of the row is Peter
There is no 'original' version of the row available
The proposed version of the row is Peter
------The row's current state is Added
The current version of the row is Peter
The default version of the row is Peter
There is no 'original' version of the row available
There is no proposed version of the row available
------The row's current state is Detached
There is no 'current' version of the row available
There is no 'default' version of the row available
There is no 'original' version of the row available
There is no proposed version of the row available
------The row's current state is Unchanged
The current version of the row is
The default version of the row is
The original version of the row is
There is no proposed version of the row available
------The row's current state is Modified
The current version of the row is Gary
The default version of the row is Gary
The original version of the row is
There is no proposed version of the row available
------The row's current state is Deleted
There is no 'current' version of the row available
There is no 'default' version of the row available
The original version of the row is
There is no proposed version of the row available
------The row's current state is Unchanged
The current version of the row is
The default version of the row is
The original version of the row is
There is no proposed version of the row available
All done. Press Enter to exit
```

Figure 4-6. The sample application now displays complete information about row states and versions.

Sorting and Searching DataTables

The DataTable's **Select()** method is incredibly powerful. In its many overloaded forms, it lets you grab data from a table in a specific order, grab a subset of the records in a table, and even grab all rows matching a specific version. In fact, Select() will also let you use any combination of these conditions to get at just the rows you need. In all cases, Select() will return to you an array of DataRow objects, leaving the original table intact.

The simplest way to use Select() is to just call it, with no parameters. This will return an array of rows in the order that they were added to the table or in the order of the primary key of the table if one is set. Setting up a primary key is simple enough, so most people use this form of the Select() method to simply reorder the data in their table. Take a look at the following example (you'll be extending this in a little while to look at the other ways that Select() can be used). If you want to key this in and try it out, start a new VB .NET console project and call it TableSelects.

```vb
Option Strict On
Imports System.Console



Module Module1

    Sub Main()
        Dim peopleTable As DataTable = New DataTable("People")
        peopleTable.Columns.Add("FirstName", System.Type.GetType("System.String"))
        peopleTable.Columns.Add("LastName", System.Type.GetType("System.String"))
        peopleTable.Columns.Add("Email", System.Type.GetType("System.String"))

        ' Use a calculated field to work out a simple email address
        ' (not a good way of doing things in a live app
        ' thanks to the risk of duplicates)
        peopleTable.Columns("Email").Expression = _
            "LastName + substring(FirstName,1,1) + " + _
            "'@apress.com'"

        ' Set up the primary key to be a combination of lastname and firstname
        peopleTable.PrimaryKey = New DataColumn() _
            {peopleTable.Columns("LastName"), _
            peopleTable.Columns("FirstName")}
```

```
' Add some rows to the table
Dim newPerson As DataRow = peopleTable.NewRow()
newPerson("FirstName") = "Joe"
newPerson("LastName") = "McAllister"
peopleTable.Rows.Add(newPerson)

newPerson = peopleTable.NewRow()
newPerson("FirstName") = "Mike"
newPerson("LastName") = "Zebra"
peopleTable.Rows.Add(newPerson)

newPerson = peopleTable.NewRow()
newPerson("FirstName") = "Zara"
newPerson("LastName") = "Armadillo"
peopleTable.Rows.Add(newPerson)

' Use select to grab the rows in primary key order
' (since we have a primary key) and print out the information
For Each newPerson In peopleTable.Select()
    WriteLine(newPerson("Email").ToString() + " " + _
        newPerson("FirstName").ToString() + _
        " " + newPerson("LastName").ToString())
Next

WriteLine("All done. Press Enter to exit")
ReadLine()

End Sub

End Module
```

The majority of the program should be quite easy to follow, so I've highlighted the new bits in bold. Since you want the program to select all the rows of data in primary key order, the first new thing you need to do is set up the primary key. In this trivial example, the LastName and FirstName fields are used together to form the primary, unique key.

```
peopleTable.PrimaryKey = New DataColumn() _
    {peopleTable.Columns("LastName"), _
     peopleTable.Columns("FirstName")}
```

This involves nothing more than creating an array of DataColumns and passing that array across to the table's **PrimaryKey** property. The program then goes ahead and creates a few rows of data before finally you use Select to grab the rows as an ordered array.

```
For Each newPerson In peopleTable.Select()
    WriteLine(newPerson("Email").ToString() + " " + _
        newPerson("FirstName").ToString() + _
        " " + newPerson("LastName").ToString())
Next
```

You don't even need to tell Select() that you want to select in primary key order. The fact that the table has a primary key means that Select() will use it. Without a primary key, the records would be returned in the order they were added to the table.

You are not limited to grabbing all the rows based on the primary key. By passing in a filter expression to Select(), you can choose to pull all rows matching the expression, in primary key order. Modify the For-Each loop to look like this:

```
For Each newPerson In peopleTable.Select( _
        "Firstname like 'Z%' Or Lastname like 'Z%'")
    WriteLine(newPerson("Email").ToString() + " " + _
        newPerson("FirstName").ToString() + _
        " " + newPerson("LastName").ToString())
Next
```

This will pull only "Zara Armadillo" and "Mike Zebra" from the table. This can include anything a standard column expression includes, and additionally it can make use of standard SQL keywords such as Like.

If the primary key order is unsatisfactory, you can pass in a second string to Select() to define a sort order. This is specified in the same way the sort order might be specified in a standard SQL Select statement. Change the For-Each loop once again to see.

```
For Each newPerson In peopleTable.Select( _
        "Firstname like 'Z%' Or Lastname like 'Z%'", "Lastname DESC")
    WriteLine(newPerson("Email").ToString() + " " + _
        newPerson("FirstName").ToString() + _
        " " + newPerson("LastName").ToString())
Next
```

This will pull the same two records as before (thanks to the filter expression) but sort them in descending order by last name.

Finally, you can also send Select() a DataViewRowState constant to pull only rows matching a specific state from the table. This is handy for finding out all changed, deleted, or added rows in a table in order to present them to the user for approval. Although you need to send three parameters to the Select() statement in order to retrieve using the row state, the filter expression and sort order can be omitted.

The values that can be used are Added, CurrentRows, Deleted, ModifiedCurrent (which returns current rows that have been modified from their original state), ModifiedOriginal (which returns original rows that have since been modified), OriginalRows, or Unchanged. Make the changes shown in the following code in bold to your program to see this in action.

```
                :
                :
newPerson = peopleTable.NewRow()
      newPerson("FirstName") = "Mike"
      newPerson("LastName") = "Zebra"
      peopleTable.Rows.Add(newPerson)

      peopleTable.AcceptChanges()

      newPerson = peopleTable.NewRow()
      newPerson("FirstName") = "Zara"
      newPerson("LastName") = "Armadillo"
      peopleTable.Rows.Add(newPerson)

      ' Use select to grab the rows in primary key order
      '   (since we have a primary key)
      ' and print out the information
      For Each newPerson In peopleTable.Select("", "", DataViewRowState.Added)
          WriteLine(newPerson("Email").ToString() + " " + _
              newPerson("FirstName").ToString() + _
              " " + newPerson("LastName").ToString())

      Next

      WriteLine("All done. Press Enter to exit")
      ReadLine()
```

By adding in a call to AcceptChanges() before all the rows have been added, you are left with a table containing two original rows and one added row. The change to the Select() call retrieves that Added row, with no filter or sort.

Table and Row Events

Tables support events, making it easy for you to add code to automatically track and respond to changes in the table's data. You can track when a column has changed, or is being changed, as well as when a row is changing, has been changed, is being deleted, or has been deleted.

Column Events

The **ColumnChanged** and **ColumnChanging** events let you catch the point in time that a column's data has changed or is changing. The difference between the two is that ColumnChanged typically occurs after a call to EndEdit(), and ColumnChanging occurs after a call to BeginEdit(). Both events are passed a **DataColumnChangeEventArgs** object, which provides you with access to three properties: **Column**, to get at the DataColumn being changed; **ProposedValue**, to get at the value being entered; and **Row**, to access the actual DataRow object that triggered the change. Armed with the latter you can, of course, start to use the row's state and versions to get at before and after images of the row in question.

Row Events

Four events can be triggered in response to something happening to a row: **RowChanged**, **RowChanging**, **RowDeleted**, and **RowDeleting**. Each of them is passed a **DataRowChangedEventArgs** object that provides access to two properties: **Action** and **Row**. Row is obviously the DataRow that the event occurred to, whereas Action takes a value from the DataRowAction enumeration.

The Action value is self-explanatory. It highlights exactly what caused the event, and it can take any of the following values: **Add**, **Change**, **Commit**, **Delete**, **Nothing**, or **Rollback**.

Events in Action

The events are all quite simple to use and get the hang of (providing, of course, you know how to write event handlers in your VB code), so here's a final example program to show them in action. Again, it's a VB .NET console project, and its name is TableEvents.

```
Option Strict On
Imports System.Console


Module Module1
```

```
Sub Main()

    Dim newTable As DataTable = New DataTable("TestTable")
    newTable.Columns.Add("ID", System.Type.GetType("System.Int16"))
    newTable.Columns.Add("Name", System.Type.GetType("System.String"))

    ' Add the event handlers
    AddHandler newTable.RowChanged, New _
            DataRowChangeEventHandler(AddressOf Row_Changed)
    AddHandler newTable.RowDeleted, New _
            DataRowChangeEventHandler(AddressOf Row_Changed)
    AddHandler newTable.RowChanging, New _
            DataRowChangeEventHandler(AddressOf Row_Changing)
    AddHandler newTable.RowDeleting, New _
            DataRowChangeEventHandler(AddressOf Row_Changing)

    Dim newRow As DataRow = newTable.NewRow()
    newRow("ID") = 1
    newRow("Name") = "Dog"
    newTable.Rows.Add(newRow)
    newTable.AcceptChanges()

    newRow.Delete()
    newTable.AcceptChanges()

    WriteLine("All done. Press Enter to exit")
    ReadLine()
End Sub

Private Sub Row_Changed(ByVal Sender As Object, _
            ByVal args As DataRowChangeEventArgs)
    WriteLine("EVENT : Something has happened to a row")
    If args.Row.HasVersion(DataRowVersion.Current) Then
        WriteLine(args.Action.ToString + " " + _
            args.Row("ID").ToString() + args.Row("Name").ToString())
    Else
        WriteLine("Action was " + args.Action.ToString() + _
            ", no current row available")
    End If
End Sub
```

```
Private Sub Row_Changing(ByVal Sender As Object, _
            ByVal args As DataRowChangeEventArgs)
    WriteLine("EVENT : Something is currently happening to a row")
    If args.Row.HasVersion(DataRowVersion.Current) Then
        WriteLine(args.Action.ToString + " " + _
            args.Row("ID").ToString() + args.Row("Name").ToString())
    Else
        WriteLine("Action was " + args.Action.ToString() + _
            ", no current row available")
    End If
End Sub

End Module
```

There are a couple of important things to note from the event handlers. First, it's important to check with HasVersion() before trying to access a row. There are times where the current version of a row is not available (such as when you're deleting rows), so the Row parameter of DataRowChangeEventArgs is set to Null. Try to access fields in a Null row and you'll meet up with a nasty exception.

Also, the Action parameter can be set as well as read. This is where the real power of the RowChanging and RowDeleting events comes into play. You can set the Action property to Nothing in these events and effectively cancel the operation should you so decide.

Finally, if you run the program, you'll notice that you always get a Changing and Changed event, no matter what you do. You will never be presented with just a Changing or just a Changed event.

Summary

DataTables are the staple of DataSets, and so this chapter focused on tables and practically everything to do with them. There's still more to cover, though. You can use expressions for both searching and applying constraints to columns, and there is of course the small issues of relating tables to each other in a DataSet and using DataAdapters to populate and respond to changes in DataTables. These are just the few of the things you'll learn about in the next chapter.

By now you should be more than comfortable with the following:

- Creating a table

- Creating columns in a table

- Responding to events in a table

- Adding, deleting, and updating data

- Accessing and determining row versions and states

- Setting up the primary key of a table

- Searching and sorting on a DataTable

CHAPTER 5

DataSets Inside Out: Navigating

"Procrastination is the art of keeping up with yesterday."

—Don Marquis, 1927

THE CLASSES THAT COMPRISE ADO.NET are incredibly powerful, especially when compared to the features available in previous incarnations of Microsoft's data-access technologies. They are also very circular. It's impossible to talk at any length about a DataSet without knowing anything about the DataTable class, hence the extensive coverage of that subject in the last chapter. Although it is possible to work with DataTables without the use of a DataSet, it's through using a DataSet and its extensive features that DataTables really come into their own. ADO.NET is the computer equivalent of the age-old chicken and egg question.

In this chapter you'll take a journey through the features of the DataSet that make that particular class so powerful. You'll learn about the extended set of features provided by the DataAdapter to build and work with the data contained inside a DataSet. You'll also take a look at navigating data inside a DataSet using relationships between tables.

Relations

Think back to the Pets table in the last chapter. Imagine if you will that this table came from a simple veterinary database linking owners to pets, and pets to their medical history. Before ADO.NET, if you wanted to write an application that could display the owner along with their pets and the pets' medical history, you were left with three choices.

The most common approach to this problem would be to use a query that performed a join across the three tables. This would select, as a single record set, owner information, pet information, and medical history. It certainly solves the problem of how to obtain all the relevant information for the application, but it also brings in problems of its own. One downside to using joins in queries is that the join will duplicate data, and thus it doesn't make the most efficient use of the link between the database and application. For example, take a look at this simple query:

```
SELECT Owner.Name, Pet.Name, History.Condition FROM
    Owner, Pet, History WHERE
    Pet.OwnerID = Owner.OwnerID AND
    History.PetID = Pet.PetID
```

Of course, this query could have been written more elegantly with explicit joins instead of the implicit ones shown here, but the results are the same:

```
John Doe, Fluffy, Sciattica
John Doe, Fluffy, Pregnancy
John Doe, Fluffy, Check-up
John Doe, Snuggles, Venom milking
John Doe, Snuggles, Fractured Fangs
```

The sample results here are perfectly valid. A cursory glance over them shows one owner (John Doe), who has two pets (Fluffy, and the inappropriately named Snuggles), and a variety of reasons for treatment of the two animals. A cursory glance over the data also reveals a bunch of duplicated data; John Doe's name appears on each record of the result set, Fluffy appears in three records within the result set. Imagine if the information we needed to pull from the database was more complex and contained thousands of rows; the sheer volume of duplicated data would grow quite considerably.

An alternate approach, but not necessarily a more efficient one, would be to run three queries within the application, two of them over and over. You could have your application select all owners and then navigate through the record set running a query to select all pets for the current owner. For each pet you could run yet another query to get that pet's medical history. Obviously, this approach reduces the amount of duplicated data that's returned from the database, but there's an equal amount of stress put on the database connection by the need to keep on running queries. In addition, if you only wanted to see owners and pets where there is a valid medical history in the database, you would have to write some funky code to make sure that the innermost query actually returns something before displaying the owner or pet name.

The third approach, and a far more efficient way of doing things, would be to use ADO's data-shaping language to issue the query. This, of course, requires learning the subtleties of a new scripting language that in many instances can be every bit as entangling as writing a complex SQL query. For this reason there aren't that many VB 6.0 developers out there that even know how ADO's SHAPE command works.

ADO.NET provides you with a much nicer way of doing things, and it comes in the form of the **DataRelation** class. With ADO.NET, you simply pull in all the records of both the parent and child tables that you'll need and link them with a DataRelation object. It's a simple process and nowhere near as scary as it might sound. A DataRelation has a name, and it holds a collection of fields in the parent table that should be used to match a collection of corresponding fields in the child table.

The classic example is, of course, an order entry one (such as the data in the Northwind database). In such a system you typically have an Order table that holds generic information about the order, such as the date, order number, a link to the customer placing the order, and so on. You also have an OrderDetails table, which holds each line of the order. In your average, everyday order entry system, one order from one customer could be for many different products or services.

The DataRelation object has two properties to cope with this linking: **ChildColumns** and **ParentColumns**. Both are arrays of DataColumn objects, and since a DataColumn object knows who its parent table is, the DataRelation is thus able to very easily link two tables together.

That's great for defining the relationship in a very theoretical way, but how do you actually make use of it in your code? You don't! In fact, it's the DataRow object that uses the relationship. The DataRow has two very handy methods: **GetChildRows**() and **GetParentRows**(). Both methods return an array of DataRow objects, and both need to be told the name of a relationship to use. Passing in the name of a relationship to these two methods causes them to talk to the DataSet to find the appropriate relationship and then resolve it.

So, back to the Order-OrderDetails example. Having created an appropriate relationship object to link the two tables together, you simply pull out the Order rows that you are interested in and ask each one to give you its child rows.

As always, this is so much easier to visualize if you have some code in front of you, so start up a new VB .NET console project called DataRelations and key this in:

```
Option Strict On
Imports System.Data.SqlClient
Imports System.Console

Module Module1

    Sub Main()

        ' First, create a connection that we can use to get at the two tables
        Dim connection As SqlConnection = New SqlConnection( _
            "Data Source=SARATOGA\$VSTE;" + _
            "Initial Catalog=Northwind;" + _
            "Integrated Security=SSPI")
        Try
```

```vb
        ' Create a data adapter to deal with the order records
        Dim ordersAdapter As SqlDataAdapter = New SqlDataAdapter( _
            "SELECT * FROM Orders", connection)
        ' Create a data adapter to deal with the order detail records
        Dim orderDetailsAdapter As SqlDataAdapter = New SqlDataAdapter( _
            "SELECT * FROM [Order Details]", connection)

        ' Create an empty DataSet, and then...
        Dim orderDataset As DataSet = New DataSet("Orders")
        ' ...add in the orders table and ...
        ordersAdapter.Fill(orderDataset, "Orders")
        ' ...the OrderDetails table into it.
        orderDetailsAdapter.Fill(orderDataset, "OrderDetails")

        ' Build a Datarelation to link the Orders and OrderDetails,
        ' and store that relation in the DataSet.
        orderDataset.Relations.Add(New DataRelation( _
            "OrderDetails", orderDataset.Tables("Orders").Columns("OrderID"), _
            orderDataset.Tables("OrderDetails").Columns("OrderID")))

        ' Now, find the first order and print details of all its order
        ' lines.
        Dim order As DataRow = orderDataset.Tables("Orders").Rows(0)
        Dim orderLine As DataRow
        For Each orderLine In order.GetChildRows("OrderDetails")
            Dim detailColumn As DataColumn
            For Each detailColumn In _
                    orderDataset.Tables("OrderDetails").Columns
                WriteLine(detailColumn.ColumnName + " : " + _
                    orderLine.Item(detailColumn.Ordinal).ToString())
            Next
            WriteLine()
        Next

    Catch ex As Exception
        WriteLine("Something nasty happened")
        WriteLine(ex.ToString())
    End Try

    WriteLine("All done. Press Enter to exit.")
    ReadLine()

End Sub

End Module
```

The example is very simple, and it's not particularly elegant in the approach it takes to extract data from the database (you would rarely want to Select * without a Where clause somewhere to limit the amount of data returned), but it suits your purposes. If you key in and run the program, the result is a console listing of the three child rows attached to the very first order in the Northwind database. Run the application and you should see the same output as in Figure 5-1.

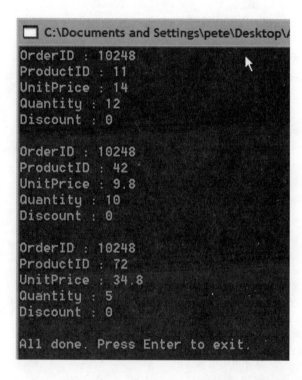

Figure 5-1. A simple enough example—the order detail records are attached to a single order, and all accessed via an offline DataSet.

Let's explore the code to see exactly how it works.

The first thing you'll notice is the return of the Imports line that brings in the appropriate data provider. This is, of course, necessary since this example hits a database, whereas the examples in the previous chapter did everything in memory. The code then starts much the same as the earlier examples by setting up a Connection object to talk to the database.

The good stuff comes now. With a Connection object set up, the next step is to create at least one DataAdapter. This will be responsible for pulling data from the connection and feeding it into your DataSet. Since this example needs to deal with two very different result sets (orders and order details), two data adapters are created.

```
' Create a data adapter to deal with the order records
    Dim ordersAdapter As SqlDataAdapter = New SqlDataAdapter( _
        "SELECT * FROM Orders", connection)
    ' Create a data adapter to deal with the order detail records
    Dim orderDetailsAdapter As SqlDataAdapter = New SqlDataAdapter( _
        "SELECT * FROM [Order Details]", connection)
```

As I mentioned in the overview in the last chapter, a DataAdapter actually holds four Command objects: one for selecting data, one for updating it, one for deleting it, and one for creating new rows. All you need to do in this example, though, is select data, so rather than to go all the hassle of creating separate **SqlCommand** objects and adding them into the **SqlDataAdapter**, the SQL statement is simply passed into the DataAdapter's constructor along with the Connection object. Constructing a DataAdapter in this way passes the burden of creating the Command object over to the DataAdapter and allows you to keep the code a little shorter.

You haven't hit the database yet, though. The process of creating a Connection object doesn't mean that the connection is opened. Similarly, passing a Connection object into a DataAdapter does not automatically open and use the connection. So, at this point, the example is really quite friendly in terms of the server resources it consumes.

The next step is to set up a DataSet. Despite the apparent complexity of DataSets and the power they offer, creating one is a relative no-brainer.

```
' Create an empty DataSet, and then...
    Dim orderDataset As DataSet = New DataSet("Orders")
```

The DataSet is, after all, just a container for other objects, notably tables and their relations. So all you're doing here is getting an empty container ready for use. It's the next two lines of code that put it to use.

```
' ...add in the orders table and ...
    ordersAdapter.Fill(orderDataset, "Orders")
    ' ...the OrderDetails table into it.
    orderDetailsAdapter.Fill(orderDataset, "OrderDetails")
```

Some people get confused here, and it's easy to see why. The DataSet relies on a data adapter to get information out of a database. So, it's easy to fall into the trap of saying **DataSet.Fill()**, and passing in the name of the adapter to use. As you can see in the code, it actually works the other way around. With a DataSet created and ready to accept information, you need to call the DataAdapter's **Fill()** method to populate the Dataset. The first parameter obviously specifies the DataSet that you want to populate, and the second parameter allows you to name the resulting table.

This somewhat innocuous little method call is actually quite a big deal. From a database point of view, calling Fill() will cause the connection to open and be authenticated in the usual way (a process that can result in an exception, don't forget). It will then run the Select command, parsing that command; wait for results from the database; pull the result set back in its entirety; create a table; populate the table with the appropriate schema; and then create rows matching that schema holding the data returned from the Select statement. In addition to all that, if the name of the table that you pass into the Fill() method already exists in the DataSet, then Fill() won't create a new DataSet object at all; telling Fill() to fill a table that already exists actually makes Fill "update" the in-memory table with any differences between the in-memory data and the data returned by the database. Handy, huh!

To summarize, the upshot of the two Fill() calls is that your DataSet now contains two DataTables: one is named Orders and the other is named OrderDetails. The database access part of the application is now complete. The connection is closed and the potentially precious database resources are freed for another user to (ab)use. Now that the tables are in place, you can build the DataRelation to link them together.

```
orderDataset.Relations.Add(New DataRelation( _
        "OrderDetails", orderDataset.Tables("Orders").Columns("OrderID"), _
        orderDataset.Tables("OrderDetails").Columns("OrderID")))
```

Again, shorthand code makes sense here since the link between the two tables is so trivial. A number of constructors can be called for the DataRelation object, and you'll look at them in turn shortly. This one, though, is probably the most commonly used. It takes a string specifying a name to assign to the relation and two DataColumn objects. The first is the parent field, and the second is the child. Here you can see the Order table's OrderID field being used to link in child fields from OrderDetails, using that table's conveniently named OrderID field. The newly created DataRelation is then instantly passed to DataSet.Relations.Add(). The DataSet has a Relations property that provides access to the collection of DataRelations that it should know about.

With all the code out of the way to get the data and build the relationship, the job of navigating that data and relationship can now get underway.

```
Dim order As DataRow = orderDataset.Tables("Orders").Rows(0)
    Dim orderLine As DataRow
    For Each orderLine In order.GetChildRows("OrderDetails")
        Dim detailColumn As DataColumn
        For Each detailColumn In _
                orderDataset.Tables("OrderDetails").Columns
            WriteLine(detailColumn.ColumnName + " : " + _
                orderLine.Item(detailColumn.Ordinal).ToString())
        Next
        WriteLine()
    Next
```

The first thing that happens is you pull up the first row from the Orders table. It wouldn't take much to write a For-Each loop to pull every row, but that doesn't really do much for this example other than clutter the output and confuse the whole thing.

GetChildRows() is then called on the selected row of data. Notice how the name of the relationship you want to use is passed to GetChildRows(). You could also just pass in the relationship object itself if you happen to have it handy. The result of calling GetChildRows() is an array of DataRow objects, which can be navigated quite nicely with For-Each.

That's all there is to it. Let's take some time now to go into a little more detail on the DataRelation class.

The DataRelation Class

The DataRelation class contains no real functionality; the class is really just a handy container for a group of properties that are used to define the relation for later use. The most important of these properties are the ChildColumns and ParentColumns properties.

These properties are both arrays, and as their names imply, one holds a set of columns that form a key on the parent table (or tables), and the other holds a set of columns that form the key used to locate the child rows matching that parent row. In the previous code example, you constructed a very simple DataRelation using just one parent column to uniquely identify an order and one child column to match the order details records against the parent order. You can, of course, use more than one column for these. In order for the relationship to be considered valid, though, you need to satisfy a number of criteria:

- For every column in the ParentColumns array there must be an identically typed column in the ChildColumns array.

- All columns in the ChildColumns array must belong to the same table.

- The parent and child tables used must be in the same DataSet.

- The parent and child columns must not refer to the same physical DataColumn object.

- All parent columns must reside in the same table.

- All child columns must reside in the same child table.

When the time comes to make use of a relation (by calling GetChildRows() or GetParentRows() on the DataRow class, a protected method on the DataRelation called **CheckStateForProperty**() is called. This will check the preceding conditions, and if it finds something amiss, it will throw a **DataException** to let you know. Building the relationship in a way that satisfies all these rules is not that hard—just use common sense. The only one that occasionally catches people out is the requirement that both the child and parent tables must reside in the same DataSet.

You can set up these properties with arrays quite easily when the object is constructed. Instead of passing in single DataColumn objects to the constructor, just pass in two arrays. You will still need to supply a string as the first parameter in order to name the relation properly.

Constraints

Working with multiple tables in a DataSet brings with it certain considerations. For example, if you delete an order from the previous order entry database, what happens to the rows of Order Details related to that Order? This is where constraints come into play. *Constraints* let you manage the integrity of the data in your tables.

There are two types of constraints in ADO.NET: **ForeignKeyConstraints**, which handle the previously discussed situation, automatically updating rows in related tables based on a change in the parent; and **UniqueConstraints**, which ensure that where values should be unique in a table neither the user nor your code can enter duplicates.

When you create a relationship between two tables, the framework will automatically create a **UniqueConstraint** and a **ForeignKeyConstraint**, unless you ask it not to. With two tables joined by a relationship, the framework assumes that the columns you specified in the parent table part of the relationship should have a UniqueConstraint applied against them. It also assumes that the child rows should automatically update themselves based on changes made to the parent columns. You can stop this happening, and then go ahead and create the constraints yourself, by adding a new parameter onto the end of the Relation constructor. For example, in the previous sample code, if you wanted to stop the framework automatically creating the constraints for the relationship, you'd change the call to the relationship constructor to look like this:

```
orderDataset.Relations.Add(New DataRelation( _
       "OrderDetails", orderDataset.Tables("Orders").Columns("OrderID"), _
       orderDataset.Tables("OrderDetails").Columns("OrderID"), False))
```

The "False" value tells the DataRelation constructor that you don't really want any relationships formed. It's wise to go ahead and build them yourself at this point.

UniqueConstraint

UniqueConstraint's constructor is overloaded to provide you with a great deal of flexibility in how you create and define the constraint in your code. Although there are many ways to call the constructor, they basically fall into two categories: constraints that are named by you and constraints that are named by the framework. It's really a matter of personal choice as to whether or not you assign a name to the constraints you create, but as you have already seen when working with other ADO.NET collections, it does make sense. It's a lot easier to find a constraint based on its name at a later point in your code than it is to find it by its position in a table's **Constraints** collection.

If you do decide to name the constraints you create, the name is the first parameter you pass to the constructor. The constructor then expects to see either a single column or an array of columns. You can also optionally pass in a True/False value as the final parameter to specify whether or not you are setting up the primary key in this constraint.

Let's take a look at a simple example to see the UniqueConstraint in action. Call this project Constraints.

```
Option Strict On
Imports System.Console


Module Module1

    Sub Main()

        ' First define a simple table
        Dim contactTable As DataTable = New DataTable("Contacts")
        contactTable.Columns.Add( _
                New DataColumn("EmpID", System.Type.GetType("System.String")))
        contactTable.Columns.Add( _
            New DataColumn("Name", System.Type.GetType("System.String")))

        ' Create a unique constraint on the employee ID column
        contactTable.Constraints.Add( _
            New UniqueConstraint("UniqueEmpID", contactTable.Columns("EmpID")))

        ' Now go ahead and add some rows of data
        Dim newContact As DataRow = contactTable.NewRow()
        newContact("EmpID") = "PJW"
        newContact("Name") = "Peter Wright"
        contactTable.Rows.Add(newContact)

        ' The following new row has the same value in EmpID as the previous
        ' row. This will throw an exception
        newContact = contactTable.NewRow()
        newContact("EmpID") = "PJW"
        newContact("Name") = "Paul John Williams"
        contactTable.Rows.Add(newContact)

    End Sub

End Module
```

If you start up a new VB .NET console project and run this code, you'll see an exception (see Figure 5-2).

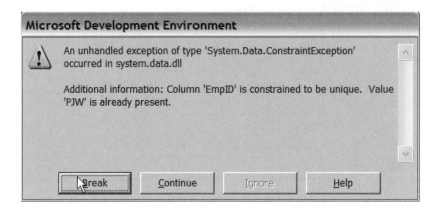

Figure 5-2. An exception is thrown if you try to violate a unique constraint.

Obviously, you'll need to write Try...Catch() exception handlers in your code when working with related tables and constraints. Remember, the .NET Framework will always raise an exception if something goes wrong instead of expecting the developer to intelligently deal with return codes from methods. Also, notice how the exception is thrown when you attempt to add the new row into the table. It isn't thrown when you write data into the offending field. In the case of editing data in a table, the exception is thrown when you call EndEdit().

ForeignKeyConstraints

ForeignKeyConstraint objects are used to control what happens to rows in child tables when a change takes place on key data in a parent table. Since a relationship links specific rows in a child table to specific rows in a parent table, data integrity becomes an issue when the value of those parent rows change. Although this sounds like it could be something terribly complicated, it actually isn't. In fact, working with ForeignKeyConstraints is a breeze and not really any harder than working with UniqueConstraints.

There are basically two conditions that a ForeignKeyConstraint looks out for and works with: when a parent row is deleted or when the key columns in a parent row are changed. When either condition occurs, the ForeignKeyConstraint can be told to cascade the changes across the child rows (so delete all child rows when the parent is deleted, or change the related columns in a child row to match the changes in the parent table), raise an exception, set the values in the child rows to null, or set the values in the child rows to their defaults (as set up in the DataColumn objects when they were created).

This is all handled through two properties of the ForeignKeyConstraint: **UpdateRule** and **DeleteRule**. All you need to do is pick a value from the Rules enumeration and set it into one or both of these properties. The values you can choose from are **Rule.Cascade**, **Rule.None**, **Rule.SetDefault**, and **Rule.SetNull**. By default, both properties are set to Cascade.

Creating the object is exactly the same as creating a UniqueConstraint. The optional first parameter is a name for the constraint, and either two columns or two arrays of columns follow this. Obviously the option to pass in a True/False value to specify whether or not the constraint is a primary key doesn't apply to ForeignKeyConstraints.

Rather than stay with dry theory, let's see how the ForeignKeyConstraint works in code. Call this project ForeignKeys.

```vb
Option Strict On
Imports System.Console

Module Module1

    Sub Main()

        ' First create two simple tables
        Dim petsTable As DataTable = New DataTable("Pets")
        petsTable.Columns.Add("OwnerName", System.Type.GetType("System.String"))
        petsTable.Columns.Add("PetName", System.Type.GetType("System.String"))

        Dim ownersTable As DataTable = New DataTable("Owners")
        ownersTable.Columns.Add("Name", System.Type.GetType("System.String"))

        ' Now set up the ForeignKeyConstraint, and add it to the parent table
        petsTable.Constraints.Add("PetsOwners", _
            ownersTable.Columns("Name"), petsTable.Columns("OwnerName"))

        ' Add the two tables to a DataSet - this lets us 'EnforceConstraints'
        Dim ds As DataSet = New DataSet()
        ds.Tables.Add(ownersTable)
        ds.Tables.Add(petsTable)
        ds.EnforceConstraints = True

        ' Now add in some data
        ownersTable.Rows.Add(New String() {"Miss Bloggs"})
        petsTable.Rows.Add(New String() {"Miss Bloggs", "Fluffy"})
        petsTable.Rows.Add(New String() {"Miss Bloggs", "Cuddles"})


        Dim ownerRow As DataRow = ownersTable.Rows(0)
```

```
                  ShowPetsTable("Before changing owner name...", petsTable)


                  ' Changing the owner name here will cause a cascading update on
                  ' the pet's table.
                  ownerRow("Name") = "Mrs Jones"


                  ShowPetsTable("After changing owner name...", petsTable)


                  WriteLine("All done. Press Enter to exit")
                  ReadLine()


            End Sub


            Private Sub ShowPetsTable(ByVal heading As String, _
                  ByVal petsTable As DataTable)
                  Dim petRow As DataRow
                  WriteLine(heading)
                  For Each petRow In petsTable.Rows
                        WriteLine(petRow("PetName").ToString() + _
                              " is owned by " + petRow("OwnerName").ToString())
                  Next
                  WriteLine("")
            End Sub


      End Module
```

The code illustrates the ForeignKeyConstraint in action, and it also highlights a few "gotchas" to be aware of. Run the code and you'll see the output in Figure 5-3.

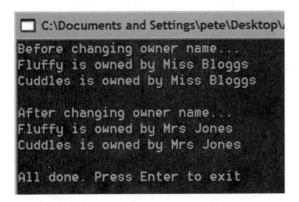

Figure 5-3. After changing a key field in the parent table, the child tables automatically update.

The application simply creates a couple of tables and builds a ForeignKeyConstraint. When the key field of the parent table (the owners table, in this case) changes (Miss Bloggs married a Mr. Jones), the child rows are automatically updated. There are a few very interesting points to note, though.

First, take a look at how the constraint is built:

```
' Now set up the ForeignKeyConstraint, and add it to the parent table
petsTable.Constraints.Add("PetsOwners", _
    ownersTable.Columns("Name"), petsTable.Columns("OwnerName"))
```

The first thing this shows is that you can get away with not actually creating a ForeignKeyConstraint at all. The DataTable.Constraints.Add() method is over-loaded. Pass it two columns from different tables and it will automatically build a ForeignKeyConstraint for you, and then add it to the Constraints collection.

Second, notice that the constraint is added to the petsTable, *not* the ownersTable. This is a major source of confusion for many people. You would think that since you are defining a constraint that specifies what should happen to child rows when a parent is updated, the constraint should be added to the parent table. To avoid the confusion, think of it this way: Constraints are added to the table whose rows are affected. So, a UniqueConstraint is added to the table whose columns need to be defined as unique. Similarly, a ForeignKeyConstraint is added to the child table because it will cause the rows in that table to change. If you try to add the constraint to the parent table, you'll get an exception at runtime, with ADO.NET telling you that it can't add the constraint since it's not "owned" by the parent table.

Some of you may be wondering as a result of this just how the child table knows when to cascade updates that have taken place on the parent. The answer is simply that it doesn't. It's the DataSet's job to make sure that the integrity of the data it manages is maintained, so it's the DataSet that actually "enforces" foreign key constraints. That's why, further down the code, a DataSet is thrown together.

```
' Add the two tables to a DataSet - this lets us 'EnforceConstraints'
Dim ds As DataSet = New DataSet()
ds.Tables.Add(ownersTable)
ds.Tables.Add(petsTable)
ds.EnforceConstraints = True
```

The DataSet is constructed in the usual way, and your two tables added to it. The DataSet's **EnforceConstraints** property is then set to True. It's now the DataSet's job to keep an eye on any changes that happen to the tables and work out which constraints should come into play as a result.

The final important bit of code to watch is the part that prints out the details of the petsTable.

```
Dim ownerRow As DataRow = ownersTable.Rows(0)

ShowPetsTable("Before changing owner name...", petsTable)

' Changing the owner name here will cause a cascading update on
' the pet's table.
ownerRow("Name") = "Mrs Jones"

ShowPetsTable("After changing owner name...", petsTable)
```

The issue here is subtle. An owner row was previously added with its Name column set to Miss Bloggs. In the block of code shown, though, the name is changed to Mrs. Jones. Even though AcceptChanges() has not been called, the ForeignKey-Constraint still kicks in and cascades that change through the child rows. When you work with DataSets, the DataSet will always try to maintain the integrity of its data, regardless of whether or not you have told the DataSet, tables, or rows to accept or reject their changes. Make a change to a row and the DataSet will instantly try to keep up with that change and run any affected constraints.

AcceptRejectRule

In the last chapter you saw that both the DataRow and DataTable classes have AcceptChanges() and RejectChanges() methods. These are in place to reset the version and state information of rows of data back to Unmodified. DataSets also have this method. Calling DataSet.AcceptChanges() will actually run AcceptChanges() on each and every table the DataSet manages.

When you start working with constraints, though, this brings into play an important question. If you accept a parent row, would you always want to automatically accept any child rows of that parent? What about the children's children? There are some times where you will, and some times when you won't, depending on the application domain that you are working in. The DataSet supports a property called **AcceptRejectRule** to let you take control of this behavior.

AcceptRejectRule can be set to either Cascade or None. Set the property to Cascade and when a parent row has AcceptChanges() called on it, either by the DataSet or by you in code, all child rows linked to the parent by a ForeignKeyConstraint will also have AcceptChanges() called on them. This is important. If you set the property to None, the child rows will not have AcceptChanges() called on them when the parent is accepted. More to the point, if the parent has RejectChanges() called, the child rows won't.

It's very important that you manually take control of just what you want the DataSet to do with this property. If the property is set to None, then you could conceivably have changes in a parent table rejected, but leave the child table looking just as it did after the previous cascading update. Alternatively, you could AcceptChanges() on the parent and then use Select() on the child rows to find out just which rows changed since their version will not be set back to Unmodified as a result of the call.

The DataAdapter

I've touched on the DataAdapter a few times, previously just showing how it's used to connect to a database to fill data in a DataSet. As you might expect by now, a DataAdapter is far more powerful than that. DataAdapters are the key to managing all aspects of a disconnected DataSet. They are able to intelligently handle updates to data and propagate those changes back to a database. They are also able to act as an incredibly powerful conduit for combining data from multiple sources into a single table. For example, if you need to extend the data in a master database with information from another database (with perhaps even a completely different format), a DataAdapter can do that for you.

Working with Updates

Before you dive into the code involved in getting a DataAdapter to send data to a database, it's worth talking through just how it all works from a theoretical point of view.

As you know from the last chapter, each row of data in a table has an associated version and state. From these it's possible to determine just whether a row has had something done to it since the original data set was loaded. Using the version and state information, you can find out whether a row has been flagged for deletion, whether it's been updated, and whether a row has been newly added.

The DataAdapter holds four Command objects (in the case of the SqlDataAdapter class, these are SqlCommand objects). When the DataAdapter's Update() method is called, the DataAdapter walks through the row of data, interrogates the version and state of each row, and then runs the appropriate Command object. Each Command needs to have parameters attached to it, and these parameters can be quite easily mapped onto named columns in the row being sent to the server. In addition, each parameter can also be mapped to a specific row version. So if an update occurred that changed a key field (not something you would want to do too often), you can set up a parameter on the update command that pulls the original version of that column up to locate the original row in the database, in order to run the Update query.

The four properties attached to the DataAdapter to handle all this are called SelectCommand, UpdateCommand, InsertCommand, and DeleteCommand. I hope their names are quite self-explanatory.

Let's take a look at a simple example of two of these commands, Select and Insert, in action. Call this project DataAdapters.

```vbnet
Option Strict On
Imports System.Data.SqlClient
Imports System.Console


Module Module1

    Sub Main()

        Try
            ' Create a data adapter to do the reading and writing
            Dim adapter As SqlDataAdapter = New SqlDataAdapter( _
                "SELECT RegionID, RegionDescription FROM Region", _
                "Data Source=localhost;" + _
                "Initial Catalog=Northwind;"   + _
                "Integrated Security=SSPI")

            ' Add in an Insert command - use the Select command's connection
            adapter.InsertCommand = New SqlCommand( _
              "INSERT INTO Region (RegionID, RegionDescription)" + _
                "VALUES (@ID, @Description)", _
                adapter.SelectCommand.Connection)

            ' Add the two parameters into the Insert command
            adapter.InsertCommand.Parameters.Add( _
              "@Description", SqlDbType.NChar, 50, _
              "RegionDescription")
            adapter.InsertCommand.Parameters.Add( _
                "@ID", SqlDbType.Int, 4, "RegionID")

            ' Create a DataSet and ask our adapter to fill it
            Dim ds As DataSet = New DataSet()
            adapter.Fill(ds)
```

```
        ds.Tables(0).Rows.Add(New Object() _
            {99, "Somewhereville"})
        adapter.Update(ds)

    Catch ex As Exception
        WriteLine("There was a serious problem... ")
        WriteLine(ex.ToString())
    End Try

    WriteLine("All done. Press Enter to exit")
    ReadLine()
End Sub

End Module
```

Run the program and you shouldn't see any output other than a message telling you that the program is complete. Take a look at Northwind's Region table through the Server Explorer and you should see that a new region has been added to the bottom of the list, as shown in Figure 5-4.

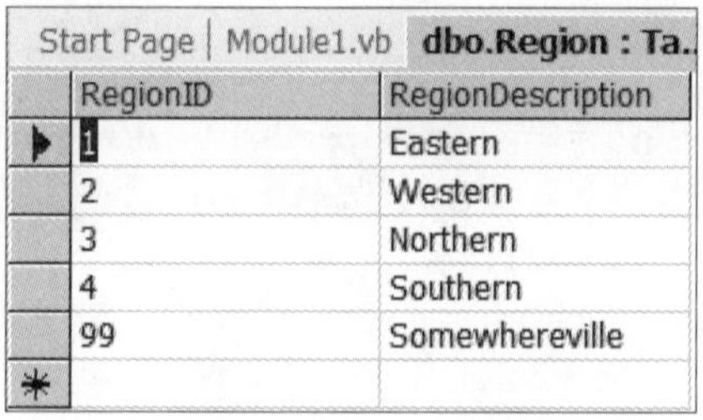

Start Page	Module1.vb	**dbo.Region : Ta.**
	RegionID	RegionDescription
▶	1	Eastern
	2	Western
	3	Northern
	4	Southern
	99	Somewhereville
✳		

Figure 5-4. Region 99 was added by the DataAdapter's InsertCommand.

The first thing that will probably strike you about the code is the shorthand approach to building the Adapter.

```
' Create a data adapter to do the reading and writing
Dim adapter As SqlDataAdapter = New SqlDataAdapter( _
    "SELECT RegionID, RegionDescription FROM Region", _
    "Data Source=localhost;" + _
    "Initial Catalog=Northwind;" + _
    "Integrated Security=SSPI")
```

Rather than go through all the effort of first creating a Connection object, then creating a command, then assigning the command to the **SelectCommand** property of the Adapter, there is a handy overload for the Adapter's constructor that lets you pass in the string for the Select command and its connect string. The Adapter is then responsible for building both the Connection object and the SqlCommand object that will be used to select data.

With the Adapter created, it's time to turn your attention to the other commands that the Adapter supports. To keep the example code quite short, I just put one additional command—the **InsertCommand**—into the code.

```
' Add in an Insert command - use the Select command's connection
adapter.InsertCommand = New SqlCommand( _
 "INSERT INTO Region (RegionID, RegionDescription)" + _
   " VALUES (@ID, @Description)", _
   adapter.SelectCommand.Connection)

' Add the two parameters into the Insert command
adapter.InsertCommand.Parameters.Add( _
    "@Description", SqlDbType.NChar, 50, _
    "RegionDescription")
adapter.InsertCommand.Parameters.Add( _
    "@ID", SqlDbType.Int, 4, "RegionID")
```

With the exception of SelectCommand, all the commands in the Adapter need to have parameters. Obviously, some way is needed of linking the parameters of a command with columns in the Dataset. The SqlParameter class has two properties for just that very purpose: **SourceColumn** and **SourceVersion**. The SourceColumn property accepts a string, the name of the column in the DataSet that the parameter should get its values from when the command is invoked. SourceVersion lets you take things a bit further by allowing you to specify the version of the DataRow to use to extract that column's data. For example, in an update you may want to allow your users to update the primary key of a row. When the UpdateCommand is run, the parameters of the command can get at the original values for the primary key by mapping onto the original version of the row.

Although there is nothing stopping you from creating the SqlParameters by hand and manually adding them to each command's Parameters collection, it's much easier to just call the overloaded Parameters.Add() method, which allows you to specify the name of the source column as the fourth method parameter. That's exactly what happens in the preceding code.

```
' Add in an Insert command - use the Select command's connection
adapter.InsertCommand = New SqlCommand( _
 "INSERT INTO Region (RegionID, RegionDescription)" + _
  " VALUES (@ID, @Description)", _
   adapter.SelectCommand.Connection)
```

The Insert command here needs to use two parameters to insert a new region into the database: @ID and @Description. These parameters are added to the Parameters collection and linked to the RegionID and RegionDescription columns in the DataSet.

```
' Add the two parameters into the Insert command
adapter.InsertCommand.Parameters.Add( _
  "@Description", SqlDbType.NChar, 50, _
  "RegionDescription")
adapter.InsertCommand.Parameters.Add( _
   "@ID", SqlDbType.Int, 4, "RegionID")
```

It really is as simple as that.

The rest of the code just adds a single row to the table and then tells the DataAdapter to Update(), passing in the name of the DataSet to update from. It's at that point that the DataAdapter starts looking at the versions and states of the rows to figure out just what changed, before calling the appropriate Command object. In this case, only one row will be flagged as not original, and that's the single row that the code manually adds. Since I didn't set up the SourceVersion property of the parameters, they will pull the values they need from the current version of the row in order to do the Insert.

Aside from showing you the syntax behind using a DataAdapter to update a database, this example also raises another interesting question. The Regions table in the Northwind database is quite small; each row consists of just two columns and there are less than ten rows in the table. What if there were 3 million rows of data and your program had still only made one change? The call to Update() could potentially take a long time to run as it chugs its way through 3 million rows, most of which require no action. More to the point, if the code doing the updates resides in the UI tier and then hands the DataSet off to a business tier class, potentially on another machine, to actually propagate the changes across to the database, won't that be a terrible drain on network resources, or at least a horrendously inefficient one? Is that really how Microsoft wants us to work?

The answer, of course, is no. The coders of the DataSet were fully aware of how important it is to keep speed up and resource drain down in an application that deals with disconnected data, and they provided a handy method called **GetChanges**() on both the DataSet and DataTable.

In the case of a DataSet, calling GetChanges() returns a brand-new DataSet object that contains just the new, changed, and deleted records from the original DataSet. The new DataSet contains everything that has happened to the original Dataset since the last call to AcceptChanges(). So, instead of passing around hideously inefficient DataSets where only a minority of records has changed, it's a no-brainer to build DataSets that consist purely of data that needs to be propagated to the database. The next example (a VB .NET console project called GetChanges) shows this in action:

```
Option Strict On
Imports System.Data.SqlClient
Imports System.Console

Module Module1

    Sub Main()

        Dim adapter As New SqlDataAdapter( _
            "SELECT * FROM Employees", _
            "Data Source=localhost;" + _
            "Initial Catalog=Northwind;" + _
            "Integrated Security=SSPI")

        Dim ds As New DataSet()
        adapter.Fill(ds)

        Dim newRow As DataRow = ds.Tables(0).Rows(0)
        newRow("FirstName") = "Pete"

        Dim newDS As DataSet = ds.GetChanges()
        WriteLine("The original dataset had " + _
            ds.Tables(0).Rows.Count.ToString() + _
            " rows of data.")
        WriteLine("The new dataset has " + newDS.Tables(0).Rows.Count.ToString())
        ReadLine()


    End Sub

End Module
```

A simple enough example—it builds a DataSet, changes one record, and then creates another DataSet with a call to GetChanges(). The resulting new DataSet has just one row of data in it, since that's all that changed in the original.

GetChanges() will by default return any row that does not have an original state. You can pass in row values from the DataRowState enumeration, though, to specify exactly the rows you are after. For example, to retrieve a DataSet consisting only of newly added rows, the call to GetChanges() could have been written as follows:

```
Dim newDS As DataSet = ds.GetChanges(DataRowState.Added)
```

The full list of values you can use here is DataRowState.Modified, DataRowState.Deleted, DataRowState.Detached, DataRowState.Added, or DataRowState.Unchanged.

CommandBuilder

If you're in a hurry and don't really want to be bothered with all the hassle of handcrafting the commands in a DataAdapter, there's an object that could suit your needs perfectly: the CommandBuilder.

There's nothing to it, really. You just create a CommandBuilder object and pass a DataAdapter to its constructor. The CommandBuilder then looks out for row modification events on tables built by the Adapter, and when it sees one, it populates the appropriate command property of the data based on the change that took place. The following short example shows you how CommandBuilders work. (I'm not going to dwell on it too long since, as the example shows you when it runs, the resulting queries are far from elegant or efficient. They do, however, get the job done if you're in a great hurry.)

```
Option Strict On
Imports System.Data.SqlClient
Imports System.Console
Module Module1

    Sub Main()

        ' Build up a really quick data adapter. Let the data adapter build the
        ' connection object, and set up the SelectCommand property
        Dim adapter As New SqlDataAdapter( _
            "Select * from Employees", _
            "Data Source=localhost;" + _
            "Initial Catalog=Northwind;" + _
            "Integrated Security=SSPI")
```

```
' Attach that adapter to a SqlCommandBuilder - it can worry about the other
' commands we'll need
Dim builder As New SqlCommandBuilder(adapter)

Dim ds As New DataSet("Employees")
adapter.Fill(ds)

' Here's where your code to make changes will go.

' Let's take a look at what the command builder did
WriteLine("The Update command...")
WriteLine(builder.GetUpdateCommand().CommandText)

ReadLine()
WriteLine("The Insert command...")
WriteLine(builder.GetInsertCommand().CommandText)

ReadLine()
WriteLine("The Delete command...")
WriteLine(builder.GetDeleteCommand().CommandText)

WriteLine("All done. Press Enter to exit")
ReadLine()


    End Sub

End Module
```

Run the application and you'll see the output in Figure 5-5.

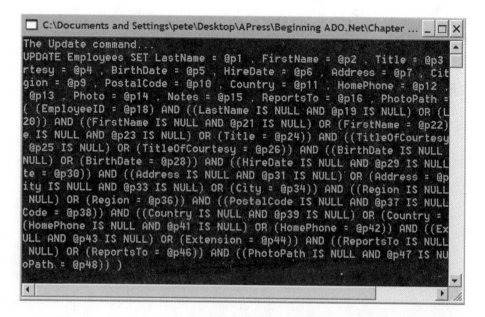

Figure 5-5. The commands built by the CommandBuilder are not very elegant.

Data Mapping

Normally, when you call the DataAdapter's Fill() method, a table is created in the DataSet with the same name as the source table, and containing columns named and defined the same as the ones you selected. This works fine for most applications. There are times, though, when it's not suitable. You might want to load data from a completely different database table into an existing table, effectively merging two data sources together. To achieve this, you'll need to let the DataAdapter know just how the source tables and columns relate to existing tables and columns in your DataSet, a process known as *data mapping*.

The first stage of mapping involves nothing more than telling the DataAdapter which DataTables to map source tables onto. This is achieved with the help of the DataAdapter's **TableMappings** collection property.

```
MyAdapter.TableMappings.Add("MyDatabaseTable", "MyDatasetTable")
```

This adds a new "table mapping" to the Adapter, and the Add() method actually returns a **DataTableMapping** object to allow you to further define the relationship by adding column mappings.

Column mappings are set up through the **DataTableMapping.ColumnMappings.Add**() method.

```
Dim tableMapping As DataTableMapping = _
          PubsAdapter.TableMappings.Add("databasetable", "datasettable")
 tableMapping.ColumnMappings.Add("sourcecolumn", "datasetcolumn")
```

As you can see, the format of setting up the column mapping is practically identical to the format of the call used to set up the table mapping; you pass in two column names to ColumnMappings.Add(), the first being the name of the column in the database and the second being the name of the column in the DataSet.

Let's see this in action with a simple example that builds a single DataTable holding employees from both the Northwind and Pubs databases:

```
Option Strict On
Imports System.Data.SqlClient
Imports System.Console
Imports System.Data.Common

Module Module1

    Sub Main()

        ' First create a dataadapter and DataSet
        ' to hold employee info from Northwind
        Dim NorthWindAdapter As New SqlDataAdapter( _
            "SELECT LastName, FirstName FROM employees", _
            "Data Source=Localhost;" + _
            "Initial Catalog=Northwind;" + _
            "Integrated Security=SSPI")

        Dim ds As New DataSet("EmployeeInfo")
        NorthWindAdapter.Fill(ds, "Employees")

        WriteLine("After selecting from Northwind, we have " + _
            ds.Tables("Employees").Rows.Count.ToString() + " employees.")
```

```
' Now create a dataadapter that maps employee info from the pubs database
' into our in memory table with employees from Northwind
Dim PubsAdapter As New SqlDataAdapter( _
    "SELECT lname, fname FROM employee", _
    "Data Source=localhost;Initial Catalog=Pubs;Integrated Security=SSPI")

Dim pubsMapping As DataTableMapping = _
    PubsAdapter.TableMappings.Add("employee", "Employees")
pubsMapping.ColumnMappings.Add("lname", "LastName")
pubsMapping.ColumnMappings.Add("fname", "FirstName")


' Finally, add the info from the pubs employee list to our own
' Northwind list
PubsAdapter.Fill(ds, "Employees")

WriteLine("After selecting from Pubs, we now have " + _
    ds.Tables("Employees").Rows.Count.ToString() + " employees.")

WriteLine("There are " + ds.Tables.Count.ToString() + " tables")

WriteLine("All done. Press Enter to exit")
ReadLine()
End Sub

End Module
```

The first thing to note is in the Imports statement at the top of the code. To work with table mappings, you'll need to reference the System.Data.Common namespace.

The first part of the code in the Main() function should be pretty easy to follow by now.

```
Dim NorthWindAdapter As New SqlDataAdapter( _
    "SELECT LastName, FirstName FROM employees", _
    "Data Source=Localhost;" + _
    "Initial Catalog=Northwind;" + _
    "Integrated Security=SSPI")

Dim ds As New DataSet("EmployeeInfo")
NorthWindAdapter.Fill(ds, "Employees")

WriteLine("After selecting from Northwind, we have " + _
    ds.Tables("Employees").Rows.Count.ToString() + " employees.")
```

It creates a simple DataAdapter the shorthand way, and then fills a DataSet with the results. In this case, that means pulling in the FirstName and LastName columns from the Employees table in the Northwind database, a total of nine records.

Adding in the data from the Pubs database starts off in similar fashion by creating a DataAdapter and specifying the Select query to run as well as details of the connection to use. Then you get into the table and column mapping details.

```
Dim PubsAdapter As New SqlDataAdapter( _
    "SELECT lname, fname FROM employee", _
    "Data Source=localhost;Initial Catalog=Pubs;Integrated Security=SSPI")

Dim pubsMapping As DataTableMapping = _
    PubsAdapter.TableMappings.Add("employee", "Employees")
pubsMapping.ColumnMappings.Add("lname", "LastName")
pubsMapping.ColumnMappings.Add("fname", "FirstName")


' Finally, add the info from the pubs employee list to our own
' Northwind list
PubsAdapter.Fill(ds, "Employees")
```

The first step is to set up a table mapping between the "employee" table in the Pubs database and the "Employees" DataTable that already exists in your DataSet. You do this by simply passing in the names of the two tables to the TableMappings.Add() method on the new DataAdapter.

The result of this is a new DataTableMapping object that you can use to set up the column mappings. The process is somewhat similar to setting up the table mapping, the obvious difference being that you are now linking the lname and fname fields in the database to the LastName and FirstName fields in our DataTable.

Finally, Fill() is called on the new DataAdapter, passing in the DataSet to fill and the name of the table mapping to make use of in that fill. When you send in a string as the second parameter to the Fill() method, the Adapter first looks to see if there is a table mapping matching the string. If there is, it's used. If there isn't, the Adapter will look for a table name matching the string and either update it or build it from scratch. In this case, a table mapping is located and it's used to add more data into the existing DataTable.

Summary

You've covered a lot of important ground in this chapter and the previous one. DataSets and the objects they work with are fundamental building blocks in ADO.NET and are probably some of the most powerful parts of the framework. In this chapter you learned

- How to work with the DataAdapter

- How to navigate relationships

- How to automatically build commands with the CommandBuilder object

- How to map parameters to columns for the DataAdapter

- How to map tables and columns to bring in data from disjointed data sources

In the next chapter you'll build on all this and introduce yet another class, the DataView, as you take your exploration of ADO.NET into the world of Windows user interface development.

CHAPTER 6

Introducing Windows Forms Applications

"One picture is worth ten thousand words."

—Frederick R. Barnard, *Printer's Ink*, 1921

VISUAL STUDIO .NET'S support for the console (text-based output into a DOS-like window) is wonderful. By using the console application templates it's dead easy to knock out programs to try out ideas, test classes and, of course, focus on learning important concepts. However, in the world of production applications, the GUI is king, whether it's deployed as part of a desktop application or over the Web using ASP.NET.

In this chapter and the next you'll look at those two things: using ADO in Windows Forms–based desktop applications and using ADO in Web-based applications. Before going any further, though, I need to evangelize a little, particularly for those of you out there who've deployed production applications prior to .NET.

You see, developers are a strange bunch. On the one hand, they all love powerful frameworks, such as .NET, and truly appreciate the amount of work a powerful, well-written framework can save them. On the other hand, there comes a point where a framework can do so much and take so much out of the hands of the programmer that many developers resist its adoption. Sometimes this resistance is well placed. Take Visual Basic, for example (not VB .NET). VB has historically included a number of controls for data binding—binding data from data sources and automatically displaying it on-screen through bound controls. Historically, this always involved something known as a *data control*. On the surface it looked neat: Stick a data control on a form, bind a number of other GUI controls to the data control, and then at runtime just load some data into the data control and you instantly have a form of data the user can view, update, and navigate, with little or no effort on the part of the developer. This power, though, also took away control from the developer. In earlier versions of VB in particular, developers taking this approach were forced to fight the data control to claw back some degree of control over how the user worked with data, and they inevitably ended up writing more code than if they had just loaded the data and manually populated the controls on the form themselves. The data control was also somewhat inefficient in the way it did things.

For these reasons, there's a lot of resistance to "bound" user interfaces. Visual Studio .NET and the user interface controls in the .NET Framework support data binding, but it is quite unlike anything you've seen before. The decision to use bound controls in .NET is not a decision to forgo control and power in the pursuit of an easy life. The bound controls in .NET do not limit the control programmers have over their data access architecture, and they do not impose unwanted restrictions on the design of the GUI. Bound controls in .NET are incredibly powerful, stunningly easy to use, and if you have experience with prior versions of ADO, DAO, and RDO, you should be pleasantly surprised by just what you can accomplish with them.

In this chapter I'll lead you through some hands-on examples of common ADO-related GUI tasks. You'll see how to use a DataGrid, how to use the Visual Studio wizards and designers to create your DataAdapters and Connections with little or no code, and how to data bind any visual control you choose. In the next chapter you'll drill down in more detail and learn how to take control of data binding through code, and also how to validate and explore data in visual bound controls, again through code.

A Simple Complex-Bound Example

Strange heading, isn't it? In a moment you're going to walk through a very simple data-binding solution, connect to a database, and display the results of a select inside a grid. The complex part of the equation is simply the name given to the type of binding that you're going to use. Windows Forms applications can make use of either **simple binding** or **complex binding**. *Simple binding*, as its name suggests, is pretty trivial; you just bind a property of a control to a column in a data source (DataSet, DataTable, or DataView). The key here, and I'm going to put this in bold just so you don't miss it, is **with simple binding you can bind ANY property of a control to a column**. Think about that for a second. Just imagine that you have a picture in a database but also store the picture's dimensions. Using simple binding, you can pull the picture itself into a picture box and then automatically set up the picture box's dimensions based on the size of the image in the database.

Complex binding is the process of linking one or more data sources into a control and allowing the user to navigate around the data. For example, the DataGrid that you're about to use has the capability to display and let the user navigate around multiple related tables. Obviously, that's quite complex.

Let's get started on the application. You're going to create a Windows Forms application that lets the user see information on employees in the Northwind table and also enables them to update the employee information.

Create a new project in Visual Studio .NET, but unlike the previous examples, select the VB .NET Windows Application as the template, as shown in Figure 6-1.

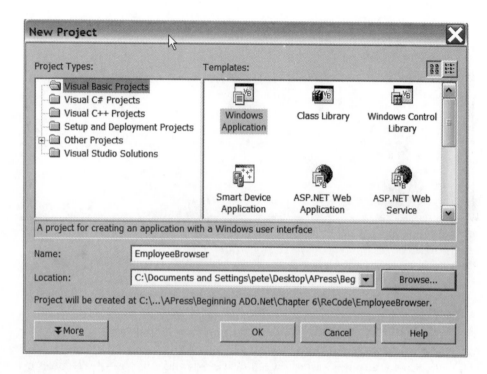

Figure 6-1. Select the VB .NET Windows Application template for the projects in this chapter.

Name your project whatever you like—I chose EmployeeBrowser just to make it obvious. After a short pause the project should be created and you'll be looking at a blank form ready to start work.

This is really just a two-tier application—all your logic is going to go behind the form, and you're going to connect straight to the database from it. In the next chapter you'll see how to add tiers to grab and validate the data, something you'll be doing a lot of when you move into the world of ASP.NET and Web service development.

Think back to the previous discussions on ADO.NET for a moment. You need to connect to the database and grab a list of employees. Once that list is grabbed, you're going to allow the user to update the data, add new items, and save it all en masse when they're done. Obviously, this is going to require a Connection, a Data-Adapter, and a DataSet. Now, you could go ahead and create these things in code, but that would be denying yourself access to some of the really powerful features of the Visual Studio .NET IDE.

Open the Toolbox at the left of the Form Designer and then select the Data tab, just like in Figure 6-2.

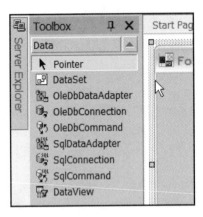

Figure 6-2. The Data tab of the Toolbox, within the VS.NET IDE

The list may surprise you. You've already done a lot of work with ADO DataSets, Connections, and Adapters, but there they all are, shown on the Data tab within the Visual Studio Designer's Toolbox. Of course, these components don't have any visual aspects to them, but double-clicking them will add them to the form in code for you. More to the point, some very handy wizards and other features come into play if you work with them this way, instead of through code.

Go ahead and double-click the SqlDataAdapter to start one such wizard—the Data Adapter Configuration Wizard—shown in Figure 6-3 in the next section.

The Data Adapter Configuration Wizard

Setting up everything you need to work with a DataAdapter and Connection in code can be a time-consuming and data entry–intensive process. The wizard can do it all for you. Now, before those with a pathological fear of anything that saves time and effort run for the hills, I should point out that the wizard is very flexible. You can override much of its operation and completely drill down into every aspect of setting the Adapter up. So, use it. The wizard in this case is your friend. Figure 6-3 shows the first page of the wizard.

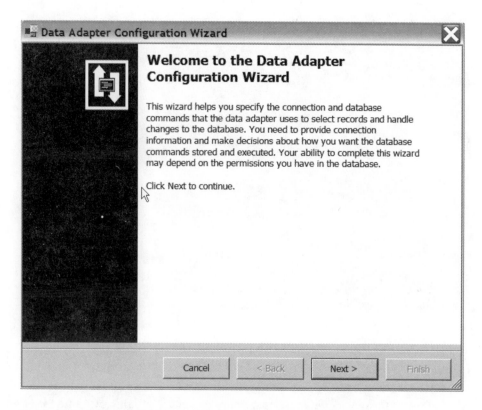

Figure 6-3. The start of the Data Adapter Configuration Wizard

Click the Next button to advance to the second page of the wizard, and you'll see a window like that shown in Figure 6-4.

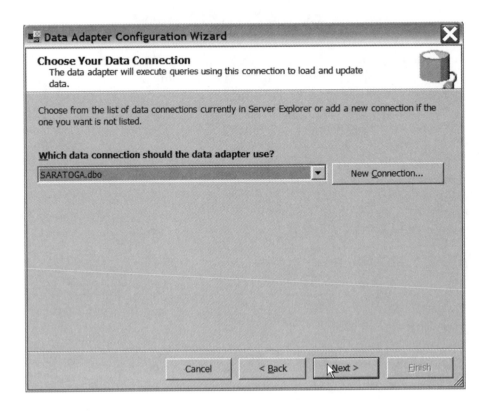

Figure 6-4. Page 2 of the Data Adapter Configuration Wizard deals with setting up the database connection that your new Adapter is going to use.

The connection part of the wizard will appear. Unless you've used the wizard before, you'll probably find that the database connection shown doesn't match the one you need. In Figure 6-4, for example, the connection that's about to be used will connect to the master database on my Saratoga (my machines are named after ships on *Star Trek*) server. This isn't a problem—just click the New Connection button to advance to the next dialog box, which is shown in Figure 6-5.

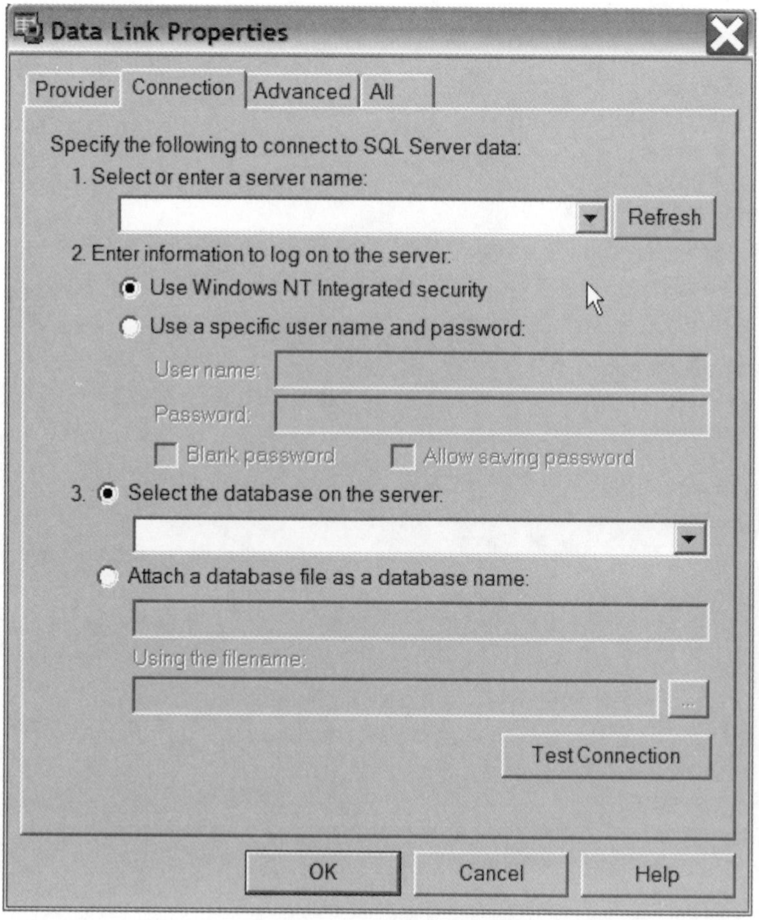

Figure 6-5. The Data Link Properties dialog box

The Data Link Properties dialog box will appear. This dialog box allows you to not only set up every aspect of the connection that you want your DataAdapter to use, but you can also use it to test the connection before it gets embedded in your code. Go ahead and choose, or enter, your own server name and the Northwind database on that server. Clicking OK will save the details you enter and return you to the second page of the Data Adapter Configuration Wizard, where you now just need to click Next to move on to the third page. (Incidentally, the connection information is saved so that the next time the wizard runs, you can just select the connection from the drop-down list on the second page of the wizard.) Your window should now look like Figure 6-6.

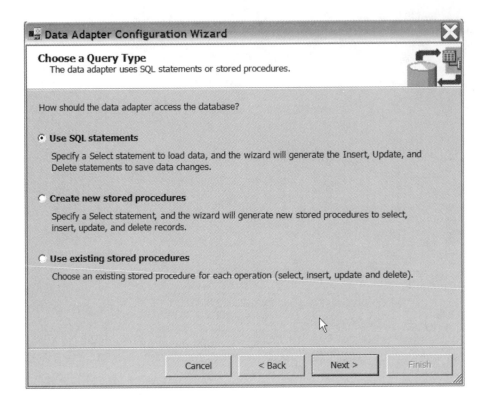

Figure 6-6. The Query Type page

The Query Type page will appear. For now, you can just click the Next button. By default the wizard expects that you're going to want to embed SQL in your code, but as Figure 6-6 shows, you can also choose to create brand-new stored procedures or use existing ones. You'll look at these options later. Clicking Next with the "Use Sql statements" option selected takes you to the Query Builder page shown in Figure 6-7.

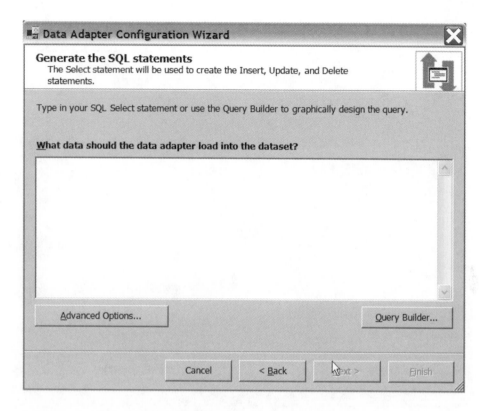

Figure 6-7. The Query Builder page of the Data Adapter Configuration Wizard

The Query Builder page has a wealth of options, although you wouldn't think so to look at it. From here you can just key in a **Select** statement and click Next to let the wizard automatically generate the **Update**, **Delete**, and **Insert** statements. The wizard can also manage concurrency issues for you by writing these new queries in such a way that they always check the database copies of records before posting new data in. If the database record changed since it was pulled into the DataSet and edited, the Insert, Update, or Delete operation will fail.

You can turn all this off, of course, and if your SQL isn't up to writing the Select statement by hand, you can use the Query Builder I touched on back in Chapter 1 to build the statement for you. That's what you're going to do now. Click the Query Builder button to see the query builder dialog box in Figure 6-8.

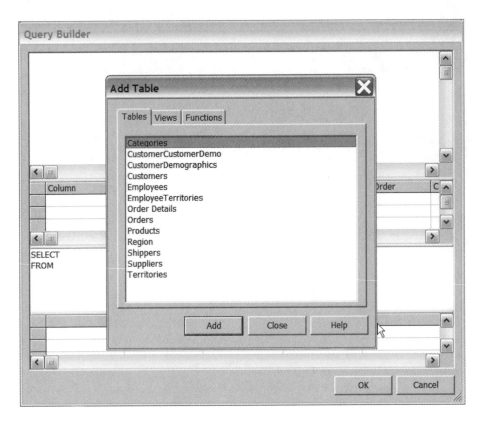

Figure 6-8. Visual Studio .NET's Query Builder is embedded in the Data Adapter Configuration Wizard.

I'm not going to go through how to use the Query Builder in detail again—just refer back to Chapter 1 if you get really lost. For now, just choose to add the Employee table into the query and then, from the list of columns that you want to pull in, select the * column to show that you want to grab all the columns. The window should look like the one shown in Figure 6-9.

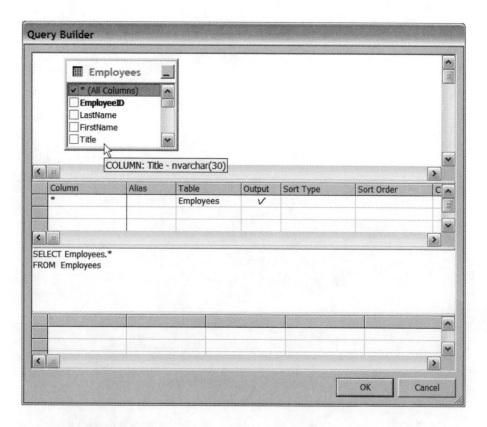

Figure 6-9. Select the * column to bring in every column of the Employee table in your Select statement.

When you are done, click OK to return to the Query Builder page of the wizard, and then click Advanced Options to take a look at the other options available to you, as shown in Figure 6-10.

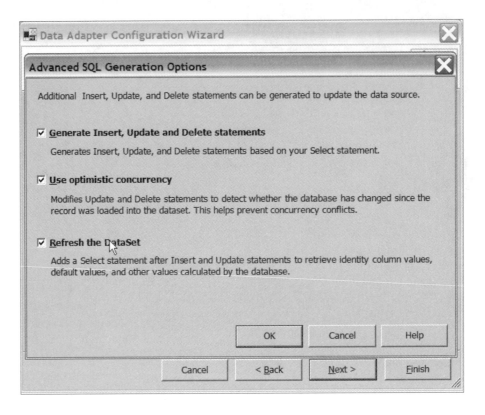

Figure 6-10. The Advanced button on the Query Builder page allows even more control over the creation of the DataAdapter.

The Advanced tab provides you with a set of options that are, by and large, quite self-explanatory. Unchecking the top option prevents the wizard from automatically generating SQL statements for the Update, Insert, and Delete commands inside the Adapter. The second option relates to the first. If you check this option, and if you have asked the wizard to build the other SQL statements for you, then that second option will cause the new SQL statements to be written such that they check the rows in the database before updating them. This is important, since you are going to be working with disconnected data in DataSets. It makes sure that if the rows in the database have in any way changed since you last grabbed them, any updates you asked to make are rejected. Finally, the "Refresh the DataSet" option extends the Update, Insert, and Delete commands even further to make them reselect data after it has been posted back to the database. You may be working with tables that have self-calculating columns, for example, and so leaving this option checked makes sure that a select is done to update the DataSet after posting new information back.

For now, just leave the settings all checked and click OK. When you return to the Query Builder page, click Next to view the wizard results shown in Figure 6-11.

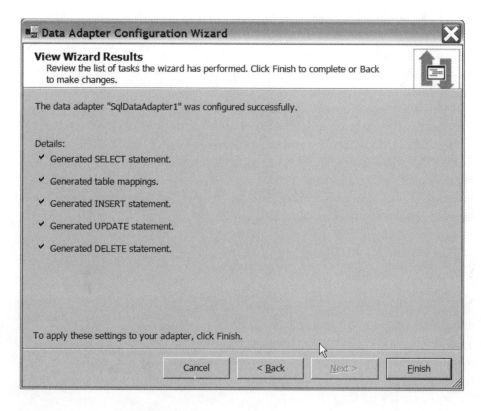

Figure 6-11. The Wizard Results page

At this point you can click the Back button to walk back through the process (most commonly to change the queries) or click Finish to create the DataAdapter. Click Finish.

You should now see two new objects underneath the form in the Visual Studio Designer: a SqlDataAdapter and a SqlConnection (see Figure 6-12). These were both created by the wizard and are ready to go. It's a good idea to change the names, though—just because you built them with a wizard doesn't mean that you have to throw clarity and naming conventions out the window.

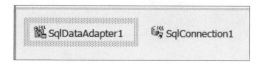

Figure 6-12. The new objects created by the Data Adapter Configuration Wizard

Click the SqlDataAdapter (just once—don't double-click it) and change its Name property in the property inspector to **employeeAdapter**. Do the same for the SqlConnection; click it and change its name in the property inspector to **northwindConnection**. Your Connection and DataAdapter are now ready for use, without you having to write a single line of code.

That whole process may have seem somewhat long-winded, but that's really only because you were reading along as you worked through the pages of the wizard. After a couple of tries with the wizard on your own, you'll find it's incredibly quick and easy to use it to get an Adapter and Connection onto your form—much easier than doing it all through code. Creating Adapters this way in particular brings another advantage with it, over and above the manual-coding approach. That advantage is the typed DataSet.

Typed DataSets

If you can take a step back for a moment and look over the DataSet code in Chapters 4 and 5 objectively, from the point of view of someone who has never ever touched .NET, it soon becomes obvious that regardless of how much power a DataSet brings to the mix, it's cumbersome to use. All that Dataset.Tables("TableName").Columns("ColumnName") hassle isn't conducive to headache-free coding.

The *typed DataSet* solves a lot of problems related to the DataSet's verbosity. With a typed DataSet you start with an XML Schema representing the data the DataSet is going to hold and use it to create a new "type." This type is then used to instantiate a class that contains all the functionality of a standard DataSet but that also adds to it by using real table and column names as properties. So, with a typed DataSet, code such as the following:

```
northwindDataSet.Tables("Employees").Rows(0).Item("LastName") = "Bloggs"
```

becomes

```
northwindDataset.Employees(0).LastName = "Bloggs"
```

I think you'll agree that the latter is far more preferable.

Building a typed DataSet manually takes a considerable amount of effort. The most time-consuming aspect is the process of producing a complete XSD schema for the tables you'll hold in the DataSet. For a complex DataSet, especially one that relies on relationships and constraints, that's not a trivial undertaking. I do cover XSD later in the book, because it is genuinely useful to know at times, but for creating a typed DataSet there's a handy tool built into the Visual Studio .NET IDE that's a lot less painful to use.

Click the DataAdapter to select it, and then right-click. A context-sensitive menu will appear that looks like the one in Figure 6-13.

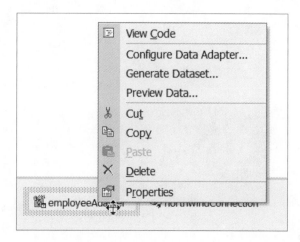

Figure 6-13. The context-sensitive menu attached to a DataAdapter

The same functionality is available through the Data menu at the top of the Visual Studio IDE. The pop-up menu lets you back into the Data Adapter Configuration Wizard through the Configure Data Adapter item and also lets you see a preview of the data that the Adapter will provide. Of most interest to you is the Generate Dataset item. Click it to bring up the Generate Dataset dialog box shown in Figure 6-14.

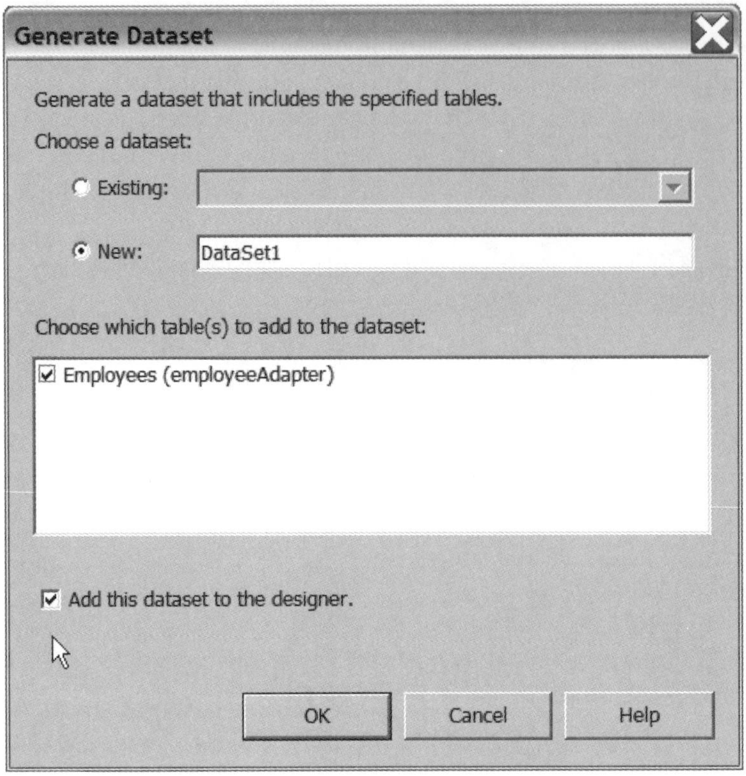

Figure 6-14. The Generate Dataset dialog box

The Generate Dataset dialog box appears quite straightforward, but it can catch you out. First, make sure that the tables you want to use in the DataSet are checked—the wizard will use these tables to build the schema that ultimately defines the DataSet type. You only have one table in the list, the Employees table, so make sure it's checked. Also, make sure the "Add this dataset to the designer" option is checked; this will cause the new DataSet to appear in the designer alongside the Connection and Adapter.

Pay attention to the name of the DataSet next in the New text box. This can be a source of confusion. The name here is not, as you might believe, the name of the DataSet that you want to create. It is the name of the type used to create the DataSet. Think of this as naming the class that you are going to create an object from. Change the name here from DataSet1 to **TEmployeeDS**, and then click the OK button.

The new type will be created, and a DataSet created from that type will appear in the designer right alongside the Adapter and Connection objects (see Figure 6-15).

Figure 6-15. The new, typed DataSet

Notice how the name is different from the type. The type you created is called **TEmployeeDS**, but the *actual* DataSet is called **TEmployeeDS1**. Select it and change its name in the property inspector to **employeeDataset** (normally you'd name it after the database or some other useful name that indicates all the data the DataSet contains—you're just working with one table, though, hence the name "employeeDataset").

At this point you have a typed DataSet in your project ready to be used. You can get at the tables in the DataSet by name, such as (don't type this)

```
Dim myTable as DataTable = employeeDataset.employees
```

You can also get at columns in the table by name—just suffix "column" onto the end of the column name:

```
Dim myColumn = myTable.myFieldColumn
```

If you do want to fiddle with the DataSet contents using code, there are a couple of things to watch out for. With a typed DataSet, you can set the value of a column on a specific row like this:

```
MyDataset.myTableName(rownumber).columnName = "columnvalue"
```

However, if you want to get or set the value of a column on the current row, you still need to go through the Items collection:

```
MyDataSet.myTableName.Item("columnName") = "columnvalue"
```

I cover this whole area in great detail in the next chapter, when you'll start exploring every feature of data binding and developing GUI-based ADO applications.

The DataGrid

The DataGrid control is huge. It has a mass of events and scads of properties, collections, and collections within collections attached. To be quite frank, it's got enough functionality to easily fill a chapter on its own. You're going to focus in this chapter on the more common things you'll want to do with it, though, and dive in deeper in the next chapter.

You should still have your blank form with its three data objects patiently waiting underneath. The next step is to add in the DataGrid and bind it to those components. Go to the Toolbox, click Windows Forms, and double-click the DataGrid component. It will appear at a default size and location within your form. Resize it so that it takes up the bulk of the form, as shown in Figure 6-16.

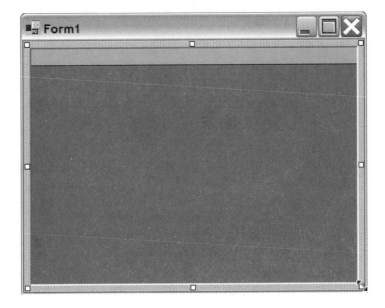

Figure 6-16. The DataGrid, unbound and naked

Binding the DataGrid is very simple: You just need to set up the **DataSource** and **DataMember** properties. DataSource is the DataSet that you want to connect to, and DataMember is the specific element that you want to bind to. Go ahead and set the DataSource property to **employeeDataset** and the DataMember property to **Employees** (see Figure 6-17). When you work with these properties in the property inspector, you'll find that you can use drop-down lists to select the elements in question. You'll also find that once you have both properties filled, the DataSet instantly changes, automatically showing a list of the columns in the Employees table. You'll see how to configure this list in a moment.

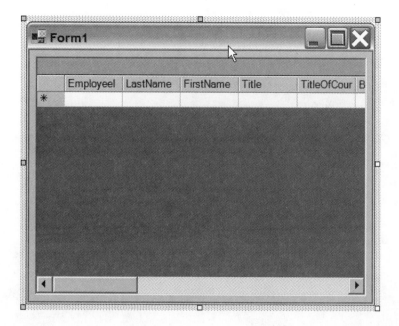

Figure 6-17. The DataGrid, bound to the Employees table in the employeeDataset DataSet

At this point you've written no code, and if you were to run the application (don't) you'd find it working perfectly, except for one small snag. The DataSet that the grid is bound to won't have been populated with any data, so when the program runs, you'll find yourself staring at an empty grid. Entering information at this point would populate the underlying DataSet, but that's hardly useful in an application that you were originally planning to use to navigate data in a database. Some code is required.

Double-click the form, not the grid, to open the code editor. You should find yourself automatically dropped into the form's Load event, which is just where you want to be. Add some code so that your form's Load event looks like this:

```
Private Sub Form1_Load(ByVal sender As System.Object, _
        ByVal e As System.EventArgs) Handles MyBase.Load
    employeeAdapter.Fill(employeeDataset)
End Sub
```

Don't forget to add the Imports System.Data.SqlClient line and Option Strict On right above the form's class definition if you want type safety and a nice, fast application. Run the program now and when the form loads, you'll see a fully populated DataGrid like the one shown in Figure 6-18.

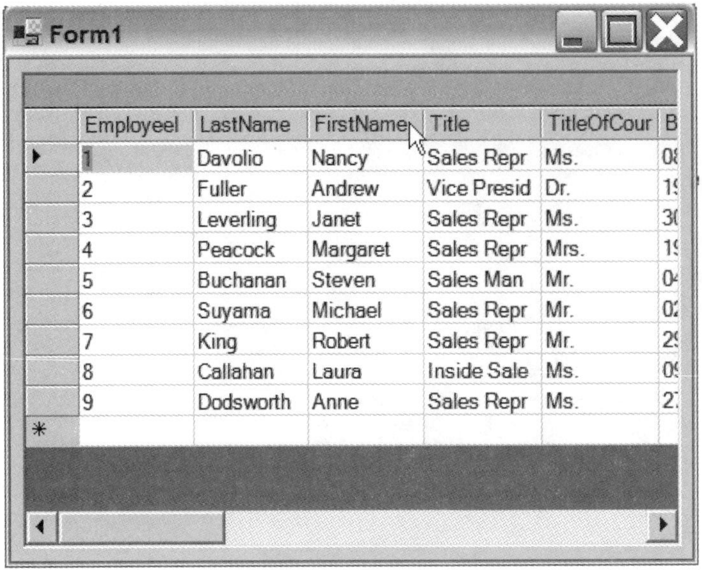

Figure 6-18. The bound grid in full flight

You can add rows to this grid, change the data already displayed in the grid, and even delete rows by clicking to the left of the row in question and then pressing the Delete key. The changes will all be replicated in the DataSet. The changes don't make their way down to the database yet, though, since that's the job of the DataAdapter; the grid just works with disconnected information in a DataSet.

Stop the application from running and change the layout of the form by adding two buttons (name them okButton and cancelButton), so that your form looks like the one shown in Figure 6-19.

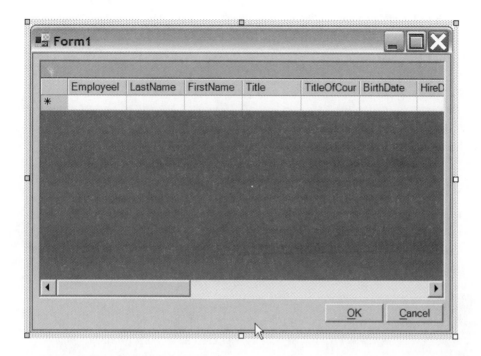

Figure 6-19. The OK and Cancel buttons will be hooked up to replicate changes to the database.

Code the Click handlers for the two buttons as follows:

```
Private Sub okButton_Click(ByVal sender As System.Object, _
        ByVal e As System.EventArgs) Handles okButton.Click
    employeeAdapter.Update(employeeDataset)
End Sub

Private Sub cancelButton_Click(ByVal sender As System.Object, _
        ByVal e As System.EventArgs) Handles cancelButton.Click
    employeeDataset.RejectChanges()
End Sub
```

When the OK button is clicked, you pass the DataSet to employeeAdapter.Update() to accept all the changes and save them to the database. Alternately, when the Cancel button is clicked, you just call **RejectChanges**() on the DataSet to put the DataSet back in the condition it was in before any changes took place. Run the application and have a play. In particular, try deleting a bunch of rows and click Cancel. Then, try adding in a new employee and click OK—pay attention to just how rapid that update is.

Customizing the DataGrid

The visual appearance, including the layout, of data in a DataGrid is controlled by a **DataGridTableStyle** object. As its name implies, the DataGridTableStyle object defines the style to apply for a specific table displayed in a DataGrid. The DataGrid actually contains a collection of these, which you can get at through the **TableStyles** collection property, and relates each one to a table of data through the **DataGridTableStyle.MappingName** property. The reason the grid stores a collection is that a DataGrid is quite capable of displaying data from multiple tables at the same time. When a new table is shown, the grid searches its Table-Styles collection for a DataGridTableStyle object and then uses its properties to define such things as the color to use for the grid lines, the font to use for the headings, and so on.

As if that weren't enough, each DataGridTableStyle object holds a collection of **DataGridColumnStyle** objects. These objects control which columns from the DataSource to show in the grid and how those grid columns should be formatted. You can see the hierarchy of the objects in Figure 6-20.

When you set the DataMember property of the DataGrid earlier, the DataGrid searched through its DataGridTableStyle objects looking for one with the same name as the table set in DataMember. When it failed to find one, it automatically mapped that table name to a default internal style that renders every field in a table a default size. You cannot customize this default style, so it's always a good idea to create your own TableStyle objects.

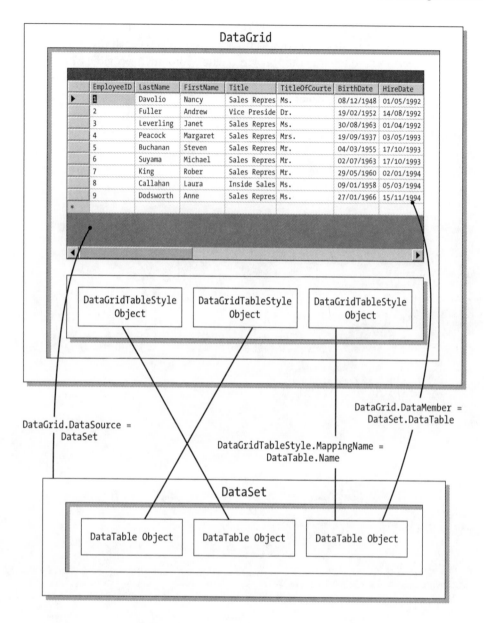

Figure 6-20. The links between the DataGrid and the information that it displays

The first step is to clear out the DataMember property of the DataGrid. Just select the text currently in the property and press the Backspace key. The grid will instantly revert back to looking the way it did when you first dropped it onto the form—with no columns defined and no data on display. Also, set the AllowNavigation property to False—I'll cover what this does later.

Still in the property window, find and click in the TableStyles property. You'll notice that within the property inspector the property shows a button containing ellipses (…) to the right of the entry area. Click this button and you'll be taken to the grid styles editor, as shown in Figure 6-21.

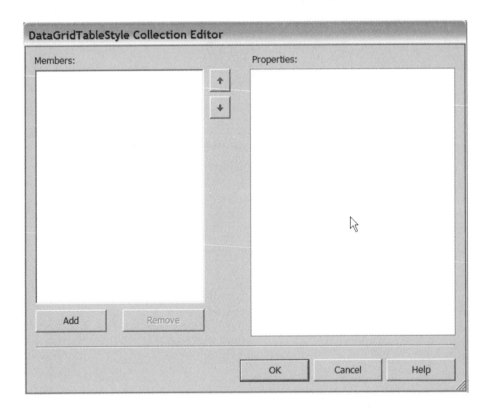

Figure 6-21. The grid styles editor allows you to add in new DataGridTableStyle objects and link them to specific table names.

When the editor appears, click the Add button at its bottom left. A new DataGridTableStyle object will be created and shown in the list on the left, while the right-hand side of the editor dialog box will change to show you a complete list of properties for that object, as shown in Figure 6-22.

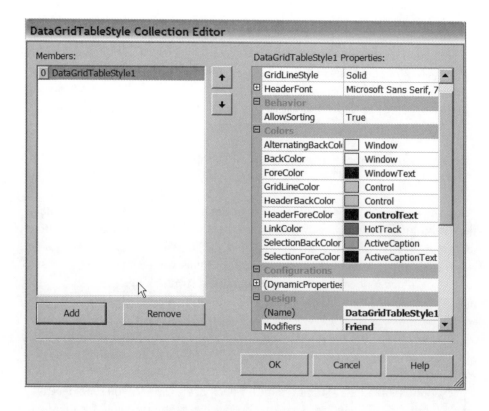

Figure 6-22. Adding a new DataGridTableStyle object causes the editor to show you all of that object's properties and allows you to edit them.

You now need to relate your new DataTableStyle object to a table. To achieve this, all you need to do is set the MappingName property to the name of the table. Click this property, drop down the list of tables, and select the Employees Table.

When you've done that, click OK to close the DataGridTableStyle Collection Editor. You have a table style defined now for the Employees table, so go ahead, click the grid and use the property explorer to set the DataMember property back to Employees.

You won't see any change on the grid when you do this, but it's a very important step. Since you've linked a table to the grid that has a matching TableStyle, the grid will start to use that new TableStyle. Any changes you make to it, including adding and deleting columns in the TableStyle, will be instantly shown in the grid. That's exactly what you're going to do now. Let me just recap the steps you've taken so far. To make the grid use your own TableStyle instead of its default, you need to do the following:

- Clear out the DataMember property of the grid.

- Open up the TableStyles Collection Editor by clicking the ellipses in the TableStyles property in the property explorer.

- Add a new TableStyle and use its MappingName property to map it to the table you are going to view.

- Close the editor down and set the DataMember property to the same table you set for the new TableStyle.

Bring up the TableStyles Collection Editor once again. When it appears, click the **GridColumnStyles** property within the editor and click the ellipses (...) button that appears in that property. This will pop open the DataGridColumnStyles editor. It should look almost exactly the same as the TableStyles Collection Editor the first time you opened it. It works in a very similar way as well. It's this editor that you use to add columns to the TableStyle object in order to let the grid know exactly which columns you want it to display and the formatting to use on those columns.

Go ahead and click the Add button to add a new column. Then, click in the MappingName property for that column and select LastName as the column you want to display, as shown in Figure 6-23.

As soon as you set the MappingName property of the column, you should see the new column appear in the grid. Set up the Header Text property to hold the column's caption. You may also want to change the Width property to make the column wider (a value of 130 works well).

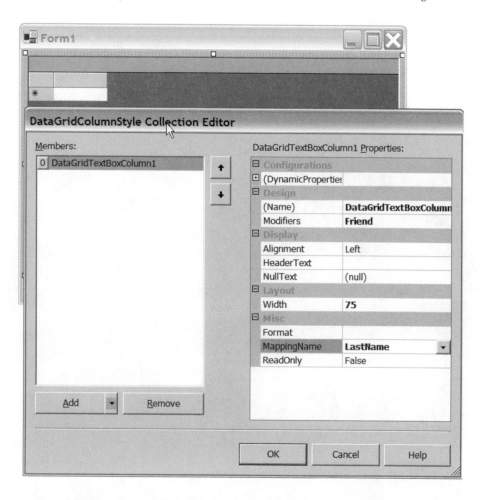

Figure 6-23. The column editor lets you add columns to a TableStyle object and map it to a specific column in the data source.

Go ahead and add in the FirstName and Title columns, as displayed in Figure 6-24.

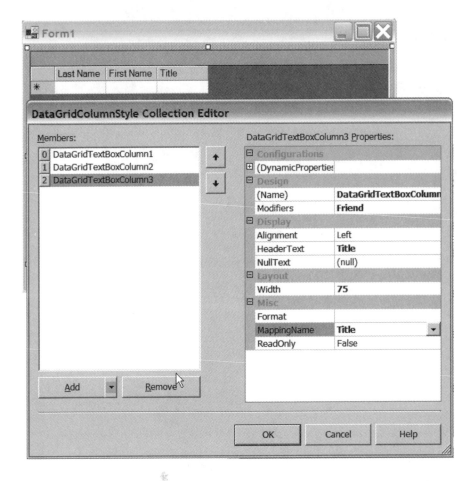

Figure 6-24. The DataGrid is set up to display just the information you need.

You're done—your grid is customized and complete. Before you finish here, though, there's another neat feature of the column editor that you should know about.

You are not limited to just adding textual columns to the grid. Notice the small drop-down arrow to the right of the Add button. If you click this arrow, you'll find that you can add either a text column or a DataGridBoolColumn. This is really just a check box, but it's useful for linking to "Bit" fields.

Also, when you added the columns to the grid, they were automatically named by the editor. The Name property is exposed within the editor, allowing you to easily assign a name that you can use in code later if you want to take control of the formatting of the grid at runtime. The same applies to the TableStyle object as well.

Reformatting the Grid

The DataGrid is pretty powerful straight out of the box, but it's also pretty plain and dull to look at. That's easily changed, and it doesn't require a great deal of clicking or typing. If you still have the application you just worked on loaded (if not, load it), right-click the grid. When the pop-up menu appears, click AutoFormat and you'll see the Auto Format dialog box appear (see Figure 6-25).

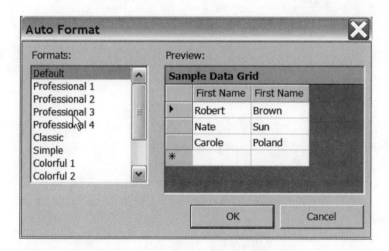

Figure 6-25. The Auto Format dialog box

If you've ever used tables in Word or Excel, you'll recognize this dialog box instantly. The list box on the left shows a list of prebuilt visual styles that can be applied to the grid, while the right-hand side shows a preview of what the selected style looks like. Take a look at each style, and when you find one you're happy with, select it and click the OK button.

The grid on your form will instantly adopt a (hopefully) more pleasing visual style. See Figure 6-26 for an example.

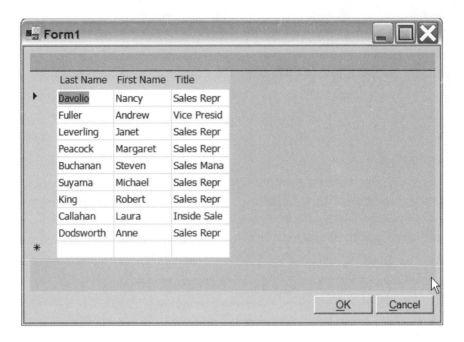

Figure 6-26. The grid with a new format applied

A Complex Complex-Binding Example

The last example was pretty simple: Just connect to a data source and display a single result set from that data source. What about something more complex? What about the master-detail problem, where selecting a row from one result set shows related rows from another result set?

The key to solving the problem lies within the XML Schema that's produced for a typed DataSet. You can easily link two tables in a typed DataSet through the schema and have Visual Studio automatically build the data relation between those two tables. Bound controls can monitor row-change events and refresh their contents when a master row changes.

Setting a Master-Child Relation

Start up a new project. Just as in the last example, select the VB .NET Windows Application template as the foundation for your new application, and call the project Master-Detail.

The first step, as in the last example, is to set up the DataAdapters you'll use to grab information. Go ahead and set up two DataAdapters called employeeAdapter and regionAdapter. For employeeAdapter, set the SQL for the select command (within the Data Adapter Configuration Wizard) to the following:

```
SELECT DISTINCT
    Employees.LastName,
    Employees.FirstName,
    Employees.Title,
    Employees.EmployeeID,
    Region.RegionID,
    Region.RegionDescription
FROM
    Employees INNER JOIN
    EmployeeTerritories ON
        Employees.EmployeeID = EmployeeTerritories.EmployeeID
            INNER JOIN Territories ON
              EmployeeTerritories.TerritoryID = Territories.TerritoryID
                  INNER JOIN Region ON
                      Territories.RegionID = Region.RegionID
```

And for the region Adapter, set the SQL for the select command to this:

```
SELECT Region.* from Region
```

The joins on the employeeAdapter's Select statement will prevent the wizard from figuring out how to write the Update, Insert, and Delete statements for the Adapter. As a result, the Results page of the wizard will contain a set of warning messages. This is quite normal, and since this application doesn't need to update the database, you can ignore the messages. In a real application, you'd respond to this by writing your own commands and dropping them into the Adapter, as you saw how to do in earlier chapters.

Before you go any further, you might want to rename the Connection object, just for completeness, to **northwindConnection**.

The next step is to build your typed DataSet. Unlike the typed DataSet in the last example, this one will include two tables, so select the Data item from the menu bar at the top of Visual Studio .NET and then choose Generate Dataset.

There are two tables listed in the Generate Dataset dialog box this time. Make sure your dialog box looks like the one in Figure 6-27, set the name to **TEmployeeRegionDS**, and click OK. As you saw earlier, this generates the type and then creates a DataSet from that type within the Visual Studio Designer. Change the name of the one in the designer to **northwindDS**.

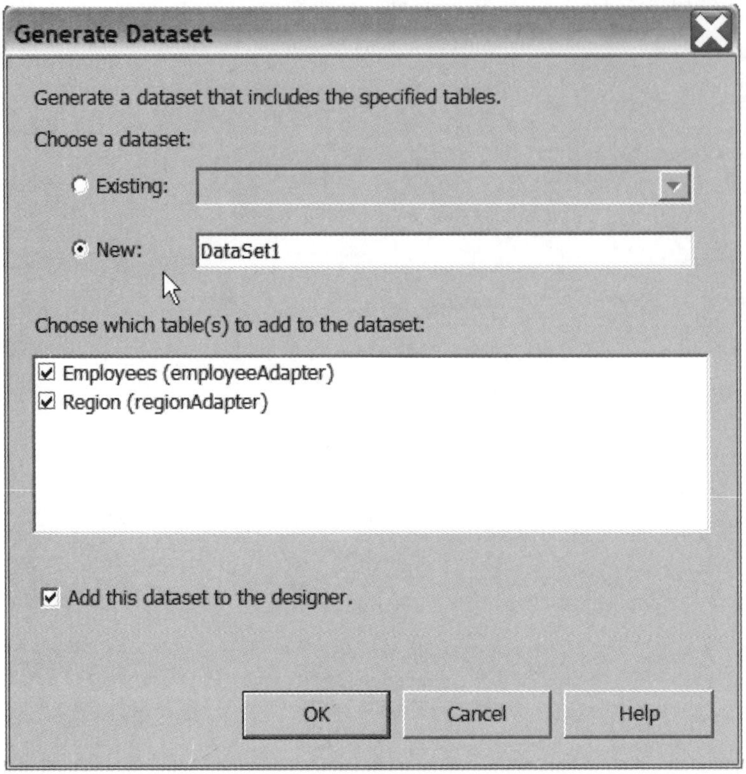

Figure 6-27. Because you have two Adapters pulling data from two data sources, the Generate Dataset dialog box shows two tables.

When you create a typed DataSet like this, an XML Schema Definition (XSD) file is added to the project, which defines the columns, tables, and so forth exposed from the DataSet. If you have a DataSet with more than one table in it, as you do now, you can also use this schema to define relationships. Look in the Solution Explorer and you'll see a file called TemployeeRegionDS.xsd. Double-click it to open the schema editor (see Figure 6-28).

It looks just like the database diagram tool, doesn't it? It works in a similar way. What you want to do here is draw a link showing that many employees can service a region.

Click the RegionID field in the Region table to select that field, and then click and drag the arrow to the left of the column across to the RegionID column on the Employees table. This will pop open a relationship editor dialog box (see Figure 6-29).

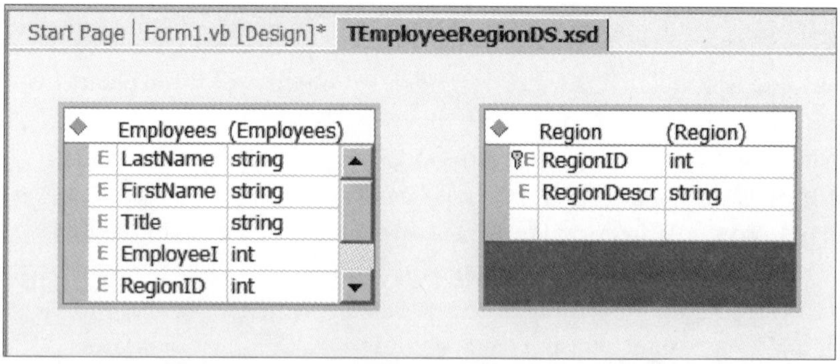

Figure 6-28. Double-clicking a schema file in Visual Studio .NET opens the schema editor.

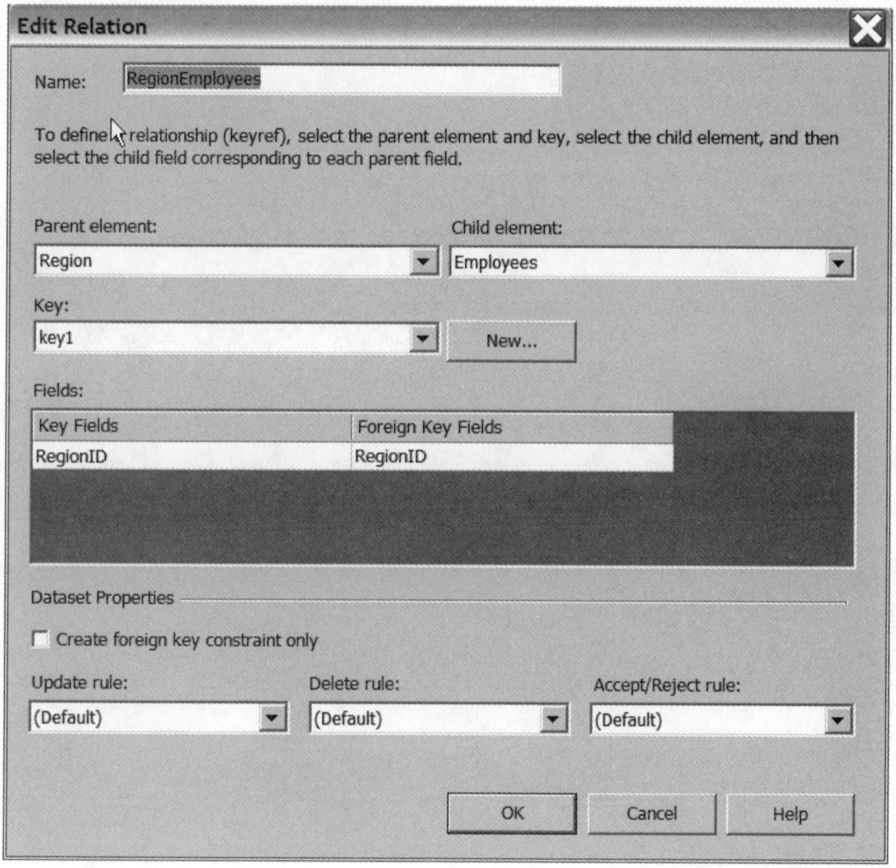

Figure 6-29. The relationship editor appears when you drag a relationship between two columns.

The relationship editor actually serves two purposes. If you leave the "Create foreign key constraint only" check box unchecked, you are actually creating a relationship between two tables. If that box is checked, then the editor will create just the constraints, not the relationship. Leave that box unchecked in this case and click OK. When the schema designer returns to view, you'll see the relationship drawn on the diagram. Time now to draw the user interface.

Drop back into the form designer (click the Form1.vb tab at the top of the designer). There is a chance that the relationship won't always return data in part because of the big join on the employee select. Since you aren't updating the database in this application, click the DataSet and set its Enforce Constraints property to False. Now drop a list box and a DataGrid onto the form, just like in Figure 6-30.

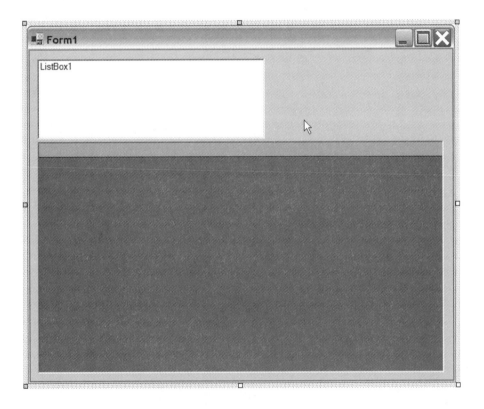

Figure 6-30. Add a list box and DataGrid to your master-detail form.

You're just going to hook these up to the relevant tables now, but you won't spend any time defining which columns to appear in the grid—you can do that yourself later as an exercise.

First up, let's set up the list box. It has a DataSource property, just like the DataGrid, and a DisplayMember property for binding to a specific column to list.

Set the DataSource to the northwindDS DataSet, and set the DisplayMember to **Region.RegionDescription**.

Next, the DataGrid. Because you're working in a master-detail form here, setting up the grid is subtly different from the previous example. Specifically, the DataMember property needs to point at the relationship you defined and not a table. In this way, the grid can track row-change events through the relationship and refresh its contents accordingly.

Set up the DataGrid's DataSource property to the northwindDS DataSet, and then for the DataMember, select Region.RegionEmployees—the relationship you built. Just as before, the grid will change to show all the columns linked through that relationship. (Note: If you didn't save the changes you made to the XSD file earlier, the relationship won't appear as a choice for the DataMember. If that's the case for you, just click the Save All button on Visual Studio's toolbar and try again.)

All that remains is to populate the DataSet. Double-click in the form to drop into the code editor and change the Form_Load event so that it reads like this:

```
Private Sub Form1_Load(ByVal sender As System.Object, _
        ByVal e As System.EventArgs) Handles MyBase.Load
    employeeAdapter.Fill(northwindDS)
    regionAdapter.Fill(northwindDS)
End Sub
```

Once again, don't forget to add Option Strict On to the top of the code.

You're all set, so go ahead and run the application. The top list shows the regions, and the grid shows the employees working within that region. If you click through the different regions in the list box, the grid will automatically update to show the relevant employees, as in Figure 6-31.

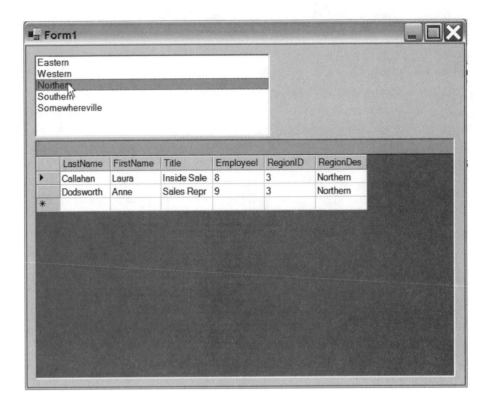

Figure 6-31. The finished master-detail application

As you've seen in this example, the DataGrid is not the only control that supports complex binding; the list box does too. Combo boxes and the checked combo box work in exactly the same fashion.

Go ahead and drop a combo box to the right of the list box. Set its DataSource to the DataSet and its DisplayMember to Region.RegionID. If you run the application now, not only does selecting a region from the list box update the grid, it also updates the text in the combo box. Similarly, selecting a RegionID from the combo box updates the selected item in the list box and also refreshes the grid.

DataGrid Navigation

Master-detail forms like the one in the previous example are very common in older-style applications. The DataGrid does provide a way to let you work with related information across tables in a DataSet without having to go to all that effort, though.

Fire up a new project in Visual Studio .NET, again making sure you choose the VB .NET Windows Application template. Call this project Navigation.

Add in three SqlDataAdapters to the form. Call them customersAdapter, OrdersAdapter, and OrderDetailsAdapter. These three adapters should all talk to the Northwind database. The Select statements for each, in order, are as follows:

```
Select * from Customers
Select * from Orders
Select * from [Order Details]
```

Name the Connection northwindConnection, just for completeness.

Now use the Data menu in Visual Studio to generate a typed DataSet. Make sure that you select all three tables to be added to the DataSet when asked. I called the type TNorthwindDataset and the DataSet itself I named northwindDataset.

Just as before, you need to define the relationships in place here, so double-click the XSD file in the Solution Explorer to fire up the schema editor. When the schema editor pops up, set up relationships between the Customers.CustomerID field and the Orders.CustomerID field (the Customers table is the parent in this relationship), and between the Orders.OrderID field and the OrderDetails.OrderID field (the Orders table is the parent in this relationship).

When you're done, click Save, return to the form designer, and add a DataGrid to the form. Set the DataSource to northwindDataset, and set the DataMember to the Customers table. Feel free to also use the AutoFormatter to change the look of the grid to something more aesthetically pleasing.

Finally, build the DataSet by coding the Form_Load event as follows:

```
Private Sub Form1_Load(ByVal sender As System.Object, _
ByVal e As System.EventArgs) Handles MyBase.Load
      customersAdapter.Fill(northwindDataset)
      ordersAdapter.Fill(northwindDataset)
      orderDetailsAdapter.Fill(northwindDataset)
    End Sub
```

When you're done, run the application. You should see a window like the one shown in Figure 6-32. Each customer will have a small plus sign (+) next to them. You can click this plus sign to view the orders of a customer. Similarly, you can expand each order to show the order details attached to that customer.

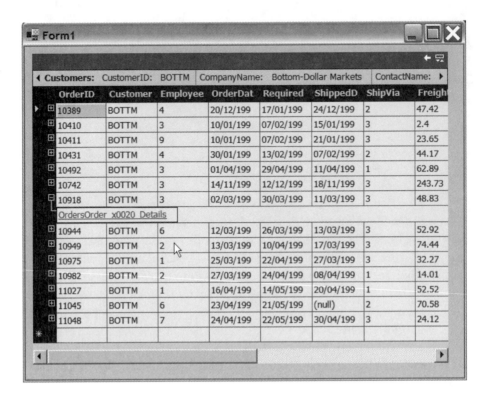

Figure 6-32. The navigable grid

The grid is able to automatically do this by examining the relations in the DataSet and allowing you to navigate through them at runtime. In fact, you don't even need to set up the DataMember property of the grid at all. If you leave it blank, when you run the application you'll need to click the plus sign and choose which table you wish to start exploring.

Simple Binding Other Controls

I mentioned earlier how any control can be bound to a column in a data source. Let's take a look at how.

Start up a new project (called SimpleBinding) and design a form like the one shown in Figure 6-33.

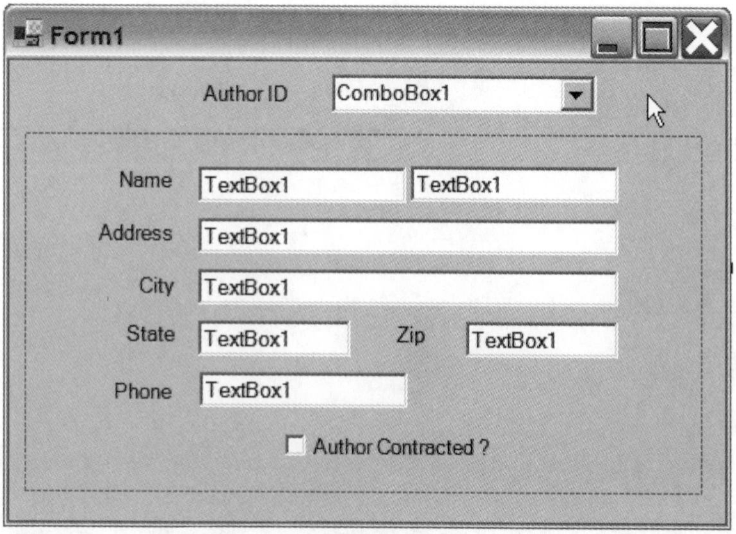

Figure 6-33. A simple data-entry/browsing form

This is quite a straightforward form. The user selects an Author ID from the combo box at the top of the form and the text boxes and check box instantly change to show the complete author information.

Once you've built your form, you'll need to add in a **SqlDataAdapter** and **SqlConnection**, and generate a typed DataSet. I'll let you work through that on your own—just make sure that the Adapter talks to the Pubs database and the Select statement for the Adapter is

```
SELECT au_id, au_lname, au_fname, phone, address, city, state, zip, contract
    FROM authors
```

For naming, I called the DataSet type TpubsDataset, and the DataSet itself pubsDataset.

Once you have the Data objects added to your form, simple binding them is quite straightforward. First, the combo box (which isn't strictly a simple bound control).

Just as with the other controls you've looked at, the combo box has **DataSource** and **DisplayMember** properties. Set the DataSource to **pubsDataset** (the DataSet you added to the form), and set the display member to **authors.au_id**.

Now, click the first text box on your form and take a look at the properties window. In the Data section you'll find a DataBindings option. Expand it to see what's underneath and your property explorer will look like the one in Figure 6-34.

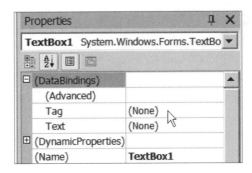

Figure 6-34. The DataBindings properties for the text box

Every visual control in the Toolbox has DataBindings collection. Expand the collection in the property window and you'll see a list of the most common properties that people want to bind to that particular control. In the case of a text box, most developers are interested in binding the Tag and Text properties. Click in the Text property, click the drop-down button that appears, and you'll see a list of data tables available to you, as shown in Figure 6-35. Go ahead and choose the fname field from the authors table.

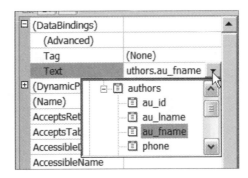

Figure 6-35. Dropping down the Text property in the DataBindings section of a text box allows you to browse and choose which field you want to bind to the text box's Text property.

You can set up the bindings on the rest of the text boxes on the form in exactly the same way, but obviously make sure you choose different fields for each text box or your form will be pretty useless at runtime.

When you're done, take a look at the DataBindings available for the check box at the bottom of the form (you can see them in Figure 6-36).

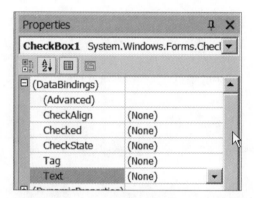

Figure 6-36. The DataBindings of a check box

There's a bunch of common properties there. You're most interested in the **Checked** property, so go ahead and choose it, drop down the list of available fields, and select the Contract field of the Authors table.

All that remains is to populate the DataSet. Add code to the Form_Load event so that it looks like this:

```
Private Sub Form1_Load(ByVal sender As System.Object, _
        ByVal e As System.EventArgs) Handles MyBase.Load
    authorAdapter.Fill(pubsDataset)
End Sub
```

Obviously, you'll need to substitute the name you gave your Adapter for authorAdapter in the code here.

Don't forget to add Option Strict On to the very top of the form's source file. When you're done, run the application and explore—your application should look like the one shown in Figure 6-37.

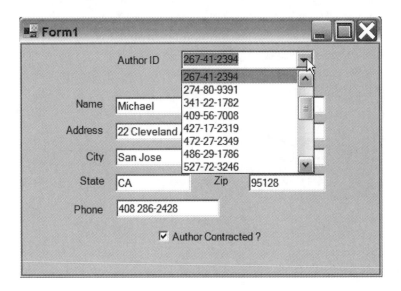

Figure 6-37. The simple bound form in action

It's worth pointing out that you can use this form to change the data on display. You don't have code in the application to update the database (authorAdapter.Update(pubsDataset)), so you won't do any damage to the database. Changes you make are only propagated as far as the in-memory tables.

Summary

This chapter focused on the concepts behind simple and complex binding, and how to put those concepts into action using the tools built into Visual Studio .NET. There was a great deal of resistance in earlier versions of Visual Basic to using the bound controls, since you ended up writing code that effectively fought against the data control at runtime to achieve the required results. There are no such problems with bound controls in .NET. The data-binding mechanisms in .NET work with you, not against you.

Specifically, you learned

- How to create a typed DataSet

- How to use the DataGrid

- How to navigate relationships in a DataSet

- How to set up simple binding on a form

In the next chapter you'll drill down into these concepts even further and explore how to take control of binding through code and add even more power to your application.

CHAPTER 7

Deeper into ADO.NET with Windows Forms

"Engage!"

—Jean Luc Picard, *Star Trek: The Next Generation*

THE LAST CHAPTER TOOK YOU on a walk-through of some of the most common things you'll want to do in ADO.NET using a Windows Forms application. You saw how to set up a simple DataGrid and how to work with master-detail forms, and you also took a brief look at simple binding. The focus in that chapter was on using the tools that Visual Studio provides to make your life as a GUI developer easier.

In this chapter you'll move a step further. Although the DataGrid and the bound controls can take a lot of the pain out of developing a user interface to work with data, there are still times when the developer will want more control. For example, there's no easy way without writing code of validating any changes a user makes in bound controls. In addition, it's not that uncommon for the developer to want to actually explore the contents of the grid at runtime to find out more about its contents, find out where the user is inside the grid, and even to change the formatting of the grid on the fly based on the actions of the user.

Using BindingContexts and CurrencyManagers

If you have come to ADO.NET from a background in any of Microsoft's earlier data-access strategies, then one thing that may have struck you by now is the absence of both traditional Recordsets and cursors. With a traditional-style Recordset, you had a single object provided by the framework that provided methods and properties to let you navigate through the rows of data and interrogate the value of fields within that data. There were methods for moving forward and backward from row to row, as well as methods to "seek" to a specific record and jump to the first and last records. This is a very common data-access model not only used within Microsoft's older development tools, but also in other development tools and frameworks, including Java and Delphi, so it may seem strange that Microsoft chose to deviate from such a "de facto" industry standard.

Cursors and Recordsets are unnecessary with ADO.NET because ADO.NET implements a very pure object-oriented data model. With ADO.NET, you have a container object such as a DataSet or DataTable, and that object provides contains a set of child objects such as DataRows and DataColumns. There's no need to provide methods to move from row to row since you can just index straight into the collection of rows to find the specific row you need or iterate through the collection with a For-Each construct.

Although this way of working undoubtedly has some benefits, it also raises some serious questions and areas for confusion. Binding is one such area. If you don't have an object such as a Recordset providing a pointer to a current row of data, how on earth can a set of bound controls keep track of just which record it is showing? If you are working with simple bound controls, how can you get those bound controls to switch to a different record in the data source?

The answer lies with a set of objects known as **BindingContexts**, **CurrencyManagers**, and **PropertyManagers**.

Every object that derives from the framework's Control object gets a **BindingContext** property. The BindingContext manages the **PropertyManager** and **CurrencyManager** objects for that control as well as for any controls that are contained within it. So, a Form's BindingContext lets you get at the CurrencyManagers in use for any and all bound controls on the form, whereas a text box's BindingContext lets you get at just the PropertyManager and CurrencyManager for that text box alone.

Despite their rather daunting names, PropertyManagers and CurrencyManagers are really quite straightforward to use. A CurrencyManager simply provides a pointer into a DataSource. This effectively gives you the same functionality as the Recordset of old. Using the CurrencyManager's properties, you can easily move from record to record, both forward and backward through a data source, as well as jump directly to any record, including the first and last.

The PropertyManager simply manages properties on controls. So, while the CurrencyManager tracks the current "object" in a data source, a PropertyManager tracks which "property" is bound to which column in the underlying data source. Let me put it a different way: A CurrencyManager says that row n is the current row in a data source, and a PropertyManager says that the "text" property is bound to the "lastname" field in the row pointed at by the CurrencyManager.

As with so many things in .NET, it's a lot easier to get your head around how these things work if you take a look at some code in action.

Fire up a new VB .NET Windows Forms project and design a form like the one in Figure 7-1. The three text boxes are named **txtFirstname**, **txtLastName**, and **txtTitle**. The two buttons are named **nextButton** and **previousButton**.

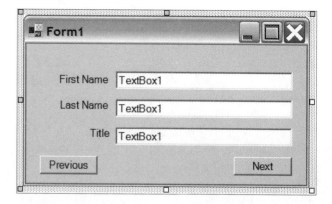

Figure 7-1. The form for the CurrencyManager example

The first thing you are going to need to do is set up a DataSet to feed some data in the form. You'll return to your old friend, the Employee table from the Northwind database.

Double-click the form to open the code editor at the form's Load event and add some code to build the DataSet:

```
' Set up the DataAdapter in the usual way.
        Dim employeeAdapter As New SqlDataAdapter( _
            "SELECT * FROM Employees", _
            "Data Source=localhost;" + _
            "Initial Catalog=northwind;" + _
            "Integrated Security=SSPI")

        ' Create a dataset for the Northwind Database
        ' and fill it with the employee info
        Dim northwindDS As New DataSet("northwind")
        employeeAdapter.Fill(northwindDS, "Employees")
```

(Don't forget to also import the System.Data.SqlClient namespace above the form's class definition and add Option Strict On.)

The next step is to set up the bindings for the text boxes. You want the txtFirstName text box to display the FirstName field, the txtLastName text box to display the LastName field, and the txtTitle text box to display the Title field. If you had added the DataSet to the form visually, this would be as simple as pointing and clicking in the last chapter. The focus in this chapter is on code, though, so go ahead and key in these three lines:

```
'----- now we can go ahead and set up the bindings
        txtFirstname.DataBindings.Add( _
        "Text", northwindDS.Tables("Employees"), "Firstname")
        txtLastName.DataBindings.Add( _
        "Text", northwindDS.Tables("Employees"), "Lastname")
        txtTitle.DataBindings.Add( _
        "Text", northwindDS.Tables("Employees"), "Title")
```

The DataBindings collection attached to every control has an **Add**() method that is used to add in a new property binding for the control. All you need to do is pass that method the name of the control's property that you want to bind, along with the name of the data source (in this case, the Employees table) and the name of the field in that data source that you want your property bound to.

When the application runs, the three text boxes will quite happily show fields from the first record in the table—in effect, the current record. What you need to do is get at the CurrencyManager, the object responsible for managing that current record pointer, so that you can work with it in the button Click events.

First, add a new member to the form's class, outside of the Form_Load event:

```
Dim currencyMgr As CurrencyManager
```

```
Private Sub Form1_Load(ByVal sender As System.Object, _
    ByVal e As System.EventArgs) Handles MyBase.Load

    ' Set up the DataAdapter in the usual way.
    Dim employeeAdapter As New SqlDataAdapter( _
            :
            :
            :
```

As you can see from the definition, this member will be used to "cache" your CurrencyManager. The next step is to set it to the actual CurrencyManager in use. To achieve this, add a line of code to the end of your form's Load event:

```
currencyMgr = CType( _
        Me.BindingContext( _
        northwindDS.Tables("Employees")), _
        CurrencyManager)
```

The form's BindingContext property is used here to retrieve the CurrencyManager. The call is actually quite misleading. What you are actually doing here is accessing the BindingContext's default property, which is an Item property. This needs to be passed a data source, as you can see. If you pass in the name of a real data source, such as a table or a DataSet, a CurrencyManager for that data source will be returned. The really misleading bit is that you can also pass in a control, at which point the BindingContext will pass back a PropertyManager— one call, two uses. You will need to use Ctype in VB .NET, though, to cast the returned object into the correct type, as you can see from the previous code.

There's not really anything complex about the CurrencyManager object. It has a **Count** property, which can be used to get at the number of records actually in the DataSource, and it has a **Position** property, which returns the index of the row currently in use and is zero based. Just to reiterate that, if your Count property told you that you have five records available in a data source, then valid values for the Position property are 0, 1, 2, 3, and 4. If you set the Position property beyond the number of records in the data source, then it will revert to showing you the last record.

Let's code the Next and Previous buttons on the form to work with that CurrencyManager object and let the user move through the records in the DataSet.

```
Private Sub nextButton_Click(ByVal sender As System.Object, _
   ByVal e As System.EventArgs) Handles nextButton.Click
      If currencyMgr.Position < currencyMgr.Count - 1 Then
         currencyMgr.Position = currencyMgr.Position + 1
      End If
End Sub
```

The code here checks to make sure you are not already positioned on the last record, and if you're not, it increments the Position property to move to the next record.

The Previous button works the converse way:

```
Private Sub previousButton_Click(ByVal sender As System.Object, _
   ByVal e As System.EventArgs) Handles previousButton.Click
      If currencyMgr.Position > 0 Then
         currencyMgr.Position = currencyMgr.Position - 1
      End If
End Sub
```

If you are not currently looking at the first record, the Position property is decremented to move you back to the previous record.

Try running the application now, and click those Next and Previous buttons. The records will change automatically each time you change the Position property— that's all thanks to the PropertyManager.

The CurrencyManager exposes a CurrentChanged event that the PropertyManager of a bound control subscribes to. When the Position property changes, so too does another property called Current, triggering the CurrentChanged event. The PropertyManager then does its thing, refreshing the values of the properties of the control that are bound according to values from the newly positioned record.

If this all seems a little too simple, then you'd be right. This approach is fine for simply moving around from row to row. If you want to do more than just move, though, you need to start paying special attention to the Current property of the CurrencyManager and to DataView and DataRowView objects.

Using DataViews and DataRowViews

Think about this for a second. What would you need to do to add a button to the previous example to delete the visible row of data? The obvious answer is access the Position property and use that to index into the Rows property of the DataSource. ADO.NET life is not that simple.

When you delete a row, as you know from the previous chapters, the row doesn't actually get deleted. Its version is changed to Deleted, but it is left in the table. When this happens, you have a bit of a problem; the position property from the CurrencyManager could conceivably point to a row that does not exist.

In fact, the problem is even subtler than that. The Position and Count properties within the CurrencyManager continue to update properly when you delete a record. If you had code like this, for example:

```
Myds.tables("mytable").Rows(currencyMgr.Position).Delete()
```

the Count property would decrease by one and the Position property would not change. The data on display would, though. The logic is quite clear here. If you wanted to delete the first record from a DataSet containing 5, you'd end up with a count of 4 and you'd still be looking at record 0—it's just that record number 0 would be a different record from the one you were looking at a moment ago. However, record 0 in your underlying table is still the original record, although it's now flagged as Deleted!

So, this raises all sorts of questions. For example, how come the data on display changes if you delete a record in this way, even though the original record is no longer ever shown in the form? Why is it that the bound form still displays valid data, but the Position property may actually relate to deleted rows in your tables?

The CurrencyManager actually makes use of a **DataView** to display its information. This is a "filtered" view of a table. You can tell a DataView to provide access to just the "current" records in a table, for example, and that's exactly how a CurrencyManager works. Its Position property points in to a DataView that only ever displays records with a RowState of Current. When you delete a record from the underlying table, the view will change to reflect that. Indexes provided by the CurrencyManager are now only valid for your new, customized view of the data, not for the underlying table.

The correct way to delete a record based on the Position property of a CurrencyManager then is

```
MyView.Item(currencyManager.position). Delete()
```

The DataView exposes a property called Item that provides access to the underlying **DataRowView** (not DataRow) objects. Even this is a pain, though, since few developers happen to have a DataView object lying around their code, unless they explicitly went to the trouble of creating one.

Instead, the CurrencyManager provides a **Current** property. When working with tables, the Current property returns the **DataRowView** object that is being used to get at the data currently on display. It supports all the methods a DataRow does, and can thus be used for the delete. If you wanted to add a Delete button to the form, the correct code for it would be as follows:

```
Private Sub deleteButton_Click(ByVal sender As System.Object, _
    ByVal e As System.EventArgs) Handles deleteButton.Click
        Dim currentRow As DataRowView = currencyMgr.Current
        currentRow.Delete()
    End Sub
```

Incidentally, **CurrencyMgr.Current** is also the correct way to get at the nderlying current record when using bound controls.

All tables have a default view attached to them that provides access only to the valid and current records in the table. All bound controls by default make use of that view to ensure that they only display current and valid data.

```
Dim tableView As DataView = myTable.DefaultView
```

You can, of course, create a view yourself and stylize it. It's actually a great way of working with data when coding the GUI.

Whenever you work with bound controls, they access data through a view; it's the easiest way for them to ensure that the data on display consists of current records only and not deleted ones or "original" ones absent of changes. DataViews not only allow you to control which versions of rows you see, they also allow you to filter tables based on their contents and change the sort order of information.

To create a view, you just need to pass in a filter string, sort string, and the row versions that you are interested in as parameters. For example:

```
Dim myView As New DataView( myTable,
    "mycolumn = myvalue", "mysortcolumn DESC", DataRowViewState.CurrentRows)
```

Notice that the row state is determined by selecting a value from the **DataRowViewState** enumeration, not the DataRowState enumeration. The two are very similar—take a look at the online help to see the complete list.

To get at the rows of data, use the DataView's **Item** property. This requires an index to be passed in to specify the number of the row that needs to be retrieved. The result passed back is the DataRowView object you saw earlier.

DataRowViews also allow you to control whether rows can be added, deleted, or updated. This is handled by the AllowEdit(), AllowDelete(), and AllowNew() methods attached to the DataView object.

Let's take a look at DataViews in code, just to wrap things up. Start up a new Windows Forms project and add two DataGrids to the default form, as shown in Figure 7-2.

Figure 7-2. Your new form

Leave the grids with their default names of DataGrid1 and DataGrid2 just to keep things simple (in a live application, of course, you'd name them according to your team's well thought out coding standards).

What you're going to do here is show a standard view of Northwind's Regions table in the top grid and in the bottom show a sorted view of deleted records only.

Double-click the form to bring up the code editor for the Form_Load event ready for code. Import the SqlClient provider and add Option Strict On. Then you can start adding code into your Form_Load event. First, you'll need to build up a DataSet to hold your data:

```
Dim regionAdapter As New SqlDataAdapter( _
            "SELECT * FROM Region", _
            "Data Source=Localhost;" + _
            "Initial Catalog=Northwind;" + _
            "Integrated Security=SSPI")
Dim northwindDS As New DataSet("Northwind")
        regionAdapter.Fill(northwindDS, "Regions")
```

Now you can set up your view:

```
Dim regionView As New DataView(northwindDS.Tables("Regions"), "", _
            "RegionDescription DESC", DataViewRowState.Deleted)
regionView.AllowDelete = False
regionView.AllowEdit = False
regionView.AllowNew = False
```

As promised, the view is created to show deleted regions from the original Regions table in reverse **RegionDescription** order. Just for good measure, the view is also set up to prevent deletions, insertions, and edits to the viewed data.

All that remains is to bind the two grids to the right data sources.

```
DataGrid1.SetDataBinding(northwindDS, "Regions")
DataGrid2.SetDataBinding(regionView, "")
```

Normally, SetDataBinding() expects to be given a data source and the name of a table to show data from. As you can see, though, you can bind directly to a DataView (or indeed to a specific table), in which case you don't need to specify a DataMember string.

Try running the application now and delete rows from the top grid. They will instantly appear in the bottom grid, sorted, as shown in Figure 7-3.

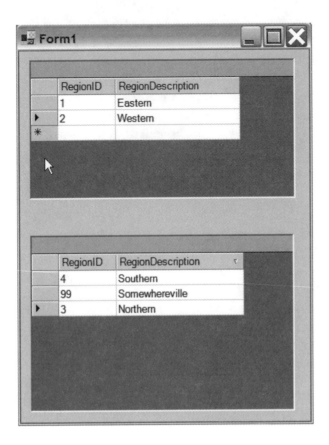

Figure 7-3. The bottom grid shows a view of the top one, in this case displaying deleted rows, sorted.

If you are going to work with bound controls in code, the DataView is your friend and can make your life a lot easier (since it can filter out unwanted row states).

Working with the DataGrid

I mentioned in the last chapter that the DataGrid is a huge control. A brief look at the sheer number of properties in the property explorer will tell you that. There are quite a few methods attached. The developers at Microsoft went to great lengths to make sure that working with a DataGrid in the point-and-click world of the Visual Studio Designer is painless, and even a little fun. The wealth of properties and methods on the grid takes a lot of the sting out of working with the grid in code as well.

Runtime Binding

Binding a grid at runtime is quite easy to achieve and gives you some flexibility in your solution when compared to doing things the point-and-click way. You may be responsible for developing the user interface of an application that has its DataSets served and managed by a separate tier, making it impossible to use the design-time tools to drop a DataAdapter and typed DataSet onto a form. However, runtime binding a grid is not as simple as just setting up the DataSource and DataMember properties directly. Setting up those properties requires at least two lines of code: one to update the DataSource and the other to update the DataMember. After each operation, the grid could potentially try to refresh its contents, causing some nasty screen glitches during the binding process.

There is a method on the grid that allows you to get around this and set up both the DataSource and DataMember in one go: **DataGrid.SetDataBinding()**. To call it, just pass in two parameters. The first parameter is the DataSource, and the second is the DataMember (usually the name of the table that you want to display in the grid). The grid will then refresh its contents after internally setting up both properties. Let's take a look at a short code example.

Start up a new VB Windows Forms project and drop a grid and a button onto the form, just as shown in Figure 7-4.

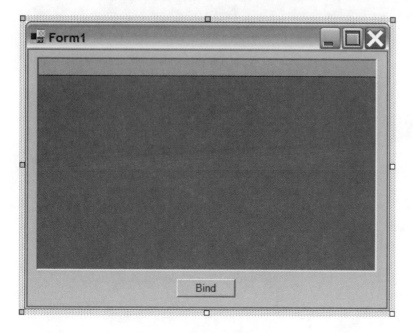

Figure 7-4. Your form should look like this.

Set the name property of the grid to **booksGrid** and the name property of the button to **bindButton**.

Double-click the button to drop into the code window, showing the button's **Click** event handler. Before you do anything else, move to the very top of the code, above the line that reads Public Class Form1, and **import** the **SqlClient** namespace.

```
Option Strict On
Imports System.Data.SqlClient
```

Back in the button's Click event, you're going to need to create a SqlDataAdapter to get the data for the grid.

```
Dim booksAdapter As New SqlDataAdapter( _
      "SELECT * FROM titles", _
    "Data Source=localhost;Initial Catalog=Pubs;Integrated Security=SSPI")
```

Obviously, you'll need to change the name of the DataSource in this code to match the name of your server from the Server Explorer within the Visual Studio IDE (this is the last time I'm going to point that out—you can figure it out yourself from this point on). I've used the shorthand method of creating a DataAdapter here to keep the code simple. It takes two parameters—the first is the SQL for the Select statement, and the second is the actual connection string that you want to use. As you can see from both parameters, this DataAdapter is going to hit the Pubs database and grab all the **titles** rows from it.

Next, you're going to need a DataSet:

```
Dim pubsDataset As New DataSet("Pubs")
```

This shouldn't need any explanation by now.

The next step is to have the DataAdapter to fill the DataSet. This will open the connection, test its properties, build a SqlCommand object, and check it and fire it at the server before waiting for a result set to come back to drop into the DataSet. Obviously, that could take a second or two to run. Since you are working in a GUI environment here, you should probably give the user some feedback that something is going on, instead of just letting the form sit there blankly. The easiest way to do this is to change the mouse pointer into an hourglass:

```
Cursor.Current = System.Windows.Forms.Cursors.WaitCursor

booksAdapter.Fill(pubsDataset, "titles")
```

CursorCurrent is a property of the form, and **System.Windows.Forms.Cursors** is an enumeration that specifies the type of cursor you want. Take a look at the online help if you want to know what all the other possible values here are.

With the mouse pointer set to an hourglass, you can fill the DataSet. It's important here that you actually tell the **DataAdapter.Fill()** method the name of the resulting table to create in the DataSet (in this case, **titles**). If you don't do this, the DataAdapter will quite happily create a table in the DataSet and give it a default name of **table**. By naming the table, you can make the binding code much more "obvious" to the reader of the source, which of course is handy from a maintenance standpoint.

The next step then is to bind the grid.

```
booksGrid.SetDataBinding(pubsDataset, "titles")
```

As you can see, SetDataBinding takes two parameters—the **Datasource** object, and the name of the element to bind to (the **DataMember**), in this case the 'titles' table. If something were to go wrong at this point an exception would occur, so in a production application it's a good idea to wrap the call to SetDataBinding with a Try-Catch handler.

SetDataBinding() has a dramatic effect at runtime. The grid's **DataSource** and **DataMember** properties will get set, and the **TableStyles** collection will be searched for a table style matching the name of the table that you are trying to show. Since you haven't gone to any effort to create a matching DataGridTableStyle object, a default one will be built and the grid will be populated with all rows and all columns of the bound table. You'll take a look in a moment at setting up a DataGridTableStyle object in code.

All that remains now is to reset the cursor back to its default state:

```
Cursor.Current = System.Windows.Forms.Cursors.Default
```

Go ahead and run the application now, and assuming you entered all the code as shown, your form will look like the one in Figure 7-5 when you click the Bind button.

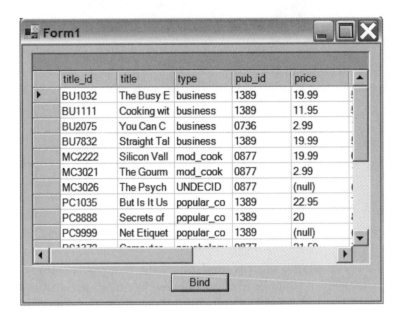

Figure 7-5. A DataGrid that is bound through code at runtime

Formatting the Grid at Runtime

Even though you may not have the data source available to you in design mode, there is nothing to prevent you from adding to the grid's TableStyles collection at design time, a process you explored in the last chapter. You can, of course, also build up the grid's table style through code.

Let's go ahead and extend the previous example to do just that. You're going to reformat the grid so that it just displays the book's title in the grid, and then adds color formatting to the grid using the table and column styles.

Add another button to the form and name it **styleButton** (see Figure 7-6).

You're going to code this button so that it can set up the grid styles separately from the binding process. One of the strengths of binding in code is that you can reformat the grid on the fly at any point in time, even after data has already been bound into the grid.

Double-click your new Style button to get coding its Click event handler. The code in this handler is going to build a new **DataGridTableStyle** object and add it to the grid's **TableStyles** collection. Since the user is free to keep on clicking the Style button as much as he or she likes in the application, the first thing you need to do is clear out the **TableStyles** collection to make sure you don't add duplicates.

```
booksGrid.TableStyles.Clear()
```

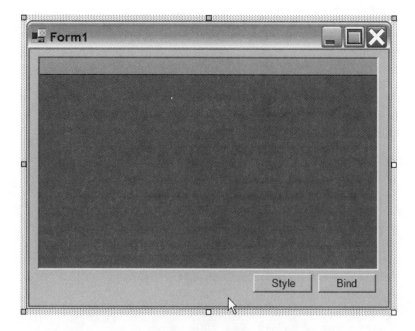

Figure 7-6. Extend the form by adding a Style button.

Next, you can start to build your new column. Now, in code you don't create a **DataGridColumn** object. Instead, you create an object derived from it. You have two choices here. You can create either **DataGridTextBoxColumn** objects or **DataGridBoolColumn** objects. The former is a column that holds text. The latter is a check box–style column ideal for representing True/False values in your DataSet. Since you need to display the book's title, a DataGridTextBoxColumn makes most sense. Add some more code to your handler:

```
Dim titlesColStyle As New DataGridTextBoxColumn()
```

This will create your column, but it won't have any effect until it is bound to a column in the DataSource, through its **MappingName** property. Now is also a good time to set up the width of the column, the column header and, if you wanted to, you could use the **Format** property to apply some formatting to the contents (such as applying the correct formatting for a date or phone number).

```
    With titlesColStyle
        .HeaderText = "Book Title"
        .MappingName = "title"
        .Width = booksGrid.Width
    End With
```

The **HeaderText** property is used to set up the title for the column in the grid. **MappingName** binds the column to the "title" column in the DataSource, and the **Width** is set to a value should let you see the entire contents of most fields.

Now that the column is created, you need a **DataGridTableStyle** object to add it to.

```
Dim newTablestyle As New DataGridTableStyle()
```

Just as when you first created the column, the DataGridTableStyle object is pretty useless until you set some of its properties.

```
With newTablestyle
    .GridColumnStyles.Add(titlesColStyle)

    .MappingName = "titles"
    .AlternatingBackColor = System.Drawing.Color.Aqua
    .BackColor = System.Drawing.Color.Azure
    .ForeColor = System.Drawing.Color.Black
    .HeaderBackColor = System.Drawing.Color.Azure
    .HeaderForeColor = System.Drawing.Color.Crimson
    .ReadOnly = True

End With
```

The first thing to do is add your new column to the table style. With that done, you can map the table style to a specific table using its **MappingName** property. In this case, the table style is mapped to the "titles" table. Note that this is the same name you used as a parameter to the SqlDataAdapter.Fill() method earlier, so you know this is going to relate to a specific table.

The remaining lines of code use the color properties of the TableStyle object to bring some color into the grid. The table style's ReadOnly property is also set to True to prevent users from editing the data at runtime.

All that remains now is to add the table style to the grid. If there is already data in the grid when this happens, the grid will check to see if the new style applies to that data. If it does, then the new style will be applied instantly.

```
booksGrid.TableStyles.Add(newTablestyle)
```

Go ahead and run the application. Click the Bind button to bring in the data, and then click the Style button to add the new style. The grid's appearance will change instantly and you should end up with a grid looking just like the one in Figure 7-7.

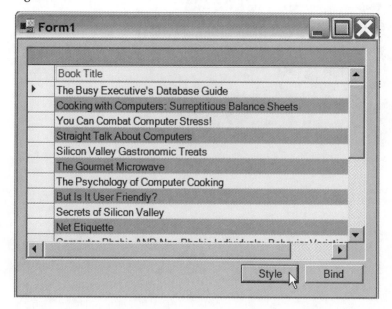

Figure 7-7. Your code-bound grid with a code-created table style attached

Exploring the Grid Through Code

The grid presents data from the bound data source and allows the user to work with it to his or her heart's content, within the constraints set down by you through the grid's properties. There will be times, though, when you want to resolve the grid's data and the user's actions on it back to the original DataRow being manipulated. This isn't as straightforward as it could be.

The DataGrid exposes a property called CurrentCell. This is a DataGridCell object, and it can be used to find out the position in the grid of the currently selected cell. This is great for finding out where in the grid the user is, but it's pretty hopeless when it comes to relating the current cell back to a specific row in a table. Try this out.

Create a new VB .NET Windows Forms project, and drop a grid onto the form and a Label control underneath the grid, as shown in Figure 7-8.

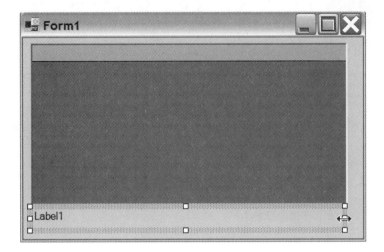

Figure 7-8. The new form with a grid and label

Don't worry about changing the names of the controls. Next, in code, import the SqlClient namespace (and set Option Strict On), and then code the Form_Load event so that it looks like this:

```
Private Sub Form1_Load(ByVal sender As System.Object, _
        ByVal e As System.EventArgs) Handles MyBase.Load
    ' Bind the grid to the employee table from Northwind
    Dim employeeAdapter As New SqlDataAdapter( _
        "SELECT * FROM Employees", _
        "Data Source=localhost;" + _
        "Initial Catalog=Northwind;" + _
        "Integrated Security=SSPI")
    Dim northwindDataset As New DataSet()
    employeeAdapter.Fill(northwindDataset, "employees")
    DataGrid1.SetDataBinding(northwindDataset, "employees")
End Sub
```

This is pretty much the same code as you saw in the earlier examples; it just sets up a binding between the grid and a data source to display a complete list of all the employees from the Northwind database.

Now, where the top of the code editor window says Form1 in the object combo, drop that down and choose **DataGrid1** as the object. Then drop down the event list and select the **CurrentCellChanged** event of the grid, as shown in Figure 7-9.

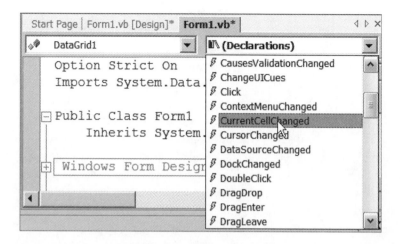

Figure 7-9. Choose the CurrentCellChanged event of the DataGrid to code.

The CurrentCellChanged event fires whenever the current cell of the grid changes. For example, this event will fire if the user clicks in another cell with the mouse at runtime, or if the user uses the cursor keys, the Tab key, or the Enter key to move around the grid that way.

Imagine a situation where when the user moved to a new cell in the grid, you wanted to be able to display the full employee name in the label control, but you didn't want to use binding. The trap that many people fall into is this one (feel free to key it into the event handler you just created to see what happens):

```vb
Private Sub DataGrid1_CurrentCellChanged( _
    ByVal sender As Object, ByVal e As System.EventArgs) _
    Handles DataGrid1.CurrentCellChanged

    Dim northwindDataset As DataSet = _
        CType(DataGrid1.DataSource, DataSet)

    ' This is not a good way to relate the grid's
    ' current cell back to the table
    ' Try deleting a row in the grid to see what happens
    Dim employeeRow As DataRow = northwindDataset.Tables("employees").Rows( _
        DataGrid1.CurrentCell.RowNumber)
    Label1.Text = employeeRow("FirstName").ToString() + _
        " " + employeeRow("LastName").ToString()
End Sub
```

The code looks like it stands a good chance of working. A DataSet object is created and set to the grid's DataSource. The **CurrentCell.RowNumber** property of the grid is then used to locate a specific row in one of the tables inside the DataSource. Finally, two fields on that row are used to set up the text of the label.

There are two problems with this. First, run the application and try moving the cursor onto a blank row, just as the user would if he or she were going to add a new record. The application will suspend with an unhandled exception. The reason for this is obvious: The user created a new row, but the code expected to find that row attached to the table. When it failed to do so, the application raised an exception.

Naturally, the obvious solution to this bijou bugette would be to either code a Try…Catch block or check the row number against the row count in the table before trying to do something.

The second problem with this approach is much more sinister.

Run the application again and delete a row. Then try moving up and down through the grid with the cursor keys. First of all, the row numbers will be out of sync, so you'll be pulling up values from rows that don't match the selected row in the grid. Second of all, you'll eventually reach a situation where a row number you get from the grid corresponds to the row you just deleted. When that happens, you'll get an exception and the application will stop running, just like in Figure 7-10.

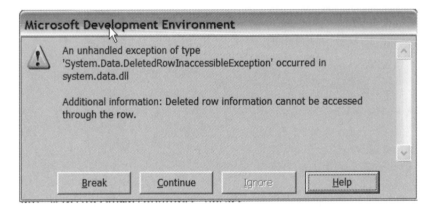

Figure 7-10. The row numbers go out of sync and navigation eventually triggers an exception.

An alternate solution is to use Select on the data table in question. Change the code in your grid's CurrentCellChanged event to this:

```
        Private Sub DataGrid1_CurrentCellChanged( _
            ByVal sender As Object, ByVal e As System.EventArgs) _
            Handles DataGrid1.CurrentCellChanged
Dim northwindDataset As DataSet = _
            CType(DataGrid1.DataSource, DataSet)
        Dim employeeRows() As DataRow = _
            northwindDataset.Tables("employees").Select( _
                "", "", DataViewRowState.CurrentRows)


        If DataGrid1.CurrentCell.RowNumber < employeeRows.GetLength(0) Then
            Label1.Text = _
                employeeRows( _
                DataGrid1.CurrentCell.RowNumber).Item("Firstname").ToString() + _
                " " + _
                employeeRows( _
        DataGrid1.CurrentCell.RowNumber).Item("LastName").ToString())
        Else
            Label1.Text = ""
        End If


    End Sub
```

Try running the application. If you move beyond the end of the grid to a new row, the application won't crash, and if you delete a row and then navigate around you should always see the correct information in the label.

What happens here is that an array of DataRows is built by calling DataTable.Select(0) on the table that's bound to the grid. The filter and sort criteria are left blank and Select is asked only to return an array of DataRows whose state is current. In this way, you can use the DataGrid.CurrentCell.RowNumber property to get a valid index into the returned array. You can even sort the grid by clicking the column names in the grid and the code will still work; sorting a grid applies sort criteria to the underlying table, so Select will still return rows in grid order.

By far the best way to relate the grid row and cell properties back to a real row of data is to use our old friend the CurrencyManager and the table's default view. Just grab the CurrencyManager for the grid or its parent container, and then use the Position property to index into the item's collection on the table's default view. Or, just pick up the value of the Current property from the CurrencyManager.

Of course, you could work direct with the grid's contents and use the properties of the grid to update the underlying data, or interrogate it, through the grid. The CurrentCell.RowNumber and CurrentCell.ColumnNumber properties can also be used to get information straight out of the grid.

The grid contains a multidimensional array property called Items. You can pass the Row and Column number properties to Items to get back the item that the grid contains. You can also change data in the grid in this way. For example:

```
DataGrid1.Items(DataGrid1.CurrentCell.RowNumber, _
    DataGrid1.CurrentCell.ColumnNumber) = "Peter"
```

Grid and Data Object Events

You've seen now how the CurrentCellChanged event works, but what about tracking other events, in particular the mouse ones? The DataGrid supports a handy little method called **HitTest**(). It expects to be passed X and Y coordinates, in that order, and in return it will pass back a DataGrid.HitTestInfo object. This can be examined to see if the user clicked nothing of value (such as the headers or borders of the grid), or more usefully, the row and column that the X and Y coordinates actually map to.

Start up a new Windows Forms project and put a grid on the form, just as before. Open up the code window, set Option Strict On and **Import** the **System.Data.SqlClient** namespace, and then set up the Form_Load event handler too look like this:

```
Private Sub Form1_Load( _
    ByVal sender As System.Object, ByVal e As System.EventArgs) _
    Handles MyBase.Load
        Dim employeesAdapter As New SqlDataAdapter( _
            "SELECT * FROM Employees", _
            "Data Source=localhost;" + _
            "Initial Catalog=Northwind;" + _
            "Integrated Security=SSPI")
        Dim northwindDataset As New DataSet()
        employeesAdapter.Fill(northwindDataset, "employees")
        DataGrid1.SetDataBinding(northwindDataset, "employees")

    End Sub
```

Just as before, this sets up the grid to display a list of employees from the Northwind database.

Next, code the grid's **MouseMove** event. What you are going to do here is write a little code that uses **HitTest**() to make the row that the mouse is currently over the current one.

```
Private Sub DataGrid1_MouseMove( _
    ByVal sender As Object, _
    ByVal e As System.Windows.Forms.MouseEventArgs) _
    Handles DataGrid1.MouseMove
      Dim hitInfo As DataGrid.HitTestInfo = DataGrid1.HitTest(e.X, e.Y)
      If Not hitInfo.Equals(DataGrid.HitTestInfo.Nowhere) Then
          DataGrid1.CurrentRowIndex = hitInfo.Row
      End If
  End Sub
```

The first thing the code does is declare a new **DataGrid.HitTestInfo** object. HitTestInfo objects are returned from calls to HitTest() and provide three properties that can be used to find out just where the user is clicking. The HitTestInfo.Row and HitTestInfo.Column properties give information on the row and column the mouse is over, whereas the Type property can be used to determine just which part of the grid (heading, borders, contents, and so forth) the mouse is over. In the example, the "hitinfo" object is set up to the hold the result of a call to your **DataGrid**'s **HitTest** method. The X and Y coordinates of the mouse are passed into the call and resolved into the three properties I just mentioned.

The code then checks to make sure that the user did actually move the mouse over a valid cell (by comparing the HitTestInfo object to HitTestInfo.Nowhere) and then sets up the CurrentRowIndex property of the grid to the row number contained within the HitTestInfo object.

If you run the application now and move the mouse over the grid, you should see the current row pointer move up and down following the mouse.

CurrentRowIndex, as its name implies, can be used to return the current row of the grid. This provides you with a more convenient alternative to grabbing the row index from the CurrentCell property of the grid. To get better acquainted with it, why not have a go at updating the example from the last section to use CurrentRowIndex instead of CurrentCell.RowNumber?

A Word on Validation

While I'm on the subject of events, it's worth pointing out that the DataGrid supports the **Validated** and **Validating** events that all controls that derive from the .NET **Control** class inherit. They are there to provide users of "normal" controls with a quick and easy way to link validation code to the GUI. For example, you may code the Validating event on a text box to check the data entered by the user, and at the end of the event set a return code that indicates whether or not the contents of the text box are acceptable. You can use these events with a DataGrid, but there is a much better way of doing things. Instead of using the Validating and Validated events on a DataGrid, just add event handlers for your DataTable and DataRow **RowChanging** and **RowDeleting** events.

Fire up yet another new VB .NET Windows Forms application, and as always drop a grid onto the form. Add an Import line just above the form's class definition to bring in the System.Data.SqlClient namespace and add Option Strict On to the line above that.

Now go ahead and add this validation method into the form:

```
Private Sub ValidateData(ByVal sender As Object, _
      ByVal e As DataRowChangeEventArgs)

      If CType(e.Row("RegionDescription", _
       DataRowVersion.Proposed), String) = "Peter" Then
          Throw New Exception( _
  "You can't set the description field of a region to 'Peter'")
      End If

    End Sub
```

This is going to be the event handler for the RowChanging event. The key parameter to the handler is the DataRowChangeEventArgs object. Objects of this class are passed through to handlers for the RowChanged, RowChanging, RowDeleting, and RowDeleted events. It has two properties: Action, which can be interrogated to find out just what action is taking place, and Row, which returns the DataRow that the event is taking place on. All you're interested in is seeing if the change being made gives you a Proposed row with a RegionDescription column value of Peter. If that happens, an exception gets thrown.

If you're coming to ADO.NET from good old-fashioned ADO, then you may be expecting to see code in here to cancel the change. You may already be wondering whether or not that Action property on the DataRowChangeEventArgs object can be used to abort the change. It can't. To cancel an update to a row or column, you have to throw an exception. It's up to the calling code to deal with that exception intelligently. If, however, you don't have error handling, as is the case when you have a DataGrid handling all the changes and updates that the user is making, a dialog box pops up telling the user that there is an problem and asking the user whether or not he or she wants to fix it.

To see this in action, code the form's Load event so that it looks like this:

```vb
Private Sub Form1_Load( _
    ByVal sender As System.Object, ByVal e As System.EventArgs) _
    Handles MyBase.Load

    Dim regionAdapter As New SqlDataAdapter( _
        "SELECT * FROM Region", _
        "Data Source=localhost;" + _
        "Initial Catalog=Northwind;" + _
        "Integrated Security=SSPI")
    Dim northwindDataset As New DataSet()

    regionAdapter.Fill(northwindDataset, "region")
    AddHandler northwindDataset.Tables("region").RowChanging, _
        New Data.DataRowChangeEventHandler(AddressOf ValidateData)

    DataGrid1.SetDataBinding(northwindDataset, "region")

End Sub
```

The code here builds a DataSet the same way as the other examples in this chapter, and then it uses **AddHandler** to tell the region table where to find its RowChanging event. In this case, it's our ValidateData method.

Run the application and try changing a region's description to Peter to see what happens (the result is shown in Figure 7-11).

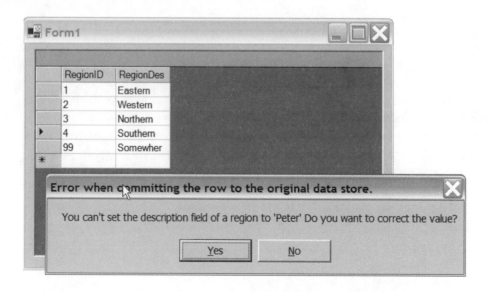

Figure 7-11. The dialog box that pops up for an unhandled exception in a RowChanging or RowChanged event

211

Here's an interesting point to ponder: What if you don't want this error to appear? Perhaps you want your own custom message to appear and for the value to be flagged as illegal for the user to clear or ignore at his or her own peril.

Batching Up Errors

DataTables, DataSets, and DataRows all have a Boolean property called **HasErrors**. You can examine this property at runtime to see if there are any problems with the rows inside a DataSet or DataTable. In the case of a DataSet, a HasErrors property set to True means that there are one or more tables within the DataSet with errors assigned to them. For a table, it means that one or more rows have errors, and for a row it means that there are errors relating to one or more columns within that row. It's up to you to set up these errors, and you can do so in the RowChanging event handler. Go ahead and change the event handler with the code highlighted in bold:

```
Private Sub ValidateData( _
    ByVal sender As Object, _
    ByVal e As DataRowChangeEventArgs)

    If CType(e.Row( _
        "RegionDescription", DataRowVersion.Proposed), String) _
        = "Peter" Then
    e.Row.SetColumnError("RegionDescription", _
                "Cannot set the description field to 'Peter'")
    End If

End Sub
```

Notice that the exception throwing code is gone, and in its place there's now a call to **SetColumnError()**, a method attached to a DataRow that allows you to set the **ErrorText** property of a specific column within that row. Since your code here just checks the RegionDescription column, SetColumnError() is used to attach the error message to that specific column.

Run your application again. Try changing a region description to Peter and see what happens (the results are shown in Figure 7-12).

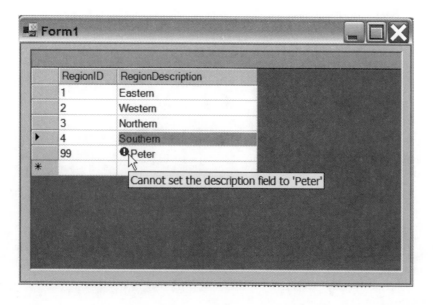

Figure 7-12. The Region Description for region 99 here has an error, as shown in the icon.

If you now hover the mouse over the field with the error, a hint box will pop up telling you just what the error in question is—the text that you passed into SetColumnError is used for the hint.

What if the user still ignores the error and tries to submit the changes to the database? Well, thankfully ADO.NET provides you with a great deal of control when this happens.

Add an Accept Changes button to your form, and then double-click it to drop into the code window. You're not going to submit the changes to the database here, but you are going to make sure that a call to AcceptChanges() only passes in valid records.

The first thing to do is to grab the DataSet from the grid and check if it has any errors.

```
Dim d Dim ds As DataSet = CType(DataGrid1.DataSource, DataSet)


If ds.HasErrors Then


End If
```

A True result from **ds.HasErrors** tells you that there are indeed errors that need fixing. DataTables have a wonderful method attached to them called GetErrors(). This will return an array of rows that have errors in them. You can iterate such an array with a simple For-Each loop:

```
Dim ds As DataSet = CType(DataGrid1.DataSource, DataSet)


If ds.HasErrors Then

    Dim errorRow As DataRow
    For Each errorRow In ds.Tables("region").GetErrors()

    Next

End If
```

Just as a DataTable can return an array of error rows, an individual DataRow can return an array of DataColumns that have errors. Again, you can iterate this with a nice, easy For-Each loop:

```
Dim ds As DataSet = CType(DataGrid1.DataSource, DataSet)

If ds.HasErrors Then

    Dim errorRow As DataRow
    For Each errorRow In ds.Tables("region").GetErrors()

        Dim errorColumn As DataColumn
        For Each errorColumn In errorRow.GetColumnsInError()


        Next

    Next
End If
```

At this point the world is your oyster. You could display an error message to the user indicating what's wrong with his or her data. You could choose to accept the changes anyway. You're going to display an error message and reject the changes, just to make sure that your DataSet is perfect before calling AcceptChanges().

```
        Dim ds As DataSet = CType(DataGrid1.DataSource, DataSet)

    If ds.HasErrors Then

        Dim errorRow As DataRow
        For Each errorRow In ds.Tables("region").GetErrors()

            Dim errorColumn As DataColumn
            For Each errorColumn In errorRow.GetColumnsInError()

MessageBox.Show("Column " + errorColumn.ColumnName + _
            " cannot be changed to " + _
            errorRow(errorColumn.ColumnName, _
            DataRowVersion.Current).ToString(), _
            errorRow.GetColumnError( _
            errorColumn.Ordinal))

            Next

            errorRow.RejectChanges()
            errorRow.ClearErrors()

        Next
    End If


        ds.AcceptChanges()
```

A message is shown to the user that displays the name of the column with the error and the value that caused the error. The error text that you set in our RowChanging event is used as the MessageBox's title. After berating the user for being so foolish, RejectChanges() is called on the row, closely followed by a call to ClearErrors(). The latter is important. Even though you have called RejectChanges(), the error text remains attached to the row. It's important to call ClearErrors() to let the DataSet know that as far as you are aware, there are no more errors attached to the row that need to be dealt with.

Finally, after all rows and columns with errors have been dealt with, AcceptChanges() is called on the DataSet.

Working with errors in this way is absolutely ideal for working with multitiered applications. The GUI can perform some validation of its own before passing the DataSet down to a business object. That object can then perform some business rule validation (such as checking if delivery slots are available in a freight shipping application). If there are problems at the business level, errors can be set and the error-ridden DataSet can be passed back up to the GUI to present to the user. If there are no errors, then the changes will be stored, the DataSet updated accordingly, and a tidy DataSet passed back to the GUI.

The error text mechanism in ADO thus makes it very easy to install multiple levels of validation in your system, and in the right places, without breaking any object-oriented architectural rules you may have in place. I think you'll agree that this approach is far nicer than the old, somewhat clunky way of managing errors across tiers.

Summary

Working with ADO.NET in a GUI is not difficult. If you've had exposure to other data-access frameworks, though (such as DAO, RDO, or even JDBC), then it's very easy to fixate on ADO.NET's lack of cursors and Recordsets and get completely lost. One such common area of confusion is the process of relating currently viewed information in bound controls back to the underlying table's rows. As you've seen in this chapter, there are plenty of ways to achieve this—the DataView and CurrencyManager approach providing the most effective combination.

With ADO.NET, GUI data binding comes back into vogue and the combination of helper properties and classes make working with bound data a dream instead of a struggle. In this chapter you saw

- How to work with DataViews

- How to use a CurrencyManager to emulate cursor-based access into data

- How to work with a DataGrid at runtime

- How to simple-bind in code

In the next chapter you'll take a look at the controls provided for those of you developing ASP.NET user interfaces and the differences between the stateless Web development model and the Windows Forms development model.

CHAPTER 8

ADO.NET and Web Forms

"Any sufficiently advanced technology is indistinguishable from magic."

—Arthur C. Clarke, *Profiles of the Future*

THERE'S SOMETHING INHERENTLY "cool" about the idea of delivering an application over the Web. You can deliver your functionality to any connected device without having to worry about cross-platform issues such as different code bases or user interfaces. You can open up your application to potentially thousands of simultaneous users and allow them to collaborate. Maintaining the application and upgrading it to handle new features or bug fixes is trivial, since the code always lives on your server, not on thousands of different computers all over the globe.

That's the "idea," anyway. The truth of the matter is that Web-based application development has always been tough—much tougher than perhaps it should be. Develop a Web application with ASP and you end up with a set of server-side pages that mix code with content. Even if you go the XML/XSL route (storing your data in XML and "translating" it into a Web page with XSL), you still end up with weird-looking ASP source that looks like a strange mix of HTML and VBScript. Switch over to the Java world in the hope that Sun will solve your problems and you'll find a wealth of powerful Web-delivery technologies backed by tools that are best described as "immature" when compared to their desktop development counterparts.

Delivering a powerful Web application that supports thousands of concurrent users and that contains a rich user interface is cool, but why on earth does it have to be so darn hard? I get the impression that's the same question the guys in Redmond asked themselves when they sat down and started to design ASP.NET.

ASP.NET is designed to solve the problems that have plagued developers wanting to deliver functionality over the Web. With ASP.NET, you can use any .NET-enabled language to write your application's code, and you can keep that code separate from the actual HTML that makes up the Web pages (the source gets held in code-behind files on the server). In addition, with ASP.NET, you can use the same design and development environment that you would use to produce a Windows desktop application, a code library, or a console application. In short, with .NET you get to use the languages that you are familiar with, in a powerful development environment that you have grown accustomed to using.

With few exceptions, Web-based applications make heavy use of database resources. By far and away the most popular type of Web application is one that exposes data for users to browse and view (an online catalog, a magazine, an intranet with corporate information) and occasionally update (ordering from the catalog, subscribing to the magazine, or posting time records to the corporate intranet). Data access then needs to play a big role, but the very model around which the Web is based brings with it additional considerations. How do you quickly get at your data? How can you effectively present that data in a Web page? What about adding functionality to let users work with that data? What about the disconnected user model?

This chapter focuses on these issues, showing you how to use ADO.NET and the ASP.NET Web server controls. It's not an exhaustive tutorial on all aspects of ASP.NET development, though, and it doesn't cover the fundamentals of building Web pages. If Web development is something you're going to be spending a lot of time doing, then take a long, hard look at the MSDN tutorials on ASP.NET in general (and of course spend a happy hour or two browsing the online Apress bookstore at `http://www.apress.com`). Also, before you dive into trying things out in this chapter, make sure that you have Internet Information Server (IIS) properly installed and ready to go, and that you've already taken a peek at the Visual Studio QuickStart tutorials on ASP.NET; at the very least, you'll pick up the basics of working with the Web that way.

The ASP.NET User Model

Developing a Web application used to be hard. Inevitably you had to choose a development model where program logic was embedded in the Web page itself, mixing content with presentation (ASP, JSP), or you were forced down a route where Web page content was embedded in the application code (Common Gateway Interface [CGI], Internet Server Application Interface [ISAPI], Servlets). The arrival of XML solved a lot of problems for the latter group, providing a way at last for developers to use a technology (XSL) to generate HTML Web pages based on the format of an XML document containing the data that needed to be displayed. The combination of XSL and XML is powerful and is supported in Visual Studio .NET, but it's far from perfect. It requires that all data to be presented by the application is contained in XML documents, and it requires that the developer be comfortable and familiar with translating HTML into XSL and then using complex XSL templates to match elements in the XML document to HTML fragments that need to be produced. No matter which Web development model you chose, though, there was one common problem with Web development that just couldn't be avoided: The development tools available were not mature and offered little of the ease of use and rapid development features that desktop developers had come to love over the years.

ASP.NET solves all these problems. In essence, ASP.NET is CGI programming, but with a mature and powerful toolset. You define a set of HTML tags to represent the Web page and then write code behind the Web page in the .NET language of your choice to add dynamic content to the page and to respond to the user's interaction with the elements on the page. When the page is requested by a Web browser, the code-behind and Web page content are compiled into a DLL (if they have not previously been compiled) and Internet Explorer then runs that DLL. This is actually the same way that ISAPI developers used to go about their business, but .NET developers have it far easier than their pioneering ISAPI ancestors. The performance of an ASP.NET application is also comparable to ISAPI's, making it far faster than the ASP technology ASP.NET was designed to replace. You can see the flow of things in Figure 8-1.

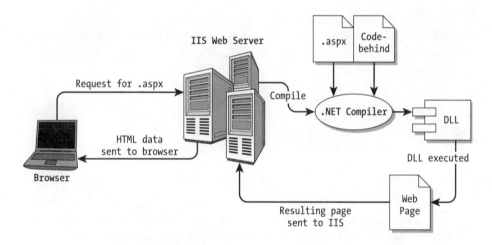

Figure 8-1. The browser requests an .aspx page. If the page has not been requested before, IIS will compile the ASPX and code-behind files to produce a DLL. That DLL then produces an HTML page, which is sent back to the browser via IIS.

Read between the lines in Figure 8-1 and you'll spot where most newcomers to ASP.NET get caught up. When a page is requested, a DLL is executed (after first being compiled, if necessary). That DLL produces HTML that is sent to IIS to send back to the browser. What happens to the DLL? It remains in memory, but since it's a DLL you can effectively think of it as running and ending. It maintains no state. Any variables you set in your code and any data you load into DataSets is lost forever as soon as the DLL finishes running. What happens to the HTML Web page? It's sent to the browser and again lost forever (IIS can cache it, but again it maintains no state, variables, and so forth).

The ASP.NET user model is a stateless one. The user requests your page, your code runs, and then it is killed. When a user clicks a button or interacts with any other "server control" on the page, a request for the same page is sent back to the server along with information about just what the user did. Think about that for a second. If you had just built an ornate DataSet with well-defined relationships and scads of data, in order to build the Web page in the first place, the user could just click a button on the page and you'd have to go through the whole process once again. It's not hard to picture a scenario where you're providing the user with a data entry form in a Web browser and the page is being re-requested once every few seconds as a result of the user moving through the controls on the page.

ASP.NET, from a database developer's point of view, requires a very different way of thinking and doing things from the traditional Windows desktop development model. Although it sounds horribly limiting, it's not. In fact, more and more Windows desktop developers are moving to the stateless programming model in their applications because it typically results in cleaner, less tightly coupled code that is easier to maintain and simpler to extend. Web services, for example, are typically used in a stateless way, and they have a valid role to play in Windows desktop-based applications.

NOTE It's worth pointing out that ASP.NET has its place, and if deploying an application automatically to a bunch of Windows machines is your goal, then ASP.NET is not necessarily the best way to go. My esteemed fellow Apress author Rob Macdonald argues that where issues of corporate-wide deployment of an application are concerned, you can have IIS serve up an executable Windows Forms–based application and then use .NET remoting to make use of functional code on other servers. This is faster than the Web services approach that's currently in vogue, and it delivers a user interface far richer than even the mighty ASP.NET can manage.

Macdonald goes on to point out that given the "x-copy" installation model supported by .NET assemblies, there is a case for only using ASP.NET and Web services when an application needs to be delivered on a wide range of platforms (including older versions of Windows and other, less commercially successful operating systems named after fruit). When designing your application architecture, bear this in mind: .NET does not give you a clear-cut binary choice in how to deploy— Windows Forms or ASP.NET—there are hybrid options available.

The Server Controls

I mentioned *server controls* in the last section, but just what are they? In a nutshell, server controls take the pain out of adding interactivity to a Web page. If you want to make a Web page do something in response to the user clicking a button, for example, you have two choices: Either you can add script into the Web page to make the user's browser do something or you can make the button call back to the Web server and have code on the server do something. Visual Studio .NET and ASP.NET support both models, but server controls are aimed at the latter.

When you drop a server control onto a Web Form (since it's not actually referred to as a "Web page" in ASP.NET), the server control automatically knows to call back to the server when the user does something. Your code sees this as an event, just like an event that may occur in a more traditional Windows Forms–based application. You write code to respond to these events and then send the same page back to the user's Web browser. As an example, you may want to show a list of employees to the user and allow him or her to click a Sort button to reorder the list. Clicking the Sort button triggers a Click event at the server, which you code to rebuild the list of employees in the desired order.

The downside to this approach is the round-trip problem. Every time the user interacts with a server control in a Web form, the browser makes a "round-trip" to the server, first sending information about the click to the server and then waiting for the server to respond with the same Web page, but with additional data or a different view on it (see Figure 8-2).

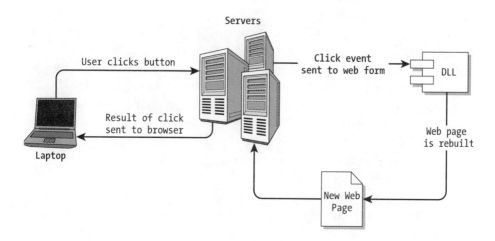

Figure 8-2. The user clicks a server control (a button, in this case). This sends a request to IIS, which fires information about the event across to the Web form DLL. Your code in the DLL responds to the event and rebuilds the Web page, which is then sent back to the Web browser.

For simple controls such as buttons, you can get around this round-trip by adding JavaScript, JScript, or VBScript to the page. This certainly stops the round-trip and speeds up the "snappy-ness" of the Web page. However, what happens when you run the Web page on a browser that doesn't support scripting? In these days of Web-born viruses and other such scripted nasties, many people are turning their browser's scripting capabilities off. Server controls don't require any scripting capability on the remote browser. They allow you to deliver a rich user interface (in many cases, one that is as rich as, or pretty darn close to, a Windows Forms application) without limiting the user base of the Web application to just those people running script-aware versions of a specific Web browser. This feature alone completely offsets the cost of the round-trip for many developers.

There are three server controls of particular interest to the ADO.NET developer: **DataGrids** (related in name only to the Windows Forms control), **Repeaters**, and **DataLists**. I'll focus on DataGrids and Repeaters here since DataLists follow the same principles employed by these two controls.

DataGrid Server Control

The DataGrid server control bears a relationship to the Windows Forms DataGrid pretty much in name only. It doesn't support hierarchical views of data the way the Windows Forms DataGrid does, and it doesn't automatically support column sorting and reordering. However, that doesn't mean the DataGrid server control is in any way limited in its functionality or, indeed, in its appearance.

Just like with the Windows Forms DataGrid, you can apply an autoformat to the grid to brighten up its appearance, but you can also make use of something called a *template* to completely customize the appearance of any aspect of the grid as you see fit. You'll take a look at templates in detail when I cover the Repeater control in a little while. In short, though, a template is an HTML block. Anything that you can define in HTML (image references, links, edit boxes, lists, tables, and even media) you can assign to any aspect of the grid. Just think about that for a second. If you were developing a video-rental Web site and bandwidth wasn't an issue, you could display a grid listing the names of the movies available and also show short video clips of the movies right there in the grid.

Another big difference with the way the DataGrid server control works is editing. You can allow your users to edit columns in the grid and even define complete forms that should appear in columns (again, with templates) when the users choose to edit. However, the grid doesn't automatically provide editing functionality to users. It's up to you to respond to events that occur in the grid and put it into edit mode through code.

There is so much functionality in the DataGrid server control that it's probably best to walk you through its feature set with an example.

 New to .NET

I mentioned this in the introduction to this chapter, but it's worth reiterating here. You won't be able to work through the examples in this chapter unless you have IIS set up and available for you to use. If you're using Windows 2000 Professional or Windows XP Professional, then this is as easy as opening up the Control Panel, choosing Add/Remove Programs, and then choosing Windows Setup. Then you can run down the list of Windows' optional extras to install IIS and/or make sure that IIS is installed.

To prevent your default localhost Web site from getting cluttered with example code, it's also a good idea to open the IIS administration tool (again from the Control Panel) and set up a new virtual directory. If you do this, you'll also need to add the FrontPage server extensions to the new virtual Web site that you create— consult IIS' online help for how to do this.

Formatting the DataGrid

Fire up Visual Studio .NET and start a Visual Basic ASP.NET Web Forms application (call it SimpleDataGrid), as shown in Figure 8-3.

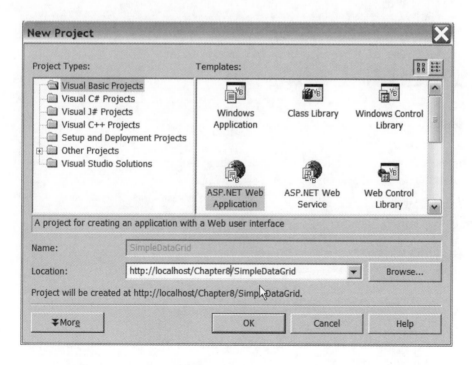

Figure 8-3. The template to use when you create an ASP.NET Web Application–based project

As I mentioned in the introduction to this chapter, I'm going to assume you have at least walked through the ASP.NET QuickStart examples in the online help. Since that's the case, I don't need to point out to you how the toolbar you get with Windows Forms applications has changed to show HTML controls and Web Forms controls, do I? You've probably also learned from your own experiences with ASP.NET that the grid layout assigned to a Web page is not really that good an idea (it wreaks havoc with style sheets and Web designers), so it's wise to set the Layout property of the page to FlowLayout. I've shown this in Figure 8-4, just in case.

link	
pageLayout	FlowLayout ▾
responseEncoding	FlowLayout
rightMargin	GridLayout
showGrid	True
smartNavigation	False

Figure 8-4. It's always a good idea to set the layout of a Web Form to FlowLayout.

With your project created, go ahead and drop a heading (just type it in, selecting the Heading 1 style from the style bar), a DataGrid, and a button on the form, just like in Figure 8-5.

A simple DataGrid

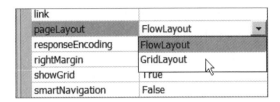

Column0	Column1	Column2
abc	abc	abc
abc	abc	abc
abc	abc	abc
abc	abc	abc
abc	abc	abc

Button

Figure 8-5. Build up your Web Form so that it looks like this.

Set the Text property of the button to New Employee, and then name the DataGrid **employeeGrid** and the button **addButton** (unlike in a Windows Forms–based application, this is achieved by changing the control's ID property). Now you're ready to start exploring the features of the grid.

If you take a look at the properties window for the grid, you'll notice straight away that the grid appears to have a lot of features. There are properties in there for controlling the paging of the data (breaking a lump of data up into smaller, more manageable pages); setting font, color, and border styles; and a whole lot more besides. You'll rarely use any of these through the properties window, though. Just as with the Windows Forms DataGrid, there are properties dialog boxes that can take the pain out of configuring and working with the DataGrid.

Right-click the DataGrid and you'll see the pop-up menu in Figure 8-6 appear.

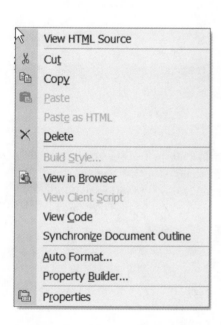

Figure 8-6. The right-click menu of the DataGrid server control

The two most interesting items on the menu (and the only two I'm going to cover here) are the **Auto Format** and **Property Builder** entries. Click the Auto Format option and the familiar Auto Format dialog box shown in Figure 8-7 will appear.

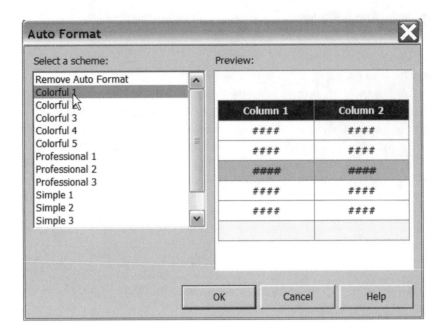

Figure 8-7. The DataGrid server control's Auto Format dialog box

Browse through the different color and style formats in the list, choose one that appeals, and then click OK. Your DataGrid will instantly adopt the selected style.

Right-click the DataGrid again, and this time choose the Property Builder option. This will bring up the far more interesting property builder dialog box shown in Figure 8-8.

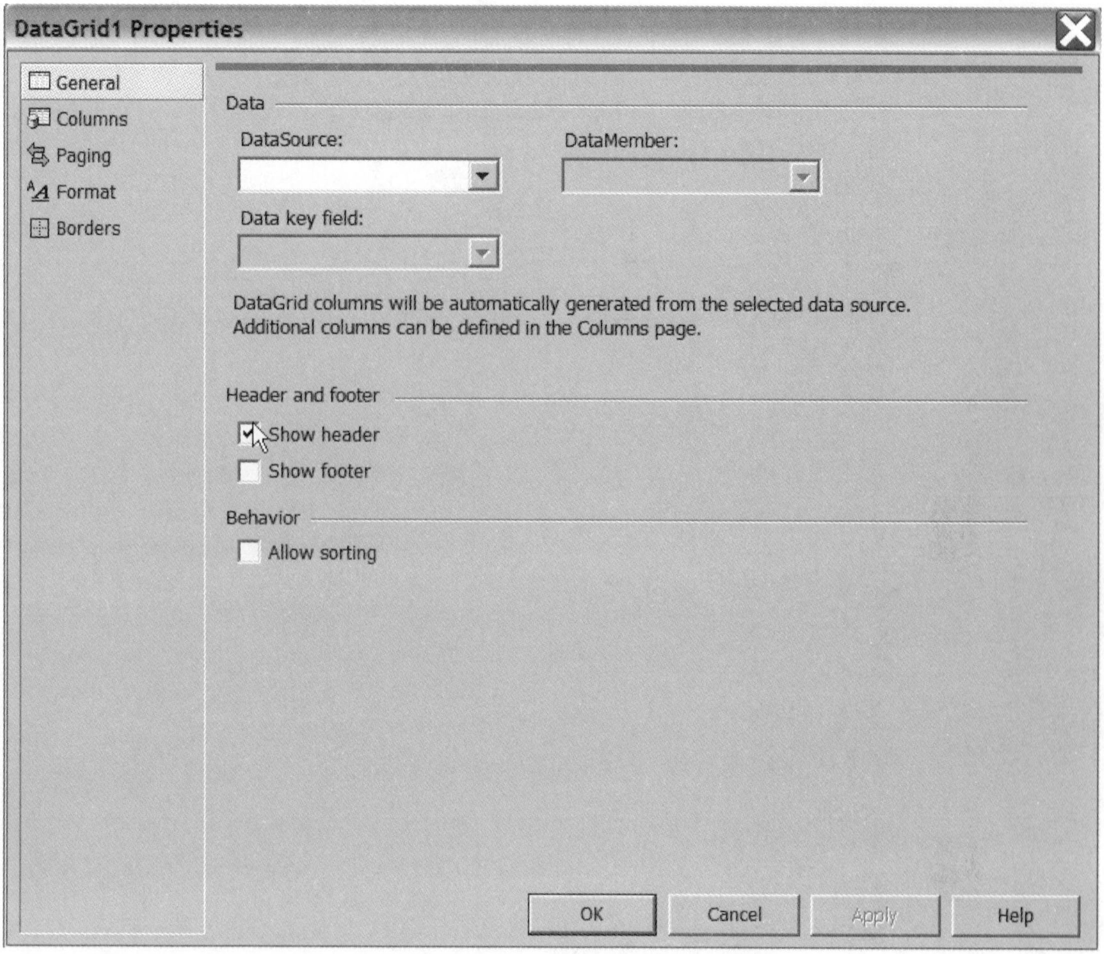

Figure 8-8. The DataGrid property builder

The list down the left-hand side of the dialog box allows you to select and configure properties of the DataGrid that relate to the columns in the grid, the paging of data, the format of the contents of the grid, the grid's borders, and other miscellaneous information under the General heading. Click the Columns option to view the columns editor shown in Figure 8-9.

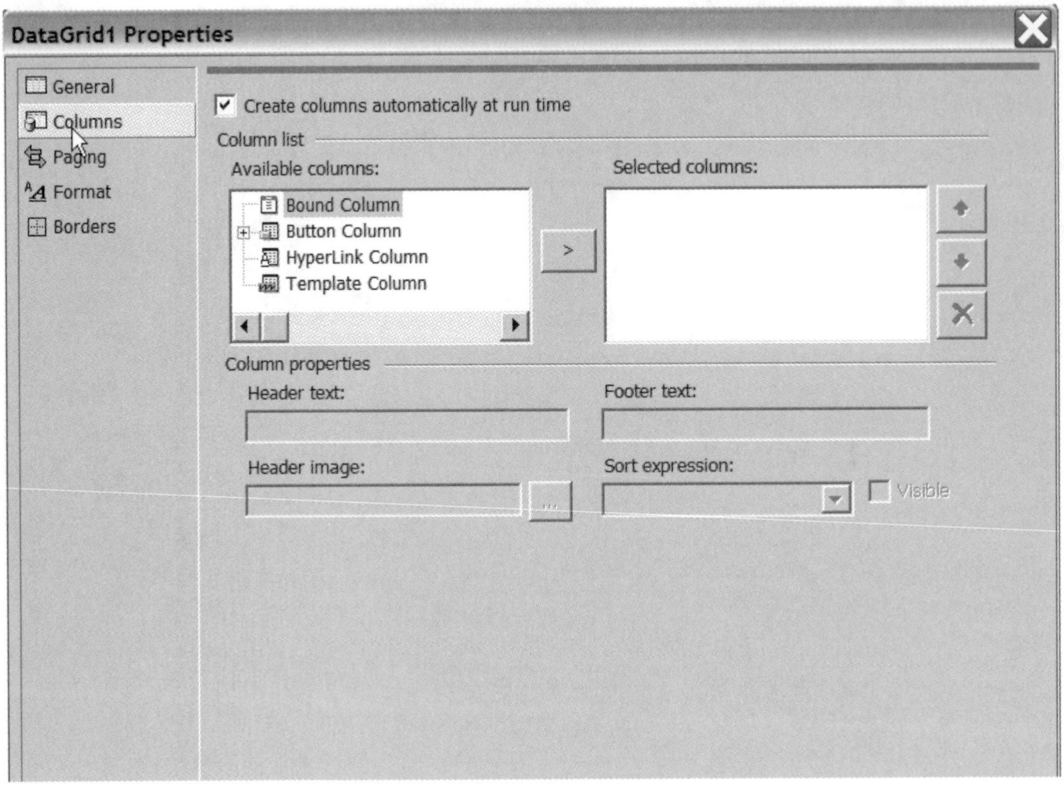

Figure 8-9. The DataGrid columns editor

This is where the really powerful properties live. Here, you select the columns that will appear in the grid and also the level of interaction that you want your users to have with the grid's data. You see, in a standard Windows Forms grid, if a user wants to edit some data, he or she simply clicks the data and starts typing. In a DataGrid server control, that's not the case; should the user decide to edit some data or delete a row, he or she needs to click a button or a link in that row to indicate that the DataGrid needs to respond. So, the columns editor is used to add in not only the rows of data that you need to present to the user, but also columns holding buttons to enable them to work with that data.

The types of columns that you can add are shown in the list box at the top left of the main dialog box area. Let's start with **Bound Column**.

As you might expect, a *bound column* is a column bound to some element of data. You're going to configure this grid to show information from the Employees table in the Northwind database, so you're going to need some bound columns to display the employee information. Go ahead and select Bound Column, and then click the ">" button four times to create four bound columns, as shown in Figure 8-10.

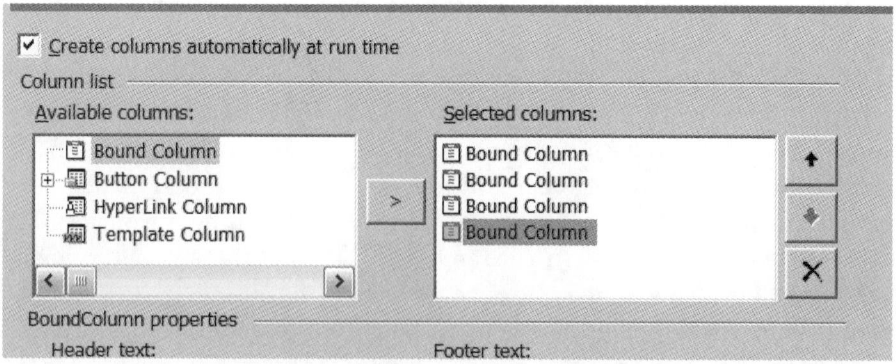

Figure 8-10. Columns are added by selecting the column type and then clicking the ">" button.

Now that you've created the columns, the next step is to add some detail to them. Specifically, you need to set the header text for the column and bind it.

Click the first column you added and fill in the dialog box so that it looks like the one shown in Figure 8-11.

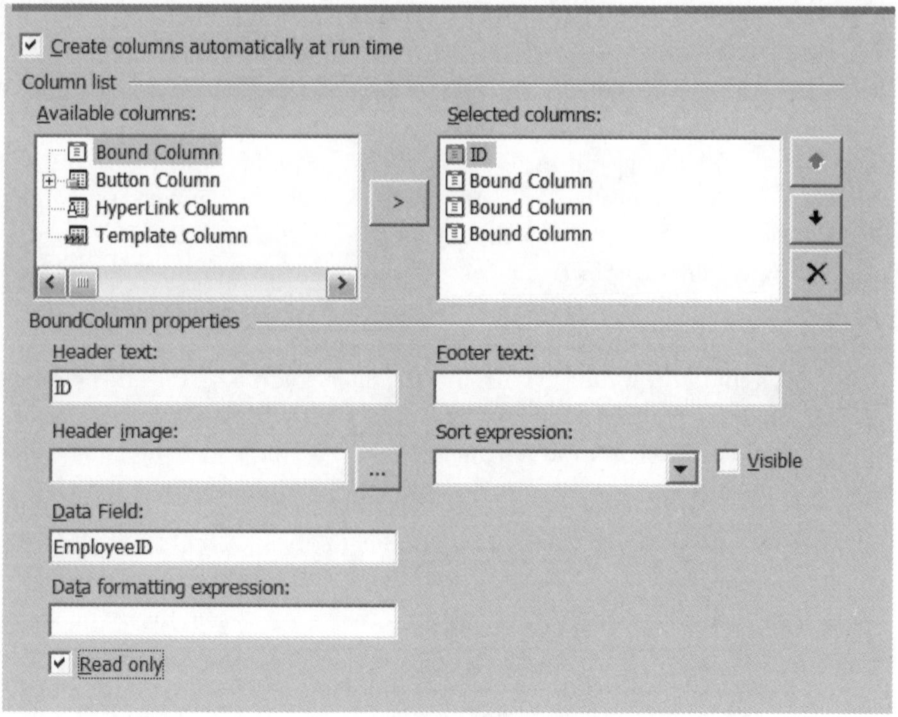

Figure 8-11. The ID column, fully defined

Here I set the "Header text" to **ID**, made the column not visible, set it to read-only, and bound it to the EmployeeID field. If you worked through the DataGrid examples back in Chapter 6, then you may have a few questions at this point.

First, how can you bind a column when you haven't yet set a DataSource or DataMember into the DataGrid server control? In ASP.NET, you typically set the grid's DataSource and DataMember properties at runtime with code. In this example, you're going to add a little code later to hit the database and build a DataSet for the grid to bind to. In a live application, though, that's not a very good level of separation between the user interface tier and the business rules and data access tiers. Most Web applications get their DataSets from some business class in the application, or even from a Web service, leaving the nasty data-access code to some lower-level class. For that reason, although you can bind the grid at design time, it's not a good habit to get into.

Second, why was the column set to invisible? With a Windows Forms DataGrid, it's fairly easy to determine just which row of data a user is working with. You could index into the underlying view based on the row index in the grid, or you could use a CurrencyManager (the eminently preferable approach). More to the point, though, why would you want to? A Windows Forms DataGrid is perfectly capable of running with very little help from your code, automatically updating the underlying DataSet and generally doing all the hard work for you. A DataGrid server control, on the other hand, can do none of those things.

The user needs to click a link to put the grid into edit mode. In the subsequent Click event you can find out just which row in the grid the user was working with, but you have no real way of relating that row to an actual database row. Remember, the grid is built, populated, and sent to the user, and then the DataSource you bound is destroyed, along with any other variables and objects you may have hanging around. Theoretically, days could elapse between the time you send the grid of data to the user and the time the user decides to click an Edit button, a gap of time during which it's perfectly conceivable that new rows will have been added to the database and old ones deleted. Knowing which row number in the grid the user clicked in that scenario is pretty much useless to you.

Instead, a common approach is to embed hidden columns in the grid holding key values. In the Northwind database, the EmployeeID field is the primary key for locating an employee record. You can put this value into the grid, hide it, and then extract it from the grid when the form gets posted back with an edit request. It sounds terribly unsophisticated, I know, and really it is. However, some people (myself included) prefer things working this way—it affords your code a level of complete control that you just don't get with a fully disconnected Windows Forms DataGrid. (This is because it works with a DataSet always held in memory. With ASP.NET, you'll need to hit the database again to grab the data the user wants to edit.)

The rest of the columns need to be left visible and editable. Go ahead and set the header text of the three columns to "First name," "Last name," and "Title," respectively, and set the Data Field properties to "FirstName," "LastName," and "Title."

If you click the Apply button at this point (not the OK button—you're not done yet), your grid should change to look like the one shown in Figure 8-12.

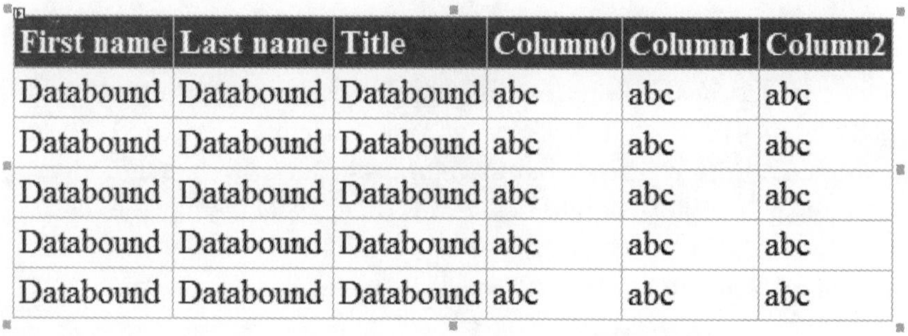

First name	Last name	Title	Column0	Column1	Column2
Databound	Databound	Databound	abc	abc	abc
Databound	Databound	Databound	abc	abc	abc
Databound	Databound	Databound	abc	abc	abc
Databound	Databound	Databound	abc	abc	abc
Databound	Databound	Databound	abc	abc	abc

Figure 8-12. The grid after the columns have been added

There are still three unnecessary columns in the grid, though—columns that you didn't create. The reason for this is that by default the DataGrid will automatically generate three columns as placeholders, and at runtime it will automatically generate columns matching the bound data source. To prevent this from happening, uncheck the "Create columns automatically at run time" check box at the top of the dialog box and click the Apply button once again. The DataGrid will instantly change to show only the columns that you just created.

The next step is to add in some button columns to allow the user to edit and delete data at runtime (you can't create an Add button in the grid, which is why you put an Add Employee button on the form at the start of this walk-through).

Expand the Button Column list in the dialog box, as shown in Figure 8-13.

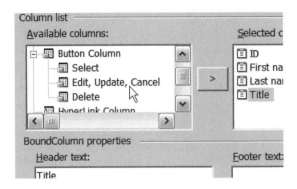

Figure 8-13. The bound column types that can be added to a grid

As you can see, there are three types of button that you can add: a **Select** button that provides the user with some means of selecting rows of data, an **Edit/Update/Cancel** button that deals with all aspects of editing data, and a **Delete** button. Go ahead and add a Delete button column and an Edit/Update/Cancel button column to the list of columns in the grid. Then, select them in the column list and use the arrow buttons to the right of the column list to move the two new columns near to the top of the list, with Delete first. This is shown in Figure 8-14.

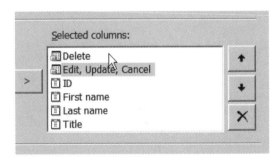

Figure 8-14. The button columns in the correct position

Click your newly created Delete button column and take a look at its properties (see Figure 8-15).

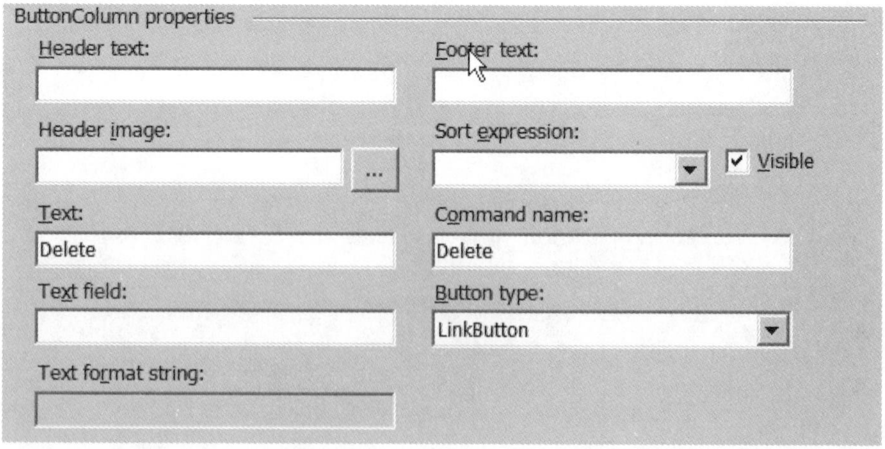

Figure 8-15. The properties for the Delete button column

Just as with a normal bound column, there are properties in there to set up the header and footer text (the text displayed at the top and bottom of the grid, respectively), as well as an image to appear in the header for the column to really jazz up the appearance of the grid.

There are also **Text** and **Text field** properties. The former is static text to display, and for a Delete button, the word "Delete" is probably just fine. The Text field property lets you specify a column to use as the caption of the button. Incidentally, you can also feed HTML into the Text property, so if you wanted to use an image to signify delete instead of simply a link that reads Delete, you could do so by adding in the appropriate <Img> tag.

When a button column is clicked at runtime, the grid fires an **ItemCommand** event. You can examine the arguments passed to this event to find out the Command name property of the item that got clicked. Leave this set to its default value of **Delete** and you'll get a nice, convenient **DeleteCommand** event.

The final property of special interest is the **Button type** property. If you drop down the combo box associated with this property, you'll see that you have two choices: **LinkButton** and **PushButton**. By default all button columns are LinkButtons. This means that the buttons appear in the grid as standard clickable links in the Web page. Selecting PushButton changes this to a push button. I find this just looks awful, though, and I tend to stick with a link button, or in special cases I set the text of the link to an image reference.

Now click the Edit, Update, Cancel button column and take a look at its properties, which are shown in Figure 8-16.

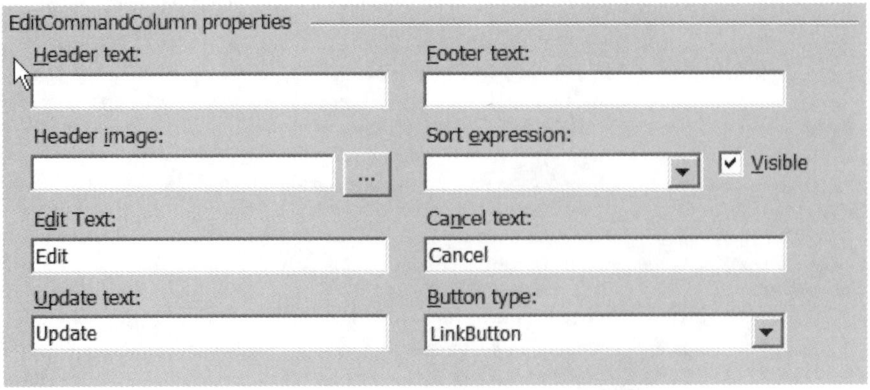
EditCommandColumn properties
Header text:
Footer text:
Header image:
Sort expression:
Visible
Edit Text:
Edit
Cancel text:
Cancel
Update text:
Update
Button type:
LinkButton

Figure 8-16. The properties for the Edit, Update, Cancel button column

The properties look similar to those for the Delete button column; however, this time there are properties for Edit text, Update text, and Cancel text. When you add a column such as this to a grid, you usually only see the Edit link appear in the grid. Go ahead and click the Apply button to see what I mean (see Figure 8-17).

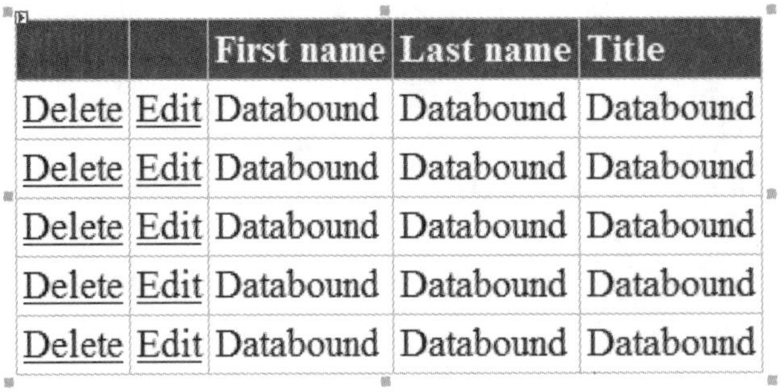
First name Last name Title
Delete Edit Databound Databound Databound
Delete Edit Databound Databound Databound
Delete Edit Databound Databound Databound
Delete Edit Databound Databound Databound
Delete Edit Databound Databound Databound

Figure 8-17. By default, an Edit, Update, Cancel button column only shows Edit.

When the user clicks the Edit link (or button, if you choose to use push buttons instead of links), your code gets an EditCommand event. It's up to you at that point to put the grid into edit mode and specify the row that needs to be edited. Once the grid drops into edit mode, the Edit link is replaced with Update and Cancel links. You'll see this in action in a little while.

You're nearly done with the grid formatting. Before you leave the properties dialog box, though, click the Format entry at the left side of the dialog box to pop open the formatting page shown in Figure 8-18.

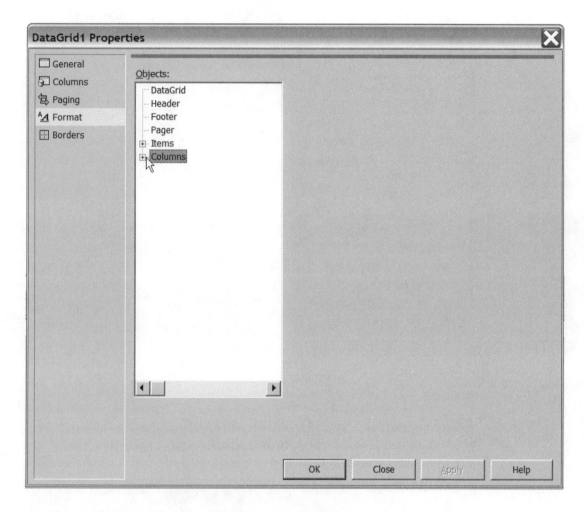

Figure 8-18. The formatting page of the properties dialog box

When the page first appears, it looks pretty sparse. There is actually a vast amount of functionality in this dialog box, though—functionality that will let you define in minute detail almost every facet of every column in the grid.

First, expand the Items entry in the list, as shown in Figure 8-19.

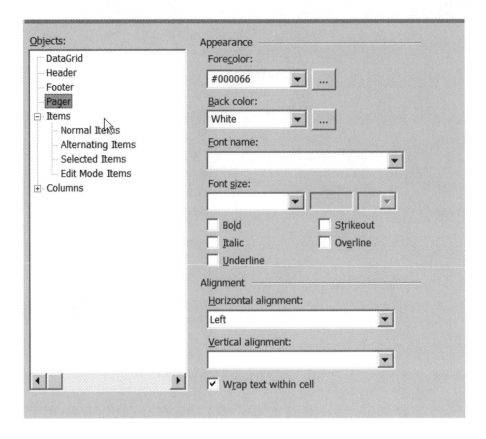

Figure 8-19. The "items" that you can format in a DataGrid server control

By selecting individual items of the DataGrid, you can customize the formatting even further. You can, for example, choose **Edit Mode Items** and specify a different set of colors, font properties, and alignment to make items being edited really stand out. Select Alternating Items and you can apply a different set of formatting to every alternate line in the grid.

You're most interested in the columns in the grid, though, so expand the Columns entry in the list, as shown in Figure 8-20.

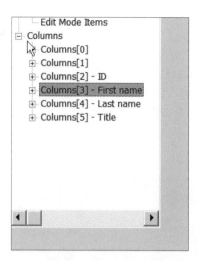

Figure 8-20. The Columns entry in the formatting page

Not only can you now see a list of all the columns in the grid, but you can also see that they're all expandable. Go ahead and select and then expand column 3 (see Figure 8-21).

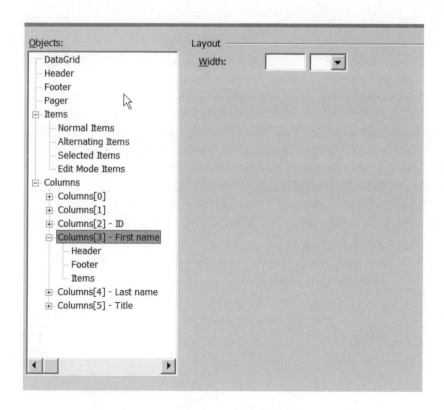

Figure 8-21. The various parts of a column that you can format

The only item that can be modified for a column itself is its width. However, you can select the **Header, Footer,** and **Items** (the content of a cell in the DataGrid) options and once again set up the font, color alignment, and so on. For now, just set the width of columns 3, 4, and 5 to 30% (you select the percent sign [%] from the drop-down list to the right of the Width text box).

When you're done, click OK and marvel at your newly formatted grid. (You can marvel at mine in Figure 8-22.)

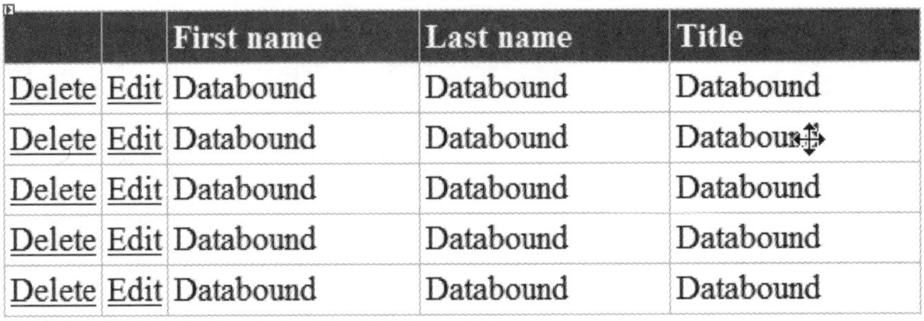

		First name	Last name	Title
Delete	Edit	Databound	Databound	Databound
Delete	Edit	Databound	Databound	Databound
Delete	Edit	Databound	Databound	Databound
Delete	Edit	Databound	Databound	Databound
Delete	Edit	Databound	Databound	Databound

Figure 8-22. The completed, formatted DataGrid

Coding the DataGrid

Now that your DataGrid is all formatted, the time has come to bring it to life. First, run the application as it is. Presuming you have IIS installed and Visual Studio .NET talks to it properly, you should see a Web page not unlike the one shown in Figure 8-23.

Server controls are also smart controls. In the case of the DataGrid, if it doesn't have any data to display, then it won't show itself. Ingrain this in your memory—it can save you hours during those late-night coding sessions when you just can't understand why the darn grid isn't showing up: no data, no grid.

Close down Internet Explorer and return to the safety of Visual Studio .NET. Once there, double-click the Web Form to open up the code window.

As always, the first step is to import the **SqlClient** namespace and turn **Option Strict On**. Move to the very top of the code and add in these two lines:

```
Option Strict On
Imports System.Data.SqlClient
```

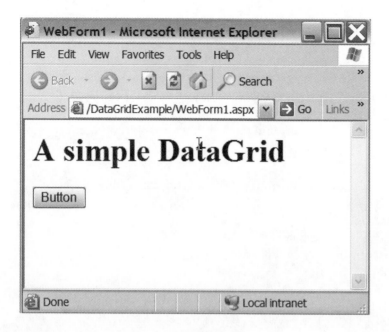

Figure 8-23. Where did your grid go?

To bind the DataGrid as soon as the Web page comes into view, you're going to need to code the **Page_Load** event. Ready for a shock? Code it so that it looks like the following code block, and then I'll explain what's going on:

```
Private Sub Page_Load(ByVal sender As System.Object, _
    ByVal e As System.EventArgs) Handles MyBase.Load
      If Not Page.IsPostBack Then
          ReBindGrid()
      End If
End Sub
```

I've highlighted the most important lines in bold.

The first line of code is probably the most vital. The page has a property called **IsPostBack**. When a user requests a Web page, this property is set to False. However, whenever an event needs to be fired on a server control, the page and all the data contained in the server controls are posted back to IIS, ready for your event code to work its magic. Whether the page was requested or posted back, the Page_Load event will always fire. The reason, of course, is that once a page has been sent to the browser, it's destroyed. For event code to run, IIS needs to re-create the page, hence the new Page_Load event.

Assuming the page is not a post back, a subroutine is called that rebinds the grid. You'll see this subroutine in a moment. What it does is hit the database (don't forget, in a live application you wouldn't want to do that—you'd use a business class to provide you with the data instead), build up a DataSet, and then bind the grid to it. This rebuilds all the data in the grid. If this was a post back, then rebinding the grid would effectively destroy its contents and replace them with whatever's in the database. Not very useful. When you work with bound controls in ASP.NET, the first line of code in your Page_Load event will almost always be If Not Page.IsPostBack Then.

Let's take a look at the **ReBindGrid**() subroutine. Go ahead and key it in.

```
Private Sub ReBindGrid()
    ' Sets up the grid bindings. This will be the first thing
    ' done when the page is loaded, and the last thing done
    ' after a page is posted back (prior to sending it out to
    ' the user's browser again).
    Dim northwindDS As DataSet = GetDataset()
    employeeGrid.DataSource = northwindDS
    employeeGrid.DataMember = "Employees"
    employeeGrid.DataBind()
End Sub
```

Not too tricky, is it? Again, I'm relying on a function later on in the code to do most of the work—in this case, a function called **GetDataset**().

The code here then just grabs a DataSet, sets the DataGrid's DataSource and DataMember properties, and then calls **DataBind**(). With server controls, simply setting the bound properties to point at a valid data source (be it a DataSet, a DataReader, or even an array or a collection) has very little effect on the control itself. You need to call DataBind() after setting up the bound properties for the server control to kick in and rebuild its contents based on the bound data.

Let's key in the GetDataset() function now:

```
Private Function GetDataset() As DataSet
    ' First create the data adapter
    Dim employeeAdapter As New SqlDataAdapter( _
        "SELECT EmployeeID, FirstName, LastName, Title FROM Employees", _
        GetConnection())
    ' Now you can build and fill the dataset
    Dim northwindDS As New DataSet("Northwind")
    employeeAdapter.Fill(northwindDS, "Employees")
    Return northwindDS
End Function
```

Again, this should be straightforward. The first real line of code sets up a DataAdapter and makes use of a function you'll see in a moment called **GetConnection**() to assign a connection to the default Select command.

With the SqlDataAdapter built, all that remains is to create a DataSet and fill it before returning it from the function.

You may be starting to wonder at this point why on earth I have so many little functions and subroutines in the code for such trivial things as building a connection or producing a DataSet. You'll see later in the code as you start to work through the DataGrid's event handlers that these functions are used quite a lot. Handling an update, for example, involves creating a new SqlCommand to do the update, and that, of course, requires a SqlConnection. Adding a new row requires adding a blank row to the end of a DataSet, hence the need for a handy GetDataset() function.

Let's code GetConnection():

```
Private Function GetConnection() As SqlConnection
    ' Connections are used to build the dataset to bind to,
    ' as well as with the commands that perform database
    ' updates, so it's a good idea to contain the connection
    ' creation code in its own independent function
    Dim con As New SqlConnection( _
        "Data Source=localhost;Initial Catalog=Northwind;" + _
        "Integrated Security=FALSE;" + _
        "User id=sa;Password=MyPassword")
    Return con
End Function
```

This should be so trivial to you by now that I'm not going to walk you through it. It is worth paying attention to the connection string itself, though. In the code here, I'm assuming that you're running SQL Server and not MSDE. If you're using MSDE, then you'll need to replace the reference to localhost with the name of your MSDE instance as described in the examples in the earlier chapters in the book. I'm also assuming that you have a password set for the database administrator called MyPassword. The alternative, of course, would be to have **Integrated Security=SSPI**. That's actually the preferred way of working. If you do change the connection string to use a trusted connection in that way, you'll need to add a new login to the database called **MYMACHINE\ASPNET**, where MYMACHINE is the name of your machine.

Whenever ASP.NET tries to connect to SQL Server over a trusted connection (Integrated Security=SSPI or Integrated Security=TRUE), the code will fail if there isn't a valid **ASPNET** login for the machine that's running IIS.

If you run the application at this point, you should see the browser display a page with a nicely populated grid. You can't do anything with the grid other than view it, but at least it does confirm that the data binding is working (see Figure 8-24).

Don't forget: If you're seeing three additional columns not in Figure 8-24, then you forgot to uncheck the "Create columns automatically at run time" option in the property builder. Go and do so now if that's the case.

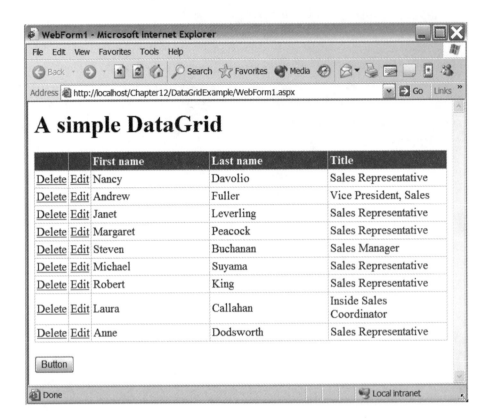

Figure 8-24. The populated DataGrid

Close the browser to stop the application running and return to the code editor in Visual Studio .NET.

Let's start to add some functionality to the grid now. Use the objects drop-down list at the top left of the code editor to select the grid (Figure 8-25).

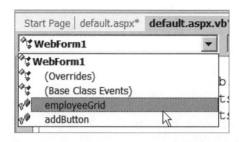

Figure 8-25. Select the DataGrid from the objects drop-down list at the top left of the code editor.

Now drop down the list of events from the combo box at the top right of the code window and choose **EditCommand**. This will create an empty EditCommand event handler. This event fires whenever the user clicks the Edit link in a row. What your code needs to do is find out which row the Edit link is in and then put that row into edit mode. The latter is achieved by setting the **EditItemIndex** property of the grid to anything other than –1 (–1 takes the DataGrid out of edit mode). You can find the row that was clicked from the **DataGridCommandEventArgs** object passed into the event handler. Go ahead and code the EditCommand handler so that it looks like mine:

```
Private Sub employeeGrid_EditCommand(ByVal source As Object, _
    ByVal e As System.Web.UI.WebControls.DataGridCommandEventArgs) _
    Handles employeeGrid.EditCommand
      ' When the user clicks on the edit command, the page
      ' is posted back. We need to set the edit row index
      ' to put the grid into edit mode
    employeeGrid.EditItemIndex = e.Item.ItemIndex

      ' Before the page is sent back to the user, rebind the
      ' grid. Failure to do this will result in the edit
      ' boxes being empty.
    ReBindGrid()
End Sub
```

The DataGridCommandEventArgs object **e** contains a property called **Item**. This actually refers to the individual row of the grid where the event was fired. It's an object of type DataGridItem. Conveniently, it has a property called **ItemIndex**, which just so happens to correspond to the row where the click occurred. Setting EditItemIndex to this value puts the correct row in the grid into edit mode.

Notice how the grid is rebound after that. Putting a row into edit mode will, by default, change the text items in the non–read-only cells to text boxes. Rebinding the grid ensures that those text boxes have the correct values in them.

NOTE I've actually done something quite bad here, but it was all in the interest of keeping the code as short as possible. In a live application, you would not want to simply put the row in question into edit mode. Instead, you'd hit the database first to determine whether the row in question had been changed since the page was last sent to the user. If it had, you'd want to throw up a dialog box to the user warning him or her of such and perhaps even pull back the new data to show the user how it had changed.

The key to remember when coding these events is that you're working in a completely disconnected model. There can be a long gap in time between your submitting a page to the browser and the user choosing to work with the data. At the very least, you should run a count query on the data in the database to check that the counts haven't changed, but as I mentioned, it makes a lot more sense to have business objects with real belt-and-braces type safety measures to handle the concurrency issues that Web applications bring with them.

If you like, go ahead and run the application now. Click an Edit link and you'll see the grid enter edit mode. Again, you won't be able to do much, since the Update and Cancel buttons aren't yet connected.

The Cancel button is actually the easiest of them all to deal with. When a user clicks Cancel, all you need to do is take the grid out of edit mode (**DataGrid.EditItemIndex = -1**) and rebind. Thus, the **CancelCommand** event handler looks like this:

```
Private Sub employeeGrid_CancelCommand(ByVal source As Object, _
    ByVal e As System.Web.UI.WebControls.DataGridCommandEventArgs) _
    Handles employeeGrid.CancelCommand
    ' When the user clicks on the Cancel button in edit
    ' mode, the page is posted back. We need to pull the
    ' grid out of edit mode, and rebind it.
    employeeGrid.EditItemIndex = -1
    ReBindGrid()
End Sub
```

Handling the UpdateCommand is a little more complex.

As you saw earlier, you can use the Item property of the DataGridCommandEventArgs object to get at the actual row of the DataGrid where the event occurred. This in turn has a Cells collection property. Each cell in that collection holds a Controls collection property. To handle an update, you need to grab the Text of each TextBox control in each cell and send that across to your database command (or business object). This is probably easier to show in code, but rather than dump the whole event handler here, let's do it piece by piece. Select the DataGrid from the objects drop-down list in the code window and then select the UpdateCommand from the event list.

```
Private Sub employeeGrid_UpdateCommand(ByVal source As Object, _
    ByVal e As System.Web.UI.WebControls.DataGridCommandEventArgs) _
    Handles employeeGrid.UpdateCommand
        ' When the employee clicks on the Update button
        ' a number of things need to happen. We need
        ' to extract the data from the text boxes in the
        ' grid in order to run an update or insert command, and
        ' then drop the grid out of edit mode.
        ' Finally, the grid needs to be rebound to pick up
        ' the changes just made to the database.

        Dim employeeID As Long
        Try
            employeeID = Long.Parse(e.Item.Cells(2).Text)
        Catch
            employeeID = -1
        End Try
```

The first thing you need to do is to grab the EmployeeID of the row being edited. For a row that the user has chosen to edit, that's not a problem. You can just grab the value of the Text property from cell 2 (cell 0 is a Delete button and cell 1 is the Edit/Update/Cancel button) and parse it into a long. If the user is editing a brand-new row, though, there won't be any valid value in that hidden cell. For that reason, a Try…Catch block is used. If there's a valid value to parse, the employeeID variable is set. If there's no valid value, then employeeID is set to −1.

With that out of the way, the next step is to grab the newly updated values of the employee's first name, last name, and title. Interrogating the text boxes in the appropriate cells in the DataGrid does this.

```
Dim newFirstName As String = _
    CType(e.Item.Cells(3).Controls(0), TextBox).Text
Dim newLastName As String = _
    CType(e.Item.Cells(4).Controls(0), TextBox).Text
Dim newTitle As String = _
  CType(e.Item.Cells(5).Controls(0), TextBox).Text
```

Since you know that there will only ever be one text box in each cell, the code just pulls the first object from each cell's Controls collection and casts it to a TextBox. The TextBox's Text property is then interrogated to drag the values entered by the user into a string variable.

From that point on, the code is quite straightforward. If this is a brand-new row (employeeID = –1), then an Insert command needs to run. If it's an existing row, then the Update command needs to run. Once again, in the interest of keeping the example short and simple, I haven't written the necessary checks into the SQL statements to check that the row hasn't been changed in the database since it was last retrieved. Don't forget to do so yourselves in your production code.

```
If employeeID > -1 Then
    ' Now for the update - best to use a parameterized command
    ' or stored procedure here, to get around problem of users
    ' entering ' symbols in the text
    Dim updateCommand As New SqlCommand( _
        "UPDATE Employees SET " + _
        "FirstName = @Firstname, LastName = @Lastname, " + _
        "Title = @Title WHERE EmployeeID = @EmployeeID", _
        GetConnection())

    With updateCommand
        .Parameters.Add("@EmployeeID", employeeID)
        .Parameters.Add("@Firstname", newFirstName)
        .Parameters.Add("@Lastname", newLastName)
        .Parameters.Add("@Title", newTitle)

        .Connection.Open()
        .ExecuteNonQuery()
        .Connection.Close()
    End With
```

```
      Else
          ' An insert is needed
          Dim insertCommand As New SqlCommand( _
              "INSERT INTO Employees (FirstName, LastName, Title) " + _
              "VALUES(@FirstName, @LastName, @Title)", _
              GetConnection())
          With insertCommand
              .Parameters.Add("@FirstName", newFirstName)
              .Parameters.Add("@LastName", newLastName)
              .Parameters.Add("@Title", newTitle)
              .Connection.Open()
              .ExecuteNonQuery()
              .Connection.Close()
          End With
      End If
```

One point worth noting about this code is the use of a parameterized command. When you work with data the user has entered, a parameterized command or stored procedure is best—it solves the problem of dealing with the users entering quotes in their data and thus damaging straight SQL statements. Of course, a stored procedure is always the ideal and preferred method of updating or retrieving data thanks to its speed.

Finally, once the commands have been executed, all that remains is to take the grid out of edit mode and rebind it.

```
      employeeGrid.EditItemIndex = -1
    ReBindGrid()
  End Sub
```

Now you'll code the Click event on that Add button and the example will be complete. This is quite straightforward. The DataSet used to bind the grid is grabbed, and a new row is added to it. The grid is then put into edit mode on that new, blank row.

```
  Private Sub addButton_Click(ByVal sender As System.Object, _
      ByVal e As System.EventArgs) Handles addButton.Click
      ' When the user chooses to add a new item into the grid,
      ' we need to rebuild the dataset, add a blank row to it,
      ' then set the grid into edit mode on the new row
      Dim northwindDS As DataSet = GetDataset()
      northwindDS.Tables("Employees").Rows.Add( _
          northwindDS.Tables("Employees").NewRow())
```

```
    employeeGrid.EditItemIndex = _
      northwindDS.Tables("Employees").Rows.Count - 1
    employeeGrid.DataSource = northwindDS
    employeeGrid.DataMember = "Employees"
    employeeGrid.DataBind()
End Sub
```

Finally, after all that, is the DataGrid's DeleteCommand handler:

```
Private Sub employeeGrid_DeleteCommand(ByVal source As Object, _
    ByVal e As System.Web.UI.WebControls.DataGridCommandEventArgs) _
  Handles employeeGrid.DeleteCommand
      ' When the delete link is clicked, we need to delete the current row
      ' (in a live app check that the user really does want to delete),
      ' and rebind the grid before sending it back to the user.
      Dim EmployeeID As Long = Long.Parse(e.Item.Cells(2).Text)
      Dim deleteCommand As New SqlCommand( _
          "DELETE FROM Employees WHERE EmployeeID = @EmployeeID", _
          GetConnection())
      With deleteCommand
          .Parameters.Add("@EmployeeID", EmployeeID)
          .Connection.Open()
          .ExecuteNonQuery()
          .Connection.Close()
      End With
      ReBindGrid()
End Sub
```

Save your project and run it, and you should find that everything works just the way it should (see Figure 8-26 for an example).

This example demonstrated a lot. You saw how to format the DataGrid, add rows to it and customize them, and add code to respond to events. You also saw a DataSet being used, when everyone out there will tell you that DataSets may be a little too "heavy" to use in an ASP.NET application.

The DataGrid will bind very easily to a DataReader. Instead of setting the DataSource and DataMember properties, just set the DataSource. However, working with a DataReader and a bound DataGrid makes adding new rows quite tricky. When you have grids that you want to allow the user to add to, a DataSet makes more sense since it's trivial to just add a new blank row and display that row in edit mode within the grid. At most other times, the light resource usage and fast operation of the DataReader is ideally suited to ASP.NET applications.

		First name	Last name	Title
Delete	Edit	Nancy	Davolio	Sales Representative
Delete	Edit	Andrew	Fuller	Vice President, Sales
Delete	Edit	Janet	Leverling	Sales Representative
Delete	Edit	Margaret	Peacock	Sales Representative
Delete	Edit	Steven	Buchanan	Sales Manager
Delete	Edit	Michael	Suyama	Sales Representative
Delete	Edit	Robert	King	Sales Representative
Delete	Edit	Laura	Callahan	Inside Sales Coordinator
Delete	Edit	Anne	Dodsworth	Sales Representative
Delete	Update Cancel	Pete	Wright	CoffeeBoy

Figure 8-26. The grid in edit mode on a new row

Repeater Server Control

The copious properties pages of the DataGrid server control make it a formidable tool for building rich user interfaces within Web applications. The Repeater control, on the other hand, has very few properties and no properties pages, and it is ideally suited to the display, rather than the entry, of data. It is, however, incredibly powerful despite its somewhat sparse appearance out of the box.

Start up a new Visual Basic ASP.NET Web application project, and call this one SimpleRepeater. Set the Web Form's layout to FlowLayout and add a heading and Repeater to the form, as shown in Figure 8-27.

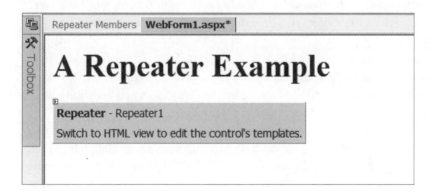

Figure 8-27. The Repeater control looks somewhat sparse when it's first created.

Before you go any further, set the **ID** property (the name of the control) to employeeRepeater so that the example code you're going to work through later works on your machine.

Take a quick glance at the rest of the properties of the Repeater (see Figure 8-28).

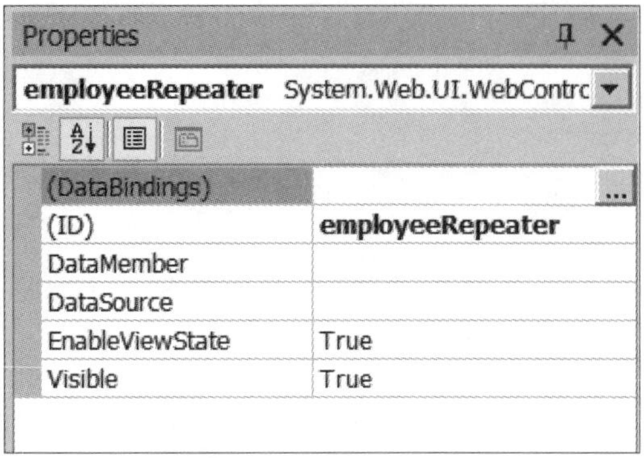

Properties	⊐ ✕
employeeRepeater System.Web.UI.WebContrc ▾	
(DataBindings)	...
(ID)	**employeeRepeater**
DataMember	
DataSource	
EnableViewState	True
Visible	True

Figure 8-28. The properties of a Repeater server control

There's a property to enable ViewState (session caching of data in a hidden field in the Web page), as well as the two standard data-binding properties, DataSource and DataMember. That's pretty much it. The DataBindings property just lets you bind the Visible property of the control to a field and specify whether or not the Repeater is bound to the page's data source or its own. You very rarely work with the DataBindings property of a Repeater control; instead, you rely on DataSource and DataMember.

If you right-click the Repeater, you'll see a pop-up menu devoid of entries such as Auto Format and Property Builder. To be quite honest, the first time you come across a Repeater control, it's hard to imagine just what use it is.

The power of the control comes from **Templates**. These are blocks of HTML markup that are used to define just how each element of the Repeater should appear. The Repeater can work with templates to define its header (**HeaderTemplate**), footer (**FooterTemplate**), items (**ItemTemplate**), alternate items (**AlternateItemTemplate**), and separators between each item of data (**SeparatorTemplate**).

It's the fact that these templates are specified in standard HTML markup that lends the control its power and versatility. Anything that you can define in HTML you can define within a template of the control. Repeaters can thus do everything from simply listing data to outputting fully formatted articles on an online magazine (the introduction would be the header template, the paragraphs would be the item templates, and the author's bio would be the footer template).

To define these templates, though, you need to switch to HTML view. I'm sure you know how to do this, but for those that need a memory refresher, just click the HTML button at the bottom left of the Web Form (see Figure 8-29).

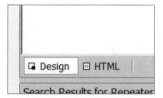

Figure 8-29. Click the HTML button to switch the Web Form into HTML markup mode.

Since the Web Form is quite simple so far, you shouldn't see too much HTML code appear. The key line to look for is this one:

```
<asp:Repeater id="employeeRepeater" runat="server"></asp:Repeater>
```

This simple tag specifies the use of a Repeater. To define templates for the Repeater, you need to add blocks of HTML inside the <asp...> and </asp...> tags.

This example is going to display the list of employees from the last example inside a table. So, the first thing to do is define the start and end of the table itself. This requires two templates: The HeaderTemplate starts the table and the FooterTemplate ends the table.

Go ahead and change the HTML so that it looks like this:

```
<asp:Repeater id="employeeRepeater" runat="server">
<HeaderTemplate>
    <TABLE id="Table1" cellSpacing="1" cellPadding="1" width="75%" border="1">
      <TR>
          <TD style="FONT-SIZE: 18pt; COLOR: yellow; BACKGROUND-COLOR: teal">
                <div align="center">Name</div>
          </TD>
          <TD style="FONT-SIZE: 18pt; COLOR: yellow; BACKGROUND-COLOR: teal">
              <div align="center">Title</div>
          </TD>
      </TR>
 </HeaderTemplate>
 <FooterTemplate>
     </TABLE>
 </FooterTemplate>
</asp:Repeater>
```

Now save the project and switch back to design view. Your Repeater should look like the one shown in Figure 8-30.

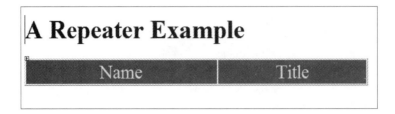

Figure 8-30. The Repeater will automatically update itself when you add templates.

As soon as you add templates to a Repeater, the Repeater will re-render itself to display those templates. In this case, you've just defined an empty table, complete with column headings, so that's just what the Repeater renders. Let's go ahead and add in a template to display items. This involves actually pulling data from the data source.

```
<ItemTemplate>
  <TR>
    <TD style="COLOR: black; BACKGROUND-COLOR: white">
      <%# DataBinder.Eval(Container, "DataItem.FirstName")%>
      <%# DataBinder.Eval(Container, "DataItem.LastName")%>
    </TD>
    <TD style="COLOR: black; BACKGROUND-COLOR: white">
      <%# DataBinder.Eval(Container, "DataItem.Title")%>
    </TD>
  </TR>
</ItemTemplate>
```

If you switch to design view now, the Repeater will have changed once again, this time to show dummy items in the list and also to indicate which of those items are data bound (see Figure 8-31).

A Repeater Example

Name	Title
Databound Databound	Databound
Databound Databound	Databound
Databound Databound	Databound
Databound Databound	Databound
Databound Databound	Databound

Figure 8-31. The Repeater will even show dummy items once you define the ItemTemplate or AlternatingItemTemplate.

It's important to note that whereas the data binding in a DataGrid is kept safely tucked away in the code behind the page, with templates (whether you use them in a Repeater or even in a DataGrid as a templated column) the data binding takes place in the page itself. Take a look over this line from the ItemTemplate:

```
<%# DataBinder.Eval(Container, "DataItem.FirstName")%>
```

The <%# tag indicates that what follows is code, not HTML markup. To bring in a bound value, you just ask the control's **DataBinder** to evaluate an expression and return a value. In this case, you're asking the DataBinder to look at the **Container** (the Repeater control, since you're defining an item inside the Repeater here) and return the **FirstName** field from the bound **DataItem**. This is standard code. You would typically just replace the name of the field with the one you need from the data source.

So, the ItemTemplate defined previously just hits the Container and pulls in the FirstName, LastName, and Title fields from the data source.

That's all there is to it. Let's add the code now to bind this Repeater to the database.

Drop out of HTML view and go back into design view of the Web Form. Then double-click the Web Form to move into the code-behind. Add the following to the very top of the code (as usual):

```
Option Strict On
Imports System.Data.SqlClient
```

Now code the Page_Load event, just as you did in the DataGrid example:

```
Private Sub Page_Load(ByVal sender As System.Object, _
    ByVal e As System.EventArgs) Handles MyBase.Load
        If Not Page.IsPostBack Then
            RebindRepeater()
        End If
End Sub
```

Just as before, you check to see if the page is a PostBack, and if it's not, you rebind the Repeater.

Add in two more routines to handle the binding (one to rebind and one to produce the SqlConnection):

```
Private Sub RebindRepeater()
    ' Set up a command to grab the data
    Dim selectCommand As New SqlCommand( _
        "SELECT Firstname, Lastname, Title From Employees", _
        GetConnection())

    selectCommand.Connection.Open()

    Dim employeeReader As SqlDataReader = _
        selectCommand.ExecuteReader()
    employeeRepeater.DataSource = employeeReader
    employeeRepeater.DataBind()
    selectCommand.Connection.Close()

End Sub

Private Function GetConnection() As SqlConnection
    Dim con As New SqlConnection( _
        "Data Source=localhost;" + _
        "Initial Catalog=Northwind;" + _
        "Integrated Security=FALSE;" + _
        "User Id=sa;Password=MyPassword")
    Return con
End Function
```

This example uses SqlDataReader to bind to, since it doesn't do any updating of the data and doesn't need to create new rows.

Once you have the code keyed in, run the application, and your page should look like the one shown in Figure 8-32.

A Repeater Example

Name	Title
Nancy Davolio	Sales Representative
Andrew Fuller	Vice President, Sales
Janet Leverling	Sales Representative
Margaret Peacock	Sales Representative
Steven Buchanan	Sales Manager
Michael Suyama	Sales Representative
Robert King	Sales Representative
Laura Callahan	Inside Sales Coordinator
Anne Dodsworth	Sales Representative

Figure 8-32. The finished data Repeater application

Some Repeater Tricks and Tips

I'm not going to dwell much longer on the Repeater; its versatility is limited only by how far you are willing or able to take the various templates that make it up. It's worthwhile pointing out some tricks and tips for using it, though.

Many people avoid the Repeater because of the amount of HTML markup that needs to be generated to get it working and looking good. There is a way around all that typing, however. Every time you drop a control onto an ASP.NET Web Form, Visual Studio .NET generates the necessary HTML markup behind the scenes. One way of building a Repeater is to first generate a form that looks exactly the way that you want it to look. When you are happy with it, drop into HTML view and cut and paste the form elements that Visual Studio .NET generated into the necessary templates. My HTML skills are somewhat lacking, and so this is the approach I took to generate the templates in the last example.

Another neat trick is to change the templates on the fly at runtime. If you generate more than one Repeater on the page and make only one visible, then you can, at runtime, reallocate templates from the invisible repeaters to the visible one. For example, you could have a button on the form that allows the user to switch between a table view of data and a straight list. Simply define two invisible repeaters, one with a table set of templates, the other with list-based templates, and when the button is clicked copy the appropriate templates into the visible repeater.

```
VisibleRepeater.ItemTemplate = HiddenGridRepeater.ItemTemplate
Etc.
```

Another off-putting feature of the Repeater is that it seems to be unable to respond to user input in the grid. This is not the case at all. If you embed a button in a column and set the ASP button's Command text appropriately, when the button is clicked the Repeater will raise an **ItemCommand** event. You can see this event in code by simply double-clicking the Repeater control in design view.

```
Private Sub employeeRepeater_ItemCommand(_
        ByVal source As System.Object, _
        ByVal e As System.Web.UI.WebControls.RepeaterCommandEventArgs) _
        Handles employeeRepeater.ItemCommand

End Sub
```

To find the Command text of the button that was pressed, just take a look at **e.CommandName**. Then you can look at **e.Item** and its properties exactly the same way that you interrogated the Item in the DataGrid's events. You could even switch the templates at that point to go into a pseudo–edit mode if you needed to. The possibilities are endless.

Summary

This has been a long chapter, and to be fair there are a lot more ADO.NET-related things I didn't cover here. For example, using Validators to validate input data, using List server controls, session state management, and so on. However, you should be completely happy with pulling data from a bound source in ASP.NET page markup, and you should know how to use the two most common ASP.NET bound server controls. The rest is really more ASP.NET-specific than ADO.NET-specific. I can't stress this enough: Take a look at the QuickStart tutorials on ASP.NET to really get up to speed with all the other issues and features of ASP.NET development.

In this chapter you focused on

- Building a DataGrid

- Binding a DataGrid

- Processing events

- Building a Repeater

- Binding to a Repeater

CHAPTER 9

Transactions and Concurrency

"No good *model ever accounted for* all *the facts, since some data was bound to be misleading if not plain wrong."*

—James Dewey Watson, from Francis Crick's *What Mad Pursuit*

I'VE SPENT A LOT OF TIME so far covering the hands-on work that you need to do to bring data access into your application, courtesy of ADO.NET. As many of you will know, though, there's a lot more to building an application that uses data access than simply hitting a database and fiddling with its data. Most of you will spend your development time working on multiuser systems for your employer, systems that have to cope with more than one user simultaneously accessing and updating data from a single data source. Some of you may be heading for the lofty heights of Web development, where the issues of multiuser development take on a whole new meaning: A popular Web application could have hundreds, even thousands, of simultaneous users, all of whom could theoretically choose to update the exact same piece of information at the exact same point in time.

This is where **concurrency management** comes into play. *Concurrency management* is, simply put, the mechanism that you build into your code to manage how multiple users access the same records at the same time. **Transactions** fall into this domain by providing an easy way to wrap a set of database operations into a single, broader operation (the transaction) that can be used to guarantee the integrity of data in the system. In fact, even if you are developing single-user solutions, concurrency management and transactions still play an important role. Transactions, for example, provide you with a means to keep your data consistent even in the event of an application or hardware crash.

Unfortunately, this whole area has become somewhat ripe for confusion. There are many developers out there who do not quite understand the big picture surrounding concurrency and transactions, and who subsequently produce systems that are at best flaky and at worst downright unreliable.

In this chapter you'll explore the theory and practice behind implementing concurrency management and using transactions in an ADO.NET application. For those of you who have historically shied away from such subjects, take solace in the fact that as with so many things in computing, the practicalities of managing this whole area are far less daunting than some would have you believe.

The chapter is split into two parts. In the first part, grab a cup of your favorite hot drink, curl up by a warm fire (in fact, a hot, sandy beach is even better), and read on. I'll cover the theory behind the whole deal in the next section. If, however, you're a seasoned data-access pro, feel free to grab Visual Studio .NET by the horns and dive into the more practical second half to see the theory put into action.

The Theory

Okay, on with the theory. Although the title of this chapter is "Transactions and Concurrency," in this section I'll dive into the theory behind concurrency management and talk about that a lot more than transactions. Transactions are simply a tool for ensuring data integrity within your chosen method of concurrency control. You'll explore them in more detail in the hands-on second half of the chapter.

Concurrency Overview

The whole point of concurrency management can be summed up very easily in just one statement: to address what happens when two users (or processes) decide to access the same piece of information in a database. The holy grail of concurrency management is to find a solution through your application design, database design, or even business processes, where two or more users will never ever want to work with the same piece of information. The holy grail of concurrency, like its ancient namespace, is actually something of a myth, and in reality you can get close by reducing the number of users actually in your system at any one point in time, but that's rarely a solution your employer will be happy with.

Concurrency management is not a complex subject, especially if you understand the underlying theory and terms that it introduces. Despite that, I still find it quite amazing just how many developers neglect to install any form of concurrency control in their applications until the very last minute. This is foolish, since as I mentioned earlier, concurrency control can be implemented at a design level with just as much effect as putting a mechanism in place through code.

Classically, there are three methods of controlling concurrency: pessimistic concurrency, optimistic concurrency, and "last in wins."

Pessimistic Concurrency Control

Pessimistic concurrency control is also known as the belt-and-braces approach. As the name implies, developers using a pessimistic approach to concurrency assume the worst. What this means from a data access point of view is that if a user decides to pull one or more records from the database, they are "locked" on the assumption that they have been selected in order to be edited. This locking prevents anyone else from reading the same records until the person who did the original selecting releases the locks.

This is certainly the safest way of addressing the problem of multiple users updating the same records, but it introduces some huge problems of its own. For example, imagine a vacation-booking system that uses pessimistic concurrency control. On the surface, it seems to be a good approach. Since a vacation can only be viewed by one person at a time from the database, and thus booked by just one person at a time, there are no issues of someone else "stealing" the dream vacation you're examining on your PC. As long as you can see the data, no one else can and the vacation is as good as yours if you choose to go for it. Sounds ideal.

What happens when your PC crashes, though? More seriously, what happens when the cat suddenly decides to pick a fight with the dog and drag you away from the computer for a few hours to clear up the mess? The result is that your dream vacation is locked, inaccessible to anyone else for the entire duration of your absence from the system. With you away from the PC, or the PC rebooting, there's no way to follow through within the application and unlock the record for others to use. There are all sorts of solutions to this problem, the most common being a lock-timeout value applied to the database. This would release the lock if nothing happens to the record within a preset period of time. That's hardly any good, though, if you're a slow reader and it takes you an hour or so to read your vacation details before deciding to book it; the vacation's lock will probably have been released in that time, so when you come to actually book the vacation it's now locked by someone else, and the whole reason for using pessimistic concurrency control is no longer valid.

This actually brings up another issue: the granularity of your concurrency mechanism. In the previous example, the record is locked for updating from the moment you decide to retrieve the record from the database. A more feasible approach would be to lock the record when you click the Book Vacation button. At that point the record is locked, loaded, updated, and stored, along with an invoice being produced and all the other steps that are involved in booking a vacation in the real world. The key is to keep the duration of the locks as small as possible.

Visual Studio .NET does not support pessimistic concurrency control because of the problems that it can introduce and because of its fairly hungry demands in terms of resources—locks are usually held open through an open connection. In addition, the disconnected data-access model of ADO.NET does not lend itself well to a pessimistic approach to data access. It can, however, be simulated, as you'll see later.

Optimistic Concurrency Control

If a pessimistic approach to concurrency always assumes the worst, an *optimistic* one assumes the best. If you've ever really used a vacation-booking system (perhaps on the Web), then you'll be very familiar with this type of concurrency control.

With an optimistic approach, you assume that the records you have chosen to update haven't already been updated. You don't lock the records when you select them, and when you decide to actually make an update, checks are put in place to determine just whether or not someone else actually did make an update before you.

In the vacation application example, you select a vacation from a list and view its details on the screen. The details may tell you that the there is one free slot available for the very week that you want to travel. You eagerly fill in your credit card details, name, and address, and click the Book Vacation button. There's a pause, and then the screen changes to tell you that there are no places available for you to book for the dates you specified. A well-written system will ease the pain by offering you other choices for dates and perhaps even different hotels or resorts. Using the optimistic concurrency control mechanism, someone else chose to look at the same record as you and clicked the Book Vacation button faster than you. When their update fired, the application didn't see any changes to the vacation information on the server and so went ahead and booked it. When your turn came around, the vacation information on the server had changed, so your request to book the vacation of your dreams failed.

In this example, optimistic concurrency is painful and inconvenient. However, it's much less costly to the vacation company than allowing you both to book the same dates and venue, or worse yet, locking vacations and limiting the number of people who can browse the online store. Optimistic concurrency is also pretty much the same way brick-and-mortar stores work.

In a brick-and-mortar operation, customers are free to wander around and browse the store's stock at their leisure. You could see a great deal on a new PC and wander off to check your credit card balance, only to return a few minutes later and find the PC sold out. The store won't "lock" the PC for you just based on your statement that you have an interest in it. Cash will need to change hands before the store even considers updating its stock (its real-world data store) just for you.

Optimistic concurrency control is the default concurrency control mechanism supported in .NET. It's ideally suited to a Web development model, where users can browse data and then inexplicably disconnect for a few hours. Data is never locked away from browsers until the moment a user actually makes an update to that data and transmits it through to the server. As you've seen, though, this approach does require a little thought at the code level, and you'll look at some of the issues surrounding it in the hands-on section in a little while.

"Last in Wins"

I love this one—I call it the slacker's approach to concurrency control. I love this approach simply because when I see it, it's usually installed in an application from a team that is now pleading for consultancy to solve their strangely unreliable data-management issues.

"Last in wins" is exactly what its name says. The last person to actually hit the database with an update wins. So, you browse your vacations online and find the one you like. I come along in a few minutes and do the same, choosing the same vacation. You go to all the effort of entering your credit card and contact details and book the vacation. A confirmation is displayed and the vacation is yours. Well done! I then click the Book Vacation button on my PC. The database updates with the information I entered and I also see a confirmation. At the airport you are turned away and I get the seat on the plane. Last in wins.

I'm not going to dwell on "last in wins" since you should already be able to see just how abhorrent and vile this approach (or lack of approach) to concurrency control really is.

The Role of the Transaction

A transaction fits into the whole concurrency story by providing a convenient way to wrap up a set of database operations into a single "atomic" unit, which is either committed to the database or rolled back and aborted.

The classic example of just where transactions should be used is in a banking system. If you wanted to transfer funds from one account to another, there are two specific operations that will need to take place: Funds will need to be debited from account A and then credited to account B. If the application crashes between the first and second operations, you have a problem. Account A will have been debited, but account B will not have been credited (actually, I believe my bank really does work that way). Your cash just vanished into the ether. More to the point, any other operations that work on account A will see a balance that is quite simply wrong.

A transaction would wrap these two operations. Until the transaction is committed, the changes made are not considered complete and stored. So, with a transaction, account A would be debited, the PC would crash, and the transaction would roll back. The result would be a completely unchanged account A balance and an unchanged account B balance—the entire operation fails, but the integrity of the data remains intact.

Here's another example back in the realm of the fictional vacation-booking system. You choose your vacation and request to book it. The availability of the vacation is set so that no one else is able to book it. A new invoice is entered into the database ready to be sent to you in the next print run. Your credit card details are then processed, and your credit is found to be wanting. With a transaction, the whole process can be rolled back based on the failure of the credit card check. The vacation will be available once more and the phantom invoice will vanish without a trace.

Transactions preserve the integrity of your data. In fact, well-designed transactions guarantee the integrity of your data.

The ACID Properties of a Transaction

Deciding what operations a transaction should encompass is made easier by the ACID properties of the transaction. Basically, to have a good transaction, you must satisfy the ACID properties of Atomicity, Consistency, Isolation, and Durability.

To be Atomic, a transaction must run once, and all operations within the transaction must depend on each other to satisfy a common goal. In an application designed to transfer funds between two accounts, the debiting of one and crediting of another are related and interdependent operations. It would be no good having each operation in its own transaction since the system could go down during the second transaction and leave the funds in the bank balances incorrect. In addition, this kind of transaction must only run once—you'd not be very happy if it repeated itself when dealing with your bank accounts.

The bank account example is actually a good example of the Consistency goal of the ACID properties. A transaction should ensure the integrity of data within the database and update that data in a manner consistent with the business rules being implemented. If you need to transfer funds between two accounts, the only consistently successful way of doing this is to decrease the balance on one account and then increase the balance on another. Wrapping those two operations up inside a single transaction ensures consistency of data in the event of a failure.

The *I* in ACID stands for Isolation, a vital ingredient of every well-designed transaction. A transaction should shield itself from any other transactions running at the same time, or more to the point, it should shield the updates it makes at least until the transaction successfully completes. I hate to return to the banking example yet again, but it's a good one: The fund transferal transaction is isolated if no other transaction or database user is able to see the changes in the account balances until the transaction is committed to the database. A dire situation could occur if halfway through a transaction some other process grabs the balance of the primary bank account just before the transferal transaction fails. In that case, the other user would have grabbed a *dirty read,* a read of data that is not committed to the database and is thus not accurate.

Finally, we come to the *D* in ACID: Durability. A transaction is your main tool when it comes to error and failure recovery. If the database connection fails, the data fails to meet some constraint, the server dies, or any of a million other nasty things occur, the transaction should roll things back to the state they were in prior to the transaction beginning. If you wrapped the debiting of one account in a transaction and the crediting of the other account in a separate transaction, you couldn't guarantee that in the event of a failure the database would be put back into the "pre–fund transfer" state. In fact, in that scenario, there's a strong possibility that a partial transaction would be stored.

The Practice

Now that you have a grasp of the basics behind transactions and concurrency, let's take a look at the issues in practice, within ADO.NET. I'm going to stick with the SQL Server data provider for the time being simply because it's the fastest and most powerful data provider in ADO.NET. The examples should work with only minor changes with the OLE DB provider (specifically, you'll need to change the names of the classes being used).

Transaction Objects

Transactions are created at runtime through the connection. The data provider's Connection class (in our case, **SqlConnection**) is equipped with a **BeginTransaction()** method that can be called to start up a transaction on that connection. The method returns a SqlTransaction object that can be used to further control the transaction. The SqlTransaction object's **Commit()** and **Rollback()** methods provide, as their names suggest, mechanisms by which work inside the transaction can be either committed or rolled back. There's also a **Save()** method, which can be passed a string to name an interim rollback point in the transaction. This same string can be passed across to the **Rollback()**, providing a means to roll back part of a transaction should you so require.

You also have a means of controlling the isolation level of the transaction through the **Isolation** property on the SqlTransaction object, and the **IsolationLevel** enumeration. You'll look at that in the next section.

Let's take a look at a simple application to show how to use SqlTransactions. Fire up Visual Studio .NET and start a new VB .NET console project. As always, start by adding the usual two Imports at the top of your source.

```
Option Strict On
Imports System.Data.SqlClient
Imports System.Console
```

The first thing to do in your **main()** function is create the connection to the database:

```
Try
    ' First set up a connection to the database - we can
    ' use this to get a transaction running
    Dim northwindConnection As New SqlConnection( _
        "Data Source=localhost;" + _
        "Initial Catalog=Northwind;" + _
        "Integrated Security=SSPI")
```

There's going to be a lot of scope in this application for failures. For example, the command that you build in a moment might specify an incorrect table name, the transaction could fail to start, and a whole host of other problems could occur. For this reason, the whole routine is wrapped in a nice Try…Catch block, as you can see.

The next step is to get your transaction under way. This can only be done using an open connection. You can't just go ahead and create a Connection object and ask it for a new SqlTransaction.

```
northwindConnection.Open()
Dim deleteTransaction As SqlTransaction = _

    northwindConnection.BeginTransaction()
```

As you can see, as soon as you start to use a transaction, you immediately run the risk of throwing all the benefits of ADO.NET's disconnected model out of the window. A transaction is pulled from an open database connection, and that connection needs to be held open for the length of the transaction. It's important then that your code only does what it needs to in order to update the database inside the transaction; the length of time spent in that transaction should be kept to the absolute minimum necessary to satisfy the ACID properties, nothing more. The transaction is not the place to write the code that will check for and work with errors in a DataSet, for example.

Now that your connection is open and a transaction started, let's hit the database and quickly find out how many rows there are in the Order Details table—you're going to delete them in a second. Add this to your code:

```
' Print out how many order details are in the database
PrintOrderDetailCount(northwindConnection, deleteTransaction)
```

PrintOrderDetailCount is a short little function that you'll use a lot in this example to keep on checking just how many rows are available in the database. It looks like this (go ahead and add it in, after the end of your Main() function):

```
Private Sub PrintOrderDetailCount(ByVal con As SqlConnection, _
    ByVal trans As SqlTransaction)
  Dim selectCommand As New SqlCommand( _
      "SELECT COUNT(*) FROM [Order details]", con, trans)
  WriteLine("There are currently " + _
    selectCommand.ExecuteScalar().ToString() + _
    " order details in the database")
End Sub
```

Notice that the function expects to be passed a SqlTransaction object. This is actually because of a slightly inconvenient way that ADO.NET works with transactions. If you have a transaction running on a connection, you can't execute any commands against that connection unless you have also explicitly passed the SqlTransaction object to the Command object. You can see that in the preceding code. The SqlTransaction is passed into the function and then passed to the SqlCommand constructor. This sets up the SqlCommand object's Transaction property. Without this, the application would simply throw an exception when run to tell you that there is a transaction in operation and the command doesn't know anything about it (strange, since to give you the error in the first place, something inside there knows about the transaction).

Back to the code in the Main() function. By now you've created a connection, started a transaction on it, and printed a count of the number of rows in the Order Detail table of the database (at runtime, you should see that there are about 2,500 records in there). Now go ahead and delete them all. This isn't as dire as it sounds—you're inside a transaction, and later in the code you're going to roll the transaction back, which will effectively cancel the delete operation.

```
' Now delete all the order detail records and print the count again
Dim deleteCommand As New SqlCommand( _
    "DELETE FROM [order details]", " + _
        northwindConnection, deleteTransaction)
WriteLine(deleteCommand.ExecuteNonQuery().ToString() + _
    " order details deleted!")
```

Once again, notice that the SqlTransaction has to be passed into the SqlCommand's constructor in order for the command to not throw an exception when it's executed. Calling ExecuteNonQuery() on a command returns a count of the number of rows affected by the command, so that's printed out to the console to show you just how many rows got deleted.

With the rows deleted, call PrintOrderDetailCount() again:

```
PrintOrderDetailCount(northwindConnection, deleteTransaction)
```

Just as you would expect at runtime, this will print 0. Within the transaction, you're able to see the updates and changes made to the database, so having just run a big Delete command recounting the records in the table gives you a grand total of zero.

Of course, you can't leave the database in that state, so the final thing to do is roll back the transaction and once again count the rows in the database.

```
' Rollback the transaction and count the order details once again
deleteTransaction.Rollback()
WriteLine("Rollback complete")
 PrintOrderDetailCount(northwindConnection, deleteTransaction)
```

That final call to PrintOrderDetailCount() will once again show you that there are 2,000 or so rows in the Order Detail table. Notice how even though the transaction is rolled back, it is still passed into the function and used in running a command. The transaction is effectively closed at that point, and the Command object is intelligent enough to know that it doesn't have to do anything special with a closed transaction. The constructor simply accepts the SqlTransaction object as a parameter and then ignores it when the command is executed.

All that remains now is to close up your Try...Catch block to finish the code, and then you can go ahead and run the application. You should see the results shown in Figure 9-1.

```
Catch ex As Exception
    WriteLine(ex.ToString())
End Try
WriteLine("All done! Press Enter to exit.")
ReadLine()
```

```
C:\Documents and Settings\pete\Desktop\APress\Beginning ADO.Net\Cha
There are currently 2155 order details in the database
2155 order details deleted!
There are currently 0 order details in the database
Rollback complete
There are currently 2155 order details in the database
All done! Press Enter to exit.
```

Figure 9-1. The output of the transaction application

Transactions and DataAdapters

The last section demonstrated that there are quite a few prerequisites when working with transactions. First, you can only start a transaction by calling the BeginTransaction() method on an open Connection object. Second, if you want to run a command against the database, you need to set the Transaction property of the Command object you intend to execute. Finally, you need to Commit() or Rollback() the transaction prior to closing the connection. If you close a connection that has an open transaction attached, ADO.NET will automatically trigger a rollback. So, how can you apply all these things when you work with DataAdapters and Commands?

The obvious answer would be to manually create the Command objects and the connections before assigning them to a DataAdapter. That approach certainly works, but at the expense of the helpful shorthand constructors that you may have gotten used to when working with DataAdapters. An alternative is to use the **SelectCommand, UpdateCommand, InsertCommand,** and **DeleteCommand** properties of a DataAdapter to get at the commands contained inside the Adapter. You can then use the Connection properties of each command to get at the connection in order to open it and start your transaction.

For example, let's say you were about to pass a DataSet down to a DataAdapter for updating, inserting, and deleting. Here's how the code might look:

```
Private Sub TransactionUpdate(ByVal sourceDataset As DataSet, _
      ByVal adapter As SqlDataAdapter)

    ' First, open the connection we're going to use - I'm assuming all
    ' commands in the adapter use the same connection
    adapter.SelectCommand.Connection.Open()
```

```vb
' Now start the transaction
Dim updateTransaction As SqlTransaction = _
    adapter.SelectCommand.Connection.BeginTransaction()

Try
    adapter.InsertCommand.Transaction = updateTransaction
    adapter.UpdateCommand.Transaction = updateTransaction
    adapter.DeleteCommand.Transaction = updateTransaction

    adapter.Update(sourceDataset)

    ' Finally, commit the transaction assuming everything went ok
    updateTransaction.Commit()

Catch ex As Exception
    updateTransaction.Rollback()
End Try

adapter.SelectCommand.Connection.Close()

End Sub
```

Don't be tempted, when working with DataAdapters, to cache the Connection object in a global variable when the Adapter is created, in order to call it later on. That approach works, but the approach in the preceding code ensures that you minimize the amount of time a connection is open; if you go ahead and cache the Connection object as soon as the Adapter is created, then it's far too tempting to open the connection and thereby negate all the disconnected benefits that come from using DataSets. If you're going to hold a connection open, you might as well walk through your data with a DataReader and fire off commands to the database as and when you need to. It's not a very elegant design, though, is it?

Isolation Levels

Isolation, one of the keys to the ACID properties of a transaction, is vitally important. Transactions need to be isolated in order to not be able to see the intermediate effects of another transaction, which could feasibly mean that your transaction reads rows that don't actually exist or values from rows that could be rolled back in a short while.

There are four values that can be used for the isolation level of a transaction: **IsolationLevel.ReadCommitted**, **IsolationLevel.ReadUncommitted**, **IsolationLevel.RepeatableRead**, and **IsolationLevel.Serializable**. You pass through the desired isolation level for your transaction to the **BeginTransaction**() method of the Connection object. For example:

```
Dim updateTransaction As SqlTransaction = _
    northwindConnection.BeginTransaction(IsolationLevel.Serializable)
```

Isolation levels can be quite confusing if they are something that you have always previously avoided working with (there are a lot of you out there—you know who you are). All the preceding isolation levels will lock the table being worked on and prevent other processes from reading from that table. The difference between the various levels is the varying degrees to which other transactions are allowed to modify the data.

The highest level of isolation is **IsolationLevel.Serializable**. With this isolation level set, the transaction will put an exclusive lock on the tables that it updates. No other process will be able to read, update, delete, or insert rows in that table. This is undoubtedly the safest way to go if you really want to isolate your transaction from everyone else connecting to the database. The downside, of course, is that for as long as your transaction is running, no one else will be able to do anything at all with the tables accessed within the transaction. It's important if you choose Serializable as your isolation level to keep the scope of your transaction as small as possible.

The **RepeatableRead** level of isolation is geared toward making any reads within your transaction repeatable. The idea here is that within your transaction, every time you hit a database and read rows from it you should always get the same data back—no one else is able to change that data until you commit or roll back your transaction. However, this level of isolation will allow phantom rows. A *phantom row* is one that another transaction that has not yet committed or rolled back is inserting or deleting. In effect, you stand a chance of reading data that doesn't actually exist, since that other transaction could roll back.

ReadUncommited is the next level down. At this level, your transaction won't share-lock anything, and it won't honor any exclusive levels. If another transaction is in the middle of inserting or deleting rows, or has made changes to data in a table, your transaction could read that data. Thus, at this level dirty reads and phantom rows are possible. It's questionable just what value this isolation level adds to any application.

ReadCommitted is slightly better, but not much. It will share-lock any data read from the database and it will honor exclusive locks, which means your transaction will wait until a more isolated transaction completes. The share locks are used to make sure that each individual read of the database's rows contains non-dirty data, but there is still a risk that you could read phantom rows.

It's pretty hard to demonstrate all these things in a sample application, but it is nonetheless useful to have a set of code around that you can use to test the various effects of the different isolation levels. For this you're going to need two projects, both VB .NET console applications. Call the first one TransactionMaker.

```vb
Option Strict On
Imports System.Data.SqlClient
Imports System.Console


Module Module1

    Sub Main()

        Dim northwindConnection As New SqlConnection( _
            "Data Source=localhost;" + _
            "Initial Catalog=Northwind;" + _
            "Integrated Security=SSPI")
        northwindConnection.Open()

        Dim updateTransaction As SqlTransaction = _
            northwindConnection.BeginTransaction(IsolationLevel.Serializable)

        Try

            Dim updateCommand As New SqlCommand( _
                "UPDATE Region SET RegionDescription = 'Some arbitrary value' " + _
                "WHERE Region.RegionId = 1", _
                northwindConnection, updateTransaction)
            updateCommand.ExecuteNonQuery()

            Dim insertCommand As New SqlCommand( _
                "INSERT INTO REGION (RegionID, RegionDescription) " + _
                "VALUES (150, 'Phantom Region')", _
                northwindConnection, updateTransaction)
            insertCommand.ExecuteNonQuery()


            WriteLine("Update complete. Press Enter to rollback")
            ReadLine()

        Catch ex As Exception
            WriteLine("Something went horribly wrong - " + ex.ToString())
        End Try
```

```
        updateTransaction.Rollback()

        WriteLine("All done! Press Enter to exit")
        ReadLine()

    End Sub

End Module
```

The code here is pretty straightforward, so I'm not going to walk you through it line by line. It simply starts a transaction with the Serializable level of isolation and then executes commands to update one row of data and insert a new row of data. After doing so, it waits for you to press the Enter key before it rolls back the changes made in the transaction.

Don't run this application just yet—build it to run it later. It doesn't make much sense to run it on its own. Don't forget to change the data source in the connection string if you're using MSDE—the examples here use SQL Server 2000.

The second application works at the opposite end of the isolation scale, using a ReadUncommitted transaction to read data from the same table that the preceding code updates. Again, this is a VB .NET console application. Call it RegionReader.

```
Option Strict On
Imports System.Data.SqlClient
Imports System.Console


Module Module1

    Sub Main()

        Dim northwindConnection As New SqlConnection( _
            "Data Source=localhost;" + _
            "Initial Catalog=Northwind;" + _
            "Integrated Security=SSPI")

        northwindConnection.Open()

        Dim readerTransaction As SqlTransaction = _
            northwindConnection.BeginTransaction(IsolationLevel.ReadUncommitted)

        Dim selectCommand As New SqlCommand( _
            "SELECT * FROM Region", northwindConnection, readerTransaction)
```

```
            Dim repeatRead As Boolean = True
        While (repeatRead)
            Try
                Dim regionReader As SqlDataReader = selectCommand.ExecuteReader()

                While (regionReader.Read())
                    WriteLine("ID : " + regionReader.GetValue(0).ToString() + _
                        ", Description : " + regionReader.GetString(1))
                End While
                regionReader.Close()

            Catch ex As SqlException
                WriteLine("The command timed out")
            End Try

            Write("Do you want to read again (Y/N) : ")
            repeatRead = (ReadLine().ToUpper() = "Y")

        End While

        readerTransaction.Rollback()
        northwindConnection.Close()

    End Sub

End Module
```

Again, don't forget to change the data source in the connection string if you're using the MSDE engine.

This example just runs a reader over and over the Region table on the Northwind database, prompting you each time to ask whether or not you want to repeat the read. Since it uses the ReadUncommitted level of SqlTransaction, it's stunningly inaccurate in the results it returns.

Run this application and you should see a nice ordered list of the data in the Region table, just like in Figure 9-2.

```
C:\Documents and Settings\pete\Desktop\APress\Beginnir
ID : 1, Description : Eastern
ID : 2, Description : Western
ID : 3, Description : Northern
ID : 4, Description : Southern
ID : 99, Description : Somewhereville
Do you want to read again (Y/N) : _
```

Figure 9-2. The Region table, before the problems start

Now run the TransactionMaker application. It will run and prompt you to press Enter to roll back the transaction. Don't! Instead, move over to the console window running RegionReader, type **Y**, and press Enter. The result is shown in Figure 9-3.

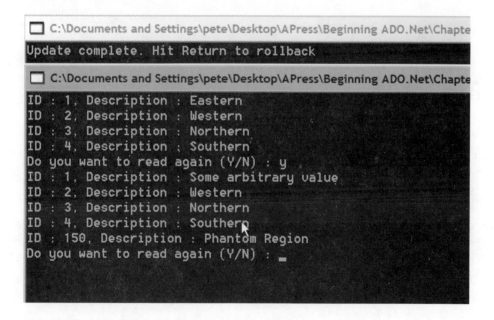

```
C:\Documents and Settings\pete\Desktop\APress\Beginning ADO.Net\Chapte
Update complete. Hit Return to rollback
```
```
C:\Documents and Settings\pete\Desktop\APress\Beginning ADO.Net\Chapte
ID : 1, Description : Eastern
ID : 2, Description : Western
ID : 3, Description : Northern
ID : 4, Description : Southern
Do you want to read again (Y/N) : y
ID : 1, Description : Some arbitrary value
ID : 2, Description : Western
ID : 3, Description : Northern
ID : 4, Description : Southern
ID : 150, Description : Phantom Region
Do you want to read again (Y/N) : _
```

Figure 9-3. Dirty reads and phantom rows in full flow

Hardly a repeatable read, is it? The second time the reader runs, it returns one dirty row and one phantom row. Bear in mind the transaction that created that data has not yet committed, and is in fact about to roll back. That's hardly the kind of result you should aim for in your own application. Feel free to change the isolation levels in both sets of code to explore the different results they give.

Managing Concurrency in ADO.NET

So, now you know the transaction's role in things. Let's take a look at actually managing concurrency in ADO.NET-based applications.

I mentioned earlier that ADO.NET actually supports optimistic concurrency. It's actually the DataAdapter that supports optimistic concurrency, geared as it is to populating and working with disconnected DataSets. The DataAdapter expects the commands you supply for handling updates, insertions, and deletions to also include a Where clause that can confirm the identity of the data in the database. In a version-based update, for example, the update command might look like this:

```
Update myTable Set MyField = @myNewFieldValue
    Where myTable.Timestamp = @myOriginalTimestamp
    And myTable.myPrimaryKey = @primaryKeyValue
```

The command would expect to be passed the timestamp on the original row from the database and would only update the row if both the timestamp and primary key in the database match the parameters passed in. The DataAdapter issues such queries against the database by calling the Command object's ExecuteNonQuery() method, a method that returns a count of the number of rows affected. If that return value is 0, the DataAdapter will automatically trigger a **DBConcurrencyException**. You can prevent it from doing this by coding the DataAdapter's **RowUpdated** event handler.

The RowUpdated event will pass in an object of type **SqlRowUpdatedEventArgs**, which contains a **Status** flag to show what happened, as well as **Row** property that can be used to get hold of the row with the error. By examining and overriding the Status flag, you can prevent the exception from occurring and instead tell the DataAdapter to continue with the rest of the records, but flag the one in error by calling **SetColumnError**() on the row.

Strangely, the DataAdapter does not expose a similar event for catching deletions that have a problem. Instead, the call to the DataAdapter's Update method will trigger a **DeletedRowInaccessible** exception. Let's take a look at these things with a simple example. You're going to inflict some damage on your old friend the Region table again, simply because it doesn't have a lot of fields to work with.

First, create a VB .NET Windows Forms application, and populate the form with a grid and button as shown in Figure 9-4.

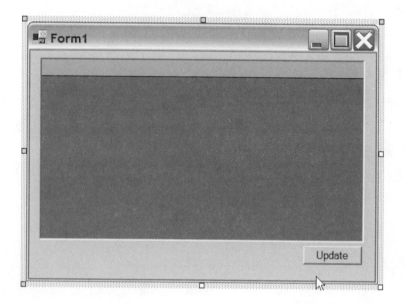

Figure 9-4. Place a grid and a button on the form so that it looks like this.

Set the name of the button to **updateButton** and set the name of the grid to **regionGrid**.

Next, add a DataAdapter to the form in the usual designer-based way (set it up to pull all values from the Region table) and call it **regionAdapter**. The resulting connection object should be named **northwindConnection**.

Finally, generate a DataSet based on the Adapter called **northwindDS**. You can see these three data components in Figure 9-5.

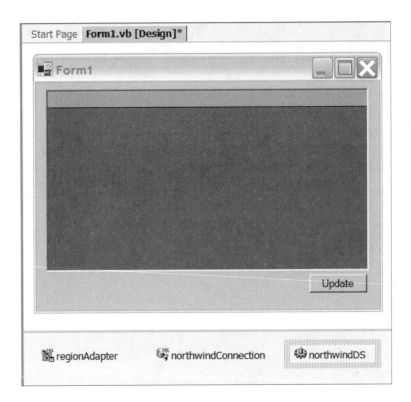

Figure 9-5. The generated DataAdapter, DataSet, and Connection added to the form

You're going to simulate some concurrency problems with this application by changing some existing data in the database, adding in a new row before populating the DataSet, and then reversing those changes immediately after the DataSet has been built. This will effectively give you a grid with a dirty read and a phantom row.

Code the form's Load event so that it looks like this:

```
Private Sub Form1_Load(ByVal sender As System.Object, _
    ByVal e As System.EventArgs) Handles MyBase.Load
    ' Add a region into the database - this will be propagated into the dataset
    northwindConnection.Open()

    Dim insertCommand As New SqlCommand( _
                "INSERT INTO REGION ( RegionID, RegionDescription ) " + _
                "VALUES ( 501, 'Delete Me' )", northwindConnection)
    insertCommand.ExecuteNonQuery()
```

```
    Dim updateCommand As New SqlCommand( _
        "UPDATE REGION SET RegionDescription='Change Me' WHERE RegionID = 1", _
        northwindConnection)
    updateCommand.ExecuteNonQuery()


    regionAdapter.Fill(northwindDS)
regionGrid.SetDataBinding(northwindDS, "Region")


    ' Now delete that new region and reverse the
    ' change made - this will cause a concurrency error if
    ' the user updates that region in the GUI
    Dim deleteCommand As New SqlCommand( _
        "DELETE FROM REGION WHERE RegionID = 501 ", northwindConnection)
    deleteCommand.ExecuteNonQuery()


    updateCommand.CommandText = _
      "UPDATE REGION SET RegionDescription = 'Eastern' " + _
        " WHERE RegionID = 1"
    updateCommand.ExecuteNonQuery()


End Sub
```

You'll need to import the System.Data.SqlClient namespace at the head of the form's class for this code to compile.

Still in the code window, select the DataAdapter from the list of objects at the top left, and select the RowUpdated event from the list of events in the drop-down list to the top right of the editor window. Code the RowUpdated handler like this:

```
Private Sub regionAdapter_RowUpdated( _
      ByVal sender As System.Object, _
      ByVal e As System.Data.SqlClient.SqlRowUpdatedEventArgs) _
      Handles regionAdapter.RowUpdated
    If e.Status = UpdateStatus.ErrorsOccurred Then
        MessageBox.Show("Couldn't update region " + e.Row.Item(0).ToString())
        e.Row.SetColumnError(1, "Concurrency error: Value already updated")
        e.Status = UpdateStatus.SkipCurrentRow
    End If
End Sub
```

I'll walk you through what's going on here. Each time the DataAdapter updates a row in the database, this event will fire. You can check the value of the **e.Status** to see just what the result of the update was. Obviously, you're most interested in errors occurring, so the If block is coded to catch that. When an error does occur, the event handler shows a message box to the user and then sets some error text on the column. Finally, to prevent the error from manifesting itself as DBConcurrencyException at runtime, the **Status** is set to **SkipCurrentRow**. You could also set it to **SkipAllRemainingRows** to drop straight out of the update—a useful strategy in some applications where you wouldn't want partial data saved to the database.

Finally, code the Click handler for the Update button to look like this:

```
Private Sub updateButton_Click(ByVal sender As System.Object, _
        ByVal e As System.EventArgs) _
        Handles updateButton.Click
    Try
        regionAdapter.Update(CType(regionGrid.DataSource, DataSet))
        CType(regionGrid.DataSource, DataSet).AcceptChanges()
    Catch ex As DeletedRowInaccessibleException
        MessageBox.Show(ex.Message)
        CType(regionGrid.DataSource, DataSet).RejectChanges()
    End Try
    regionGrid.Refresh()

End Sub
```

I'm expecting a **DeletedRowInaccessibleException** when I ask the DataAdapter to update, so it's caught, the exception's error message is displayed, and all changes made to the DataSet are rejected.

With all the code done, run the application. Change the description of the first region in the grid, delete the last region in the grid, and then click Update. You should see two error message boxes, one to deal with the concurrency exception on update and one to deal with the user's attempt to delete a row that doesn't exist. The result should be that the changes are backed out and the top row is flagged with an error, as shown in Figure 9-6.

Just how a concurrency exception is identified, though, depends on whether you choose to use version-based updates or all-value updates in your code.

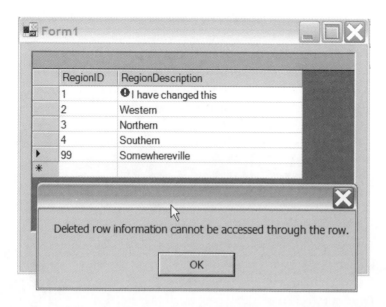

Figure 9-6. An exception occurs when you delete a row that doesn't exist.

All-value updates represent probably the least common type of update in a live system. With an all-value update, when a row needs updating the value of every field that could be changed is passed into the command as a parameter, and the value of every single field in the original row is also passed in. The command updates a row by attempting to find a row matching every original value. Few stored procedures are written this way because of the sheer volume of data that needs to be shifted over the network just to update a single row. However, this is the approach that you've taken with every example that updates from a DataSet so far in the book.

When you create a DataAdapter in the designer using embedded SQL statements, the default functionality of the DataAdapter wizard is to build an all-value update. Here's how you'd set up an all-value update for the Region table:

```
Dim updateCommand As New SqlCommand( _
    "UPDATE Region (RegionID, RegionDescription) " + _
    "VALUES (@RegionID, @RegionDescription) " + _
    "WHERE RegionID = @origRegionID " + _
    "AND RegionDescription = @origRegionDescription", _
    northwindConnection)
```

```
updateCommand.Parameters.Add("@RegionID", SqlDbType.Int, 4, "RegionID")
updateCommand.Parameters.Add("@RegionDescription", _
    SqlDbType.NChar, 50, "RegionDescription")
updateCommand.Parameters.Add("@origRegionID", SqlDbType.Int, 4, "RegionID")
updateCommand.Parameters( _
  "@origRegionID").SourceVersion = DataRowVersion.Original
updateCommand.Parameters.Add("@origRegionDescription", _
    SqlDbType.NChar, 50, "RegionDescription")
updateCommand.Parameters("@origRegionDescription").SourceVersion = _
    DataRowVersion.Current
```

Each parameter to the command is mapped to a source column in a DataSet. In addition, the parameters that are used to locate the original record, and thus manage concurrency, are mapped to the original version of the fields in question.

Even on a table as simple in structure as Northwind's Region table, you can see that the code to set up an all-value update is quite big.

Version-based updates work exactly the same way, but instead of passing in each and every value of the original row, you just pass in a timestamp parameter. This does, of course, require a bit more effort at the database, but it results in much nicer code and is usually the way things are done with stored procedures. A trigger is used on the database to timestamp rows as they are created or modified, and this timestamp is usually passed back to your code through the stored procedure used to select data. This original timestamp value is then passed back to the update and create stored procedures to assist them in locating the correct record to update. The actual process of creating and mapping the parameters is virtually identical to the previous code.

Summary

Managing concurrency and using well-designed transactions in a live production version of an application is vital, especially in these days of Web-based applications where the potential for conflicts and concurrency failures can be huge. Thankfully, managing concurrency in ADO.NET is a relative no-brainer.

In this chapter you looked at

- The theory behind transactions and concurrency

- The Transaction object and how to use it

- How to set up the isolation level of a transaction

- How to work with concurrency in a DataAdapter

- How to build commands that map parameters to manage concurrency

CHAPTER 10

The OLE DB Data Provider

"Egad, I think the interpreter is the hardest to be understood of the two!"

—Richard Brinsley Sheridan, *The Critic*, act 1, scene 2

AT THE TIME OF THIS WRITING, the .NET Framework ships with just two data providers: the highly optimized System.Data.SqlClient provider and the slower **System.Data.OleDb** provider. The latter was provided to allow developers to get at their existing database servers without having to wait for the database vendor in question to come out with a .NET-optimized data provider of their own. Incidentally, there is mention in the online help of an ODBC data provider, and Microsoft's own Compact Framework for mobile device development does include a SqlServerCE database provider. These two providers were not complete or fully documented in time to be included in this edition.

The idea behind the .NET data providers is quite simple: By inheriting functionality and interfaces from standard objects such as **DBDataAdapter** and **DBConnection**, developers can be assured that all .NET data providers will work exactly the same way. However, data provider developers are free to add extra functionality if they so desire. The OLE DB data provider is a good example of this. As well as supporting all the functionality you've grown used to with the standard SqlClient data provider, the OLE DB data provider brings with it extra features, such as support for reading from ADO Recordsets, support for reading OLE DB schemas into DataSets, and support for such old friends as Universal Data Link (UDL) files.

Introducing the OLE DB Provider

The OLE DB provider's classes are contained in the System.Data.OleDb namespace—just import that namespace into your code instead of System.Data.SqlClient and you will have access to the objects that it provides.

The namespace contains OLE DB classes for Connections, Commands, Parameters, DataAdapters, and CommandBuilders, DataReaders, and Transactions, as well as security model objects borrowed from the world of ADO.

These objects are all named the same as their SQL Server counterparts, but they're prefixed with **OleDb** instead of SQL. So a Connection is an **OleDbConnection**, a DataAdapter is an **OleDbDataAdapter**, and so on. They all work exactly the same way as their SQL Server counterparts.

OLE DB Connections and Data Providers

Some of you will be familiar with the term "provider" when talking about data access. OLE DB and ADO introduced the term "provider" in relation to connection strings. You would simply build up a connection string and name the provider that you want OLE DB to use, and thus ADO was able to provide a single interface to a wealth of behind-the-scenes data providers. The same concept applies to ADO.NET's OLE DB data provider.

The OLE DB data provider uses the same format for connection strings, providing access to SQL Server, the OLE DB data shaping service, the indexing service, Visual FoxPro, Jet, Oracle, and a host of other back-end data sources from a single .NET data provider. Just as with the SQL Server data provider, the connection string is defined when creating the Connection object. In the case of the OLE DB data provider, this is the System.Data.OleDb.OleDbConnection object. Try this VB .NET console application out:

```
Option Strict On
Imports System.Data.OleDb
Imports System.Console


Module Module1

    Sub Main()

        Dim northwindConnection As New OleDbConnection( _
            "Provider=SQLOLEDB;Data Source=localhost;Intial Catalog=Northwind;" + _
            "Integrated Security=SSPI")

        northwindConnection.Open()

        WriteLine("Provider is " + northwindConnection.Provider)
        WriteLine("Database is " + northwindConnection.Database)
        WriteLine("Data source is " + northwindConnection.DataSource)
        WriteLine("Connection state is " + northwindConnection.State.ToString())
```

```
northwindConnection.Close()

WriteLine("All done! Press Enter to exit")
ReadLine()

End Sub

End Module
```

As you can see, the format of the connection string is almost identical to that used with the SQL Server data provider. The difference, of course, is the addition of the provider string, which is used to identify the underlying OLE DB provider to use.

```
Dim northwindConnection As New OleDbConnection( _
    "Provider=SQLOLEDB;Data Source=localhost;Intial Catalog=Northwind;" + _
    "Integrated Security=SSPI")
```

This provider is then exposed through the **OleDbConnection.Provider** property. This part of the connection string is also required. If you attempt to create an OLE DB Connection object without a provider named in the connection string, you will get an exception. If you wanted to connect to a Jet data source (an Access database), the provider would be **Microsoft.Jet.OLEDB.4.0,** whereas for Oracle it would be **MSDAORA**. Those of you who have done a lot of development with OLE DB prior to .NET will probably be asking why the provider for SQL Server is SQLOLEDB and not MSDASQL. The reason is that MSDASQL connects you to the OLE DB provider for ODBC, and that's not currently supported in .NET. Microsoft has made an ODBC-specific data provider available for download at http://msdn.microsoft.com/downloads in the future. This is not included "in the box" with Visual Studio .NET, though.

It's worth pointing out that whereas you could set up dynamic properties of the underlying provider in "old-fashioned" ADO, you can't do that with the OleDBConnection object in ADO.NET. You can only set up properties of the underlying data provider that can be specified in the connection string.

Universal Data Link Files

If you are already deeply familiar with OLE DB, and in particular SQL Server 2000, then it may come as a pleasant surprise to learn that you can still use Universal Data Link (UDL) files with the OLE DB data provider in ADO.NET. A UDL file wraps up all the information about a connection in a convenient file external to the application assembly, which makes deployment to desktops using different data sources a dream. Just deploy the correct UDL file depending on the data source that you want the application to use. Although UDL files are not strictly ADO.NET, they are a useful tool to work with when using the OLE DB Data provider, so let's take a look at how they work.

Creating a UDL file is a snap. Open Notepad and save the blank document to a file called MyConnection.UDL (or anything else you choose, just so long as it ends in .UDL). Incidentally, when you use Notepad to create these things, make sure that the Save As box in Notepad shows the file type as All Files, as shown in Figure 10-1. If you don't do this, Notepad will save a file called MyConnection.UDL.txt.

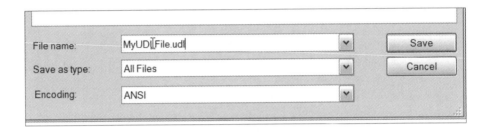

Figure 10-1. When you save a UDL file, make sure Notepad's "Save as type" box is set to All Files. Otherwise, you will end up with a filename.UDL.TXT file.

Once the file is saved, close Notepad. Open Windows Explorer, find the UDL file you just created, and double-click it. This will cause the Data Link Properties Wizard to appear, just as in Figure 10-2.

Use the wizard to set up the properties of your connection and test it, and then click OK when you are done. Make sure you select the correct provider from the Provider tab—by default the wizard will want you to use the OLE DB provider for ODBC, which won't work. Also, if you want to embed a password in the UDL file, make sure you click the "Allow saving password" check box. If you store the UDL file in the same directory as the compiled application, you can change your connection string to this:

```
Dim northwindConnection As New OleDbConnection("File Name=MyConnection.UDL")
```

Using UDL files in this way, you can deploy the application with a different UDL file to automatically force the application to connect to whichever database is most appropriate (development, testing, production, and so on). More to the point, though, if you happen to have UDL files lying around for your DTS packages or from other applications, they can be used without changes with ADO.NET's OLE DB data provider.

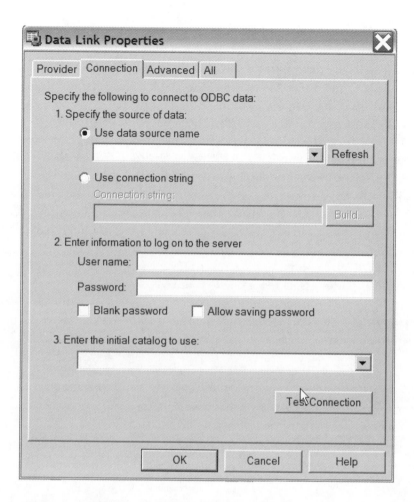

Figure 10-2. The Data Link Properties Wizard

NOTE UDL files are a great way to deploy an application with connection information contained external to the application's assemblies. They are just text files, though, so you can use the UDL files as a way of building complex connection strings, testing those connections, and then simply cutting and pasting the contents of the UDL file into your application. The disadvantage of this, of course, is that you lose the flexibility that comes with having connection information stored externally to the application.

Old-Fashioned ADO

In a little while, you'll see a really neat feature of the OLE DB data provider that allows you to mix ADO and ADO.NET code together. The first stage of this is to actually write old-style ADO code within your .NET application.

This isn't as strange as it sounds, particularly from VB .NET's point of view. There are millions of lines of tested, deployed, and quite happily running code out there that were written in VB using ADO. Migrating an application to the .NET platform does not have to be an all or nothing exercise. You can just front-end your existing applications with Web services, or you can dive in and rewrite the whole thing. A more sensible approach, though, is to use what code you can from the existing application in the new one, particularly if your budget won't quite stretch to a full re-architecture of your existing systems.

Using ADO in .NET is as simple as including a reference to ADO in your .NET solution and then importing its namespace into your code.

Fire up a new VB .NET console application—call it ADOInDotNet. In the Solution Explorer, right-click the References heading and select Add Reference to pop open the Add Reference dialog box, as shown in Figure 10-3.

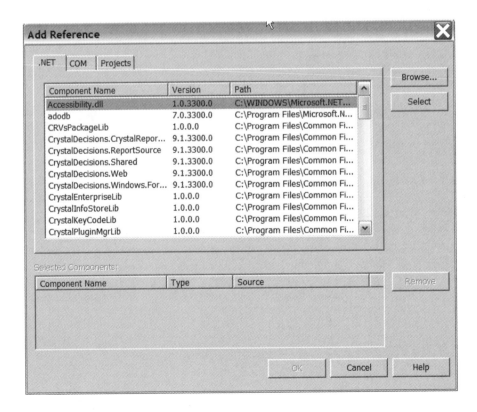

Figure 10-3. The Add Reference dialog box

Click the COM tab at the top of the dialog box and there will be a short pause while your system takes stock of all the COM servers installed on your machine before presenting you with a list. Scroll down the list and choose Microsoft ActiveX Data Objects 2.7 Library, as shown in Figure 10-4. Then click Select followed by OK.

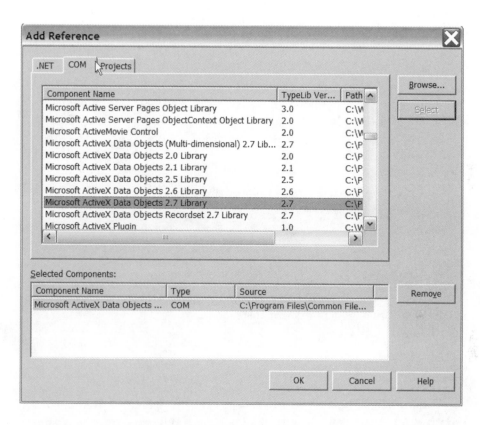

Figure 10-4. Find the ActiveX Data Objects reference and select it.

You will now have a reference to ADO included in your project. Drop into the code window and import ADO with this statement:

```
Imports ADODB
```

Now you can write code just as you would back in the days of VB 6.0.

```
Sub Main()

    Dim adoRecordset As New ADODB.Recordset()
    adoRecordset.Open("SELECT * FROM Region", _
        "Provider=SQLOLEDB;" + _
        "Data Source=localhost;" + _
        "Initial Catalog=Northwind;" + _
        "User ID=sa;Password=MyPassword")

    Do While Not adoRecordset.EOF
        System.Console.WriteLine( _
        adoRecordset.Fields("RegionDescription").Value)
        adoRecordset.MoveNext()
    Loop

    adoRecordset.Close()
    System.Console.WriteLine("All done! Press Enter to exit")
    System.Console.ReadLine()



End Sub
```

Don't forget when keying this in to change the name of the server, the username, and the password to match your own installation.

Mixing ADO with ADO.NET

You may have noticed by now that in this chapter I talk a lot about good old-fashioned ADO. The OLE DB data provider uses connection strings that are very similar to standard ADO ones, and you can even use UDL files. With a little "interop" you can use ADO within .NET. It might not surprise you then to learn that you can make ADO and ADO.NET work together, courtesy of a special feature of the OleDBData-Adapter class.

The **Fill**() method of OleDBDataAdapter can be passed an ADO Recordset along with a data table to fill. It then extracts the data from the Recordset and places it into the table. This is a one-way operation, though; you can't use the DataAdapter to then go ahead and update the Recordset. For that reason, this is a valuable tool for extending the life of existing COM objects with .NET. If those COM objects expose Recordsets, then you can grab them and manipulate them with the far more powerful tools embedded in ADO.NET. Let's take a look at this in action.

Start up a new VB .NET Window Forms application and add a reference to COM ADO just as you did earlier in this chapter.

Next, drop a grid on the form (don't worry about renaming it), and then add the following code in bold to your form:

```
Option Strict On
Imports ADODB
Imports System.Data.OleDb


Public Class Form1
    Inherits System.Windows.Forms.Form

            :
            :
            :

    Private Sub Form1_Load(ByVal sender As System.Object, _
        ByVal e As System.EventArgs) Handles MyBase.Load
        Dim adoRecordset As New ADODB.Recordset()
        adoRecordset.Open("SELECT * FROM Employees", _
            "Provider=SQLOLEDB;" + _
            "Data Source=localhost;" + _
            "Initial Catalog=Northwind;" + _
            "User ID=sa;Password=MyPassword")

        Dim employeeTable As New DataTable("Employees")
        Dim employeeAdapter As New OleDbDataAdapter()
        employeeAdapter.Fill(employeeTable, adoRecordset)
        adoRecordset.Close()

        DataGrid1.SetDataBinding(employeeTable, "")

    End Sub
End Class
```

The code should be quite easy to follow. A simple ADO Recordset is built that pulls employees from the Northwind database. A new table is then created and passed with the Recordset to an OleDBDataAdapter to fill. The resulting filled table is bound to the DataGrid. Getting data from ADO into ADO.NET is trivial, as you can see.

OLE DB Types and Literals

Given the wealth of data sources covered by OLE DB, it's easy to get confused as to just what literals to use in SQL statements for common things such as wildcards. OLE DB also supports slightly different data types just to confuse things even further.

The **OleDBLiteral** enumeration should help you out with the literals side of things. For example, the standard wildcard symbol to use in a select is held in **OleDBLiteral.Like_Percent**, whereas the single character wildcard is held in **OleDBLiteral.Like_Underscore**.

The data types are exposed through the **OleDBType** enumeration, which provides a list of types that can be used to set up the type in an OleDBParameter for a command.

Using these enumerations is relatively straightforward, and each enumeration contains a host of different values—far more than I could list here, so take a look at the online help for a complete list.

Summary

This is probably the shortest chapter in the book, and for good reason. The design of ADO.NET makes it easy for developers to add new data providers to the framework that should work exactly the same way as any other. As you've seen in this chapter, though, data provider developers are free to add their own features to these providers, such as the OLE DB provider's support for ADO Recordsets.

In this chapter you learned

- Which namespace to use to get at the OLE DB data provider

- How to use ADO within a .NET application

- How to import ADO Recordsets into a DataSet

- How to specify underlying OLE DB providers in the connection string

- How to work with UDL files for connection mapping

CHAPTER 11

Introducing System.Xml

"Standards are always out of date. That is what makes them standards."

—Alan Bennett, *Forty Years On*

THE *EXTENSIBLE MARKUP LANGUAGE* (XML) and the entire family of technologies surrounding it were originally conceived from the need to separate business presentation logic from data, a problem that even today clogs the Web and reduces its real-world usefulness at times to near zero. XML has grown far beyond even its own lofty ambitions. Referred to by some as the lingua franca of the Internet, XML has now been adopted as the standard format for pretty much any and all types of data by Microsoft. It's used as the standard format for data interchange across process and machine boundaries by the .NET Framework, it's the format used to define assembly manifests and, of course, it's the format that ADO.NET uses internally to maintain DataSets in memory and allow the simple merging of data from multiple sources and multiple formats into a single whole.

This chapter is not an exhaustive study of the XML language or its family of technologies (including XSLT and XPath). Instead, in this chapter you will take a brief look at the **System.Xml** namespace and the facilities that the .NET Framework provides for working with XML data. I will inevitably touch on some of the basics of XML itself, if only to establish a common framework of understanding for what at times can be a quite confusing subject. If you are already an XML expert, then bear with me through such discussion.

You may be wondering why I'm even bothering to go to all the effort of describing the XML manipulation facilities in .NET in a book about database development. The answer, of course, is that in .NET you can't escape XML. XML is pervasive across every single part of Visual Studio, and if you're working with ADO.NET, chances are that at some point you're going to need to work with XML natively. As I mentioned earlier, a DataSet is represented in memory as an XML document. The DataSet also provides methods to allow its easy serialization to and from disk. In addition, if you want to work with typed DataSets, then you have to work with *XML Schemas,* an XML document that effectively describes other XML documents and constrains the data they can hold.

XML is here to stay, its impact is profound, and you need to get used to it now.

XML 101

As I noted, this chapter does not contain an exhaustive description of all that XML is and does—that's a whole book on its own and a quick browse through Amazon will show you that there are plenty of other authors out there who feel the same way. It's worth looking over the basic components of XML though, just to make sure we're all working from the same foundation.

Chances are that many of you reading this will already have come across XML and perhaps used it in your own applications prior to the move to .NET. Despite the much-touted benefit of XML being that it allows a Web developer to separate content from presentation (XML for the content, XSLT for the presentation), XML is a versatile enough technology that it has found uses in a wide range of problem domains unrelated to the Web. In real-time financial trading applications, XML is typically used to wrap up information about bids, offers, and deals before throwing those mini XML documents around the network for client applications to pick up. Application configuration is also an area where XML is ideally suited thanks to XML's capability to apply a formal structure to almost any type of data. Microsoft jumped on the XML bandwagon very quickly with the release of their MSXML COM components, giving Visual Basic 6.0 developers a powerful set of tools to work with XML in their applications, and that's probably how most of you came across XML in the first place.

Despite the widespread uptake of XML, there are still a lot of people out there who don't know the names of the various components of XML. Knowing them is essential if you don't want to get lost with .NET, though, since the .NET Framework's System.Xml namespace conforms very closely to the World Wide Web Consortium's (W3C's) XML standards.

The Components of XML

XML is a large, but uncomplicated, subject that covers a number of areas. XML itself is the name given to a way of putting order around any kind of data. Think of it as a database format, but without a database engine. You can create and work with XML files with nothing more than Microsoft Notepad and Internet Explorer. An XML file is textual, just the same as an HTML file, and it can thus be created with any capable text editor, and most Web browsers, including Internet Explorer, are able to automatically recognize and display XML files (see Figure 11-1). For an example of this, do a search of your hard disk for files ending in .XML (there will be quite a few in your Visual Studio directories) and double-click one to display it in Internet Explorer.

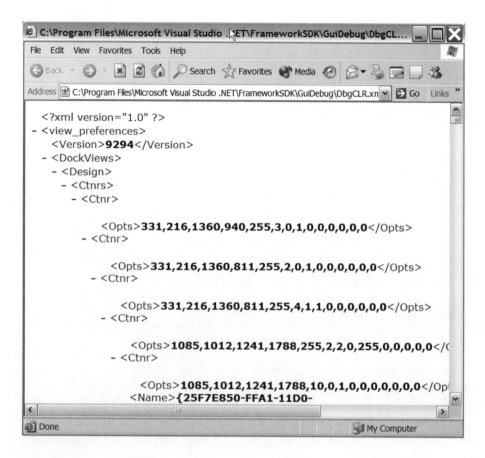

Figure 11-1. Internet Explorer is able to automatically recognize XML files and display them in an intelligent way.

An XML file is made up of *tags,* user-defined strings enclosed within angle brackets (< and >), just the same as tags in an HTML document. Unlike an HTML document, an XML document is only valid if all tags are closed. For example, if you have a tag in an XML document called <Name>, there must be a closing </Name> tag somewhere else in the document for it to be valid. You can also create "empty" tags by adding a / to the end of the tag's name. For example, <Name/> is both the open and close <Name> tag in one.

XML can be confusing for newcomers since there appear to be an awful lot of tags to learn. The names of the tags, though, are completely up to you. There is no standard for naming tags and no predefined set of commands to learn. If I wanted to catalog my collection of DVDs, for example, I could just fire up Notepad or Visual Studio's built-in XML editor and create a document called Dvds.xml that looks like this:

```
<?xml version="1.0" encoding="utf-8" ?>
<dvd-collection>
  <DVD SoundFormat='DTS' Title='Mission Impossible'>
    <Star>
      <Actor>Tom Cruise</Actor>
      <Character>Ethan Hunt</Character>
    </Star>
  </DVD>
  <DVD SoundFormat='5.1' Title='Hackers'>
    <Star>
      <Actor>Angelina Jolie</Actor>
      <Character>Acid Burn</Character>
    </Star>
    <Star>
      <Actor>Johnny Lee Miller</Actor>
      <Character>Crash Override</Character>
    </Star>
  </DVD>
</dvd-collection>
```

The only all-important things to remember when naming tags is that they shouldn't contain spaces and that XML files are case sensitive (<name> is a different tag than <NAME>). You can see in the preceding document that XML documents are hierarchical. The document tag <dvd-collection> contains all the data about a DVD collection, which consists of child nodes called <DVD>, each of which contains information about the sound format of the movie and the stars within it.

In the sample, <dvd-collection> is known as the *document element,* the root element of the XML document, since it contains everything within the document. You must have a document element.

<DVD> and <Star> are both child elements of the document, and <Star> is also a child element of <DVD>. You will also notice that when a DVD is defined here, other information is included along with the tag:

```
<DVD SoundFormat='DTS' Title='Mission Impossible'>
```

These are called **Attributes**, and their values are always enclosed in either single or double quotes. SoundFormat and Title are both attributes of the <DVD> element.

Take a look at the <Star> elements:

```
<Star>
  <Actor>Tom Cruise</Actor>
  <Character>Ethan Hunt</Character>
</Star>
```

Each <Star> element here includes two child elements, <Actor> and <Character>. In the preceding example, "Tom Cruise" and "Ethan Hunt" are known as *text nodes*. They are children of the <Actor> and <Character> elements, respectively, but even though to you and me they appear to contain the real meat of the document, they are treated internally as nodes, just like any other.

This will become more important to you as you write code to work with XML data. It's tempting to look at the <Actor> element and say that its value is "Tom Cruise." It's not. The value of that element is "Actor," and it contains a child text node whose value is "Tom Cruise." It's easy to get confused with this.

Take a look at the very first line of the document:

```
<?xml version="1.0" encoding="utf-8" ?>
```

Tags that begin with <? and end with ?> are called *processing instructions*. They are there to tell the XML processor, the classes in the System.Xml namespace, something important about the document to follow. In this case, the processing instruction tells the processor that this is an XML document that conforms to version 1.0 of the XML standard, and its contents are encoded in "utf-8," a standard character set used in the western hemisphere.

There are, of course, other elements to XML documents, far more than I can cover here. For example, CDATA sections allow you to embed content inside an XML document that should not be checked by the parser. Check out the online help in Visual Studio and on MSDN online for more information.

By default, the only checking applied to the content of an XML document is the check for well-formedness. This is the basic golden rule that whatever tags you put into an XML document must all be closed and closed in order. There are two other technologies, though, that can be applied to actually apply constraints and rules to the content of an XML document in the same way that constraints and rules control the data inside a database.

The older of the two technologies is the Document Type Definition (DTD). These files typically end in the suffix .DTD, but they can also be included in the XML document itself. The DTD is now obsolete, but it uses predefined tags and processing instructions to set up how many children a node can have, required nodes, required attributes, and much more.

DTDs are quite alien to read and develop. XML Schema, however, is far friendlier. An XML Schema file typically ends in the suffix .xsd and is used extensively in Visual Studio. I touched on XML Schema files earlier when you looked at DataSets, since an XML Schema is used to define a typed DataSet and apply data constraints to the contents of that DataSet. Schemas are also used through Windows XP and .NET to define the contents of assembly manifests and configuration files. You'll take a look at just what an XML Schema is and how to define and work with them in the next chapter, which looks at the application of XML to the world of ADO.NET development.

.NET's Take on XML

The .NET Framework supports the Document Object Model (DOM) Level 1 and Level 2 standards laid down by the W3C. The DOM standards define an API for working with XML data, using both in-memory and noncached forward-only access methods. .NET supports the APIs fully, which, of course, means that if you have to port code from another platform over to .NET, the XML side of things should never prove a problem; the DOM Level 1 and Level 2 standard APIs were defined as a platform-independent framework.

Over the years of its life, the W3C's XML standards body has received many complaints about the DOM standards. Although the standards aren't supposed to favor any particular programming language, they do tend to make life a lot easier for C++ developers than for, say, Java or Basic programmers. The .NET Framework goes beyond the standard API and implements extension methods and objects to make working with XML easier and to provide features more relevant to the types of problems .NET developers face. For example, support has been added to easily push data into, and retrieve data back out of, ADO.NET objects such as the DataSet.

In the interest of ease of use, Microsoft also took something of a gamble on some other XML-related technologies that were in the design phase but not yet standardized when they started work on .NET. The System.Xml namespace includes objects that support XPath, for intelligent querying of XML data, while ADO.NET uses XML Schemas to add structure, rules, and constraints to the data inside a specific XML document. XML Schemas, for example, are used to define the structure of typed DataSets in ADO.NET.

As you've probably picked up by now, .NET's XML support lives in the System.Xml namespace—you'll need to import that namespace into your project if you want to use .NET's XML objects directly. It's worth noting that if you intend to use a technology that itself uses XML (ADO.NET, for example), you don't need to manually import the System.Xml namespace yourself. Only import that namespace if you plan on directly making use of the XML objects within your own code.

System.Xml contains an object for every component of XML and implements those objects in an object hierarchy that exactly matches the hierarchy of XML itself. At the base, you have the XmlNode object. Since everything in XML revolves around the concept of a node, this is a good place to start. Each specific type of XML node is then descended from XmlNode as an object in its own right. You can see the structure of the objects in Figure 11-2.

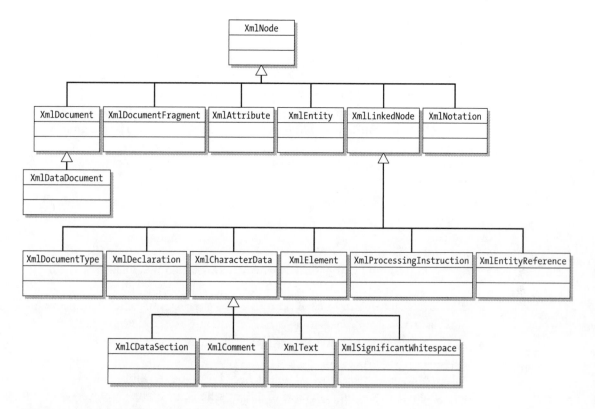

Figure 11-2. The structure of the node-based objects in System.Xml

Obviously, these objects just refer to the content of an XML document; there are other objects in the System.Xml namespace for reading and writing XML, and also for using surrounding technologies such as XSLT and XPath. You'll look at these other technologies in brief later in this chapter.

Notice in Figure 11-2 that XmlDocument is descended directly from XmlNode. As I mentioned in the overview of XML previously, an XmlDocument is itself a node, albeit a special one. XmlDocument objects, unlike other nodes, do not have parent nodes. They are used as the root of the tree, the node to start with from which you can gain access to all the other nodes that make up the document in full. The XmlDocument object in .NET also provides the methods you will use to create child nodes within the document.

Also notice how XmlAttribute is descended from XmlNode. An Attribute isn't strictly a node, since it can't have children and is usually attached to another node as a property of that node. Having XmlAttribute descend from a node in this way makes it easy for you to work with Attributes in your code; if you know how to use an XmlNode object, you know how to work with an XmlAttribute.

A final point to note that always catches newcomers to XML out is the difference between XmlText and XmlElement. It's easy to look at a fragment of XML such as this:

```
<Employee>
    <Name>John Smith</Name>
</Employee>
```

and start thinking that the Name is John Smith. That's correct from the point of view of understanding what the content of this XML fragment means, but wrong in terms of the structure of the fragment. Instead, <Name> is a child Element of <Employee>. It contains one child, an XML text node, whose value is "John Smith." Looking just at base objects here, you have an XmlNode containing an XmlNode, which contains an XmlNode. What you would actually have in code were you to come across this on its own is an XmlDocument containing a single XmlElement, which contains a single XmlText object. Simply finding the XmlElement that contains <Name> isn't enough in code to find out the name of the employee—you need to grab the element's child to do that.

The DOM

The DOM refers to an in-memory representation of an XML document, and it is in many ways analogous to the ADO.NET DataSet. When working with the DOM, you load an XML document in its entirety into memory and then disconnect from the source of the data. From the point that it's loaded, you're free to navigate the document, modify its structure, and add to or change its contents, just as you are with a DataSet. Of course, there's no support for identifying changes made to an XML document in memory other than writing the code yourself to do so, and that's where the similarities between a DOM document and ADO.NET's DataSet end.

Just as with ADO.NET, though, you do have the option of using a Reader (and a Writer) to gain forward-only access to XML data in a noncached form. I'll cover this in full later.

Loading and Working with XML Data

XML data can arrive in your application from a number of sources: a URL, a string returned from a function or Web service call, even from a variable with XML embedded in it from within your own code, and, of course, from a good old-fashioned file. Naturally, there are a number of choices open to you then for actually getting that XML data into an **XmlDocument** object that you can navigate and interrogate.

The simplest is the **XmlDocument.LoadXml**() method. Simply pass in a string containing the XML document and the method will decode the string into an in-memory, DOM-based document. Let's take a look at this in action and also explore just how to navigate around the data once it's loaded.

Start up a VB .NET console project. The first thing you're going to need to do to your project is import the System.Xml namespace by adding an Import line to the top of your code.

```
Option Strict On
Imports System.Xml

Module Module1

    Sub Main()
```

Now you are free to go ahead and create an **XmlDocument** object ready to work with the XML data.

```
Module Module1

    Sub Main()

     Dim musicDoc As New XmlDocument()
```

Now you can load some XML into your new XmlDocument object.

```
musicDoc.LoadXml( _
            "<Music>" + _
            "<Track Composer='Haydn' Date='1796'>" + _
                    "Trumpet Concerto in E Flat</Track>" + _
            "<Track Composer='Beethoven' Date='1796'>" + _
                     "Minuet in G</Track>" + _
            "<Track Composer='Beethoven' Date='1808'>" + _
                    "Symphony No. 5</Track>" + _
            "</Music>")
```

Obviously, when you work with XML in this way, you forgo the handy error-checking facilities of Visual Studio's built-in XML editor, which you'll take a look at in a little while, so be extra careful when you key in the data to make sure you don't misspell the tags.

There are a number of ways to navigate through the data in an XML document. First, the XmlNode class implements **ChildNodes** and **FirstChild** properties, which can be used to get a list of child nodes or just the first child, respectively. The latter property comes into its own when dealing with Elements that contain text nodes, such as in the previous document. To print out the name of a track, you'd find the Track node itself and then find its first child to get at the actual name of the track. To check whether there are any children of a particular node, just check the **HasChildNodes** property. There's also an **Item** property. Passing it the name of an element attempts to retrieve the first child element matching the name passed in.

Most often, you'll want to grab a bunch of child elements based on their name and then iterate through them with a For-Each loop. That's where the **GetElementsByTagName**() method comes into play. For example, to work through the tracks in your XML document in the example, just go ahead and add these few lines:

```
' Now we can iterate through the nodes within this document
Dim track As XmlElement
For Each track In _
 musicDoc.DocumentElement.GetElementsByTagName("Track")

Next
```

It should be quite easy to follow; the code defines an XmlElement object called Track, which you use to iterate through all the <Track/> elements in the XmlDocument. Interrogating the values of the attributes of each track, as well as finding out the name of each track, is equally painless.

To get an Attribute's value, just call **GetAttribute**(), passing in the name of the attribute that's required. You'll get back a string, since attributes in XML are always encoded as strings. To get the actual name of the track itself, just look at the **Value** of the element's **FirstChild** property. **FirstChild** will return an XmlNode, and its **Value** property in the case of a Text node is the text itself.

Go ahead and extend the For-Each loop with the lines of the following code shown in bold:

```
' Now we can iterate through the nodes within this document
Dim track As XmlElement
For Each track In _
    musicDoc.DocumentElement.GetElementsByTagName("Track")
    Console.WriteLine("Composer :" + _
            track.GetAttribute("Composer"))
    Console.WriteLine("Date Composed :" + _
            track.GetAttribute("Date"))

    Console.WriteLine("Title of piece : " + _
        track.FirstChild.Value)
    Console.WriteLine()
Next
```

This code could be better. For instance, you assume that each node will contain two attributes (Composer and Date) that both contain valid values. What if they don't?

Well, you can check to see if an attribute exists with a call to the element's **HasAttribute**() method. **HasAttribute**() will return True if the named attribute exists and False if it doesn't. As for the Track name, as I mentioned earlier, you can call **HasChildNodes**() to check whether child nodes exist, and assuming they do, you can examine the **NodeType** property to find out just what kind of node any child node is. **NodeType** returns a value from the XmlNodeType enumeration, and it can be any of the values shown in Table 11-1.

Table 11-1. XmlNodeType Values

XmlNodeType Value	Description
Attribute	An attribute from within an XmlNode—for example, Composer in the following Track element: `<Track Composer='Schubert'/>`
CData	A block of text that has been marked as CDATA to prevent the XML parser from attempting to interpret it as XML. It's handy for embedding HTML within other markup with an XML document: `<![CDATA[<H1>Hello, World</H1>]]>`
Comment	A comment embedded in the XML: `<!--Hello, code reader -->`
Document	The root node within an XML document.

Table 11-1. XmlNodeType Values (Continued)

XmlNodeType Value	Description
DocumentFragment	Similar to a Document, but marked as being a DocumentFragment through code.
Element	A standard XML element that usually contains attributes, other elements, or text.
EndElement	The closing tag of an element.
EndEntity	The closing tag of an Entity definition.
Entity	An Entity, defined as <!ENTITY>, defines a tag that can be expanded. It's usually found in Schemas.
EntityReference	A reference to a previously defined Entity.
Notation	A notation included within the document type element.
ProcessingInstruction	A processing instruction defined in text as <?..?>.
SignificantWhitespace	White space between tags in a document that has been declared with xml:space=preserve.
Text	The child text within an element.
Whitespace	White space between tags.
XmlDeclaration	Declares the document as an XML one, and specifies which version to adhere to (i.e., <?xml version='1.0'?>).

So, to cover all the bases in the loop, expand it with the following code shown in bold:

```
Dim track As XmlElement
For Each track In _
        musicDoc.DocumentElement.GetElementsByTagName("Track")
    If track.HasAttribute("Composer") Then
        Console.WriteLine("Composer :" + _
            track.GetAttribute("Composer"))
    End If

    If track.HasAttribute("Date") Then
        Console.WriteLine("Date Composed :" + _
            track.GetAttribute("Date"))
    End If
```

```
' The value of the node is actually 'Track'. To get at the child
' Xml Text node, we need to use FirstChild and print its value
If track.HasChildNodes() Then
    If track.FirstChild.NodeType = XmlNodeType.Text Then
        Console.WriteLine("Title of piece : " + _
            track.FirstChild.Value)
    End If
End If
Console.WriteLine()
Next
```

In a live application you'd probably want to do more with each element than simply print it out to the console. In fact, printing out an XML document to the console is really quite easy thanks to the XmlDocument's **Save**() method. The Save() method can be passed either an open stream, the name of a file, a TextWriter object, or an XmlWriter object. You'll look at creating streams and writers in a moment, but it's worth pointing out that the console itself has a property called **Out** that is an open stream. Sending data to that stream causes it to appear on the console. So, you can pass this stream to the Save method and have the XmlDocument render itself into the console with one line of code. What's actually happening here is the XmlDocument is outputting the text of the XML document itself, thinking it is being saved. It just happens that since you're working with the console stream, the document is displayed instead of being stored in a file.

Wrap up the example code with these additional lines:

```
musicDoc.Save(Console.Out)

Console.WriteLine()
Console.WriteLine("All done! Press Enter to exit")
  Console.ReadLine()
```

If you run the application now, you should see the code from earlier writing out information about the contents of the XML document, along with the

XmlDocument's own version of things at the end. You can see the results in Figure 11-3.

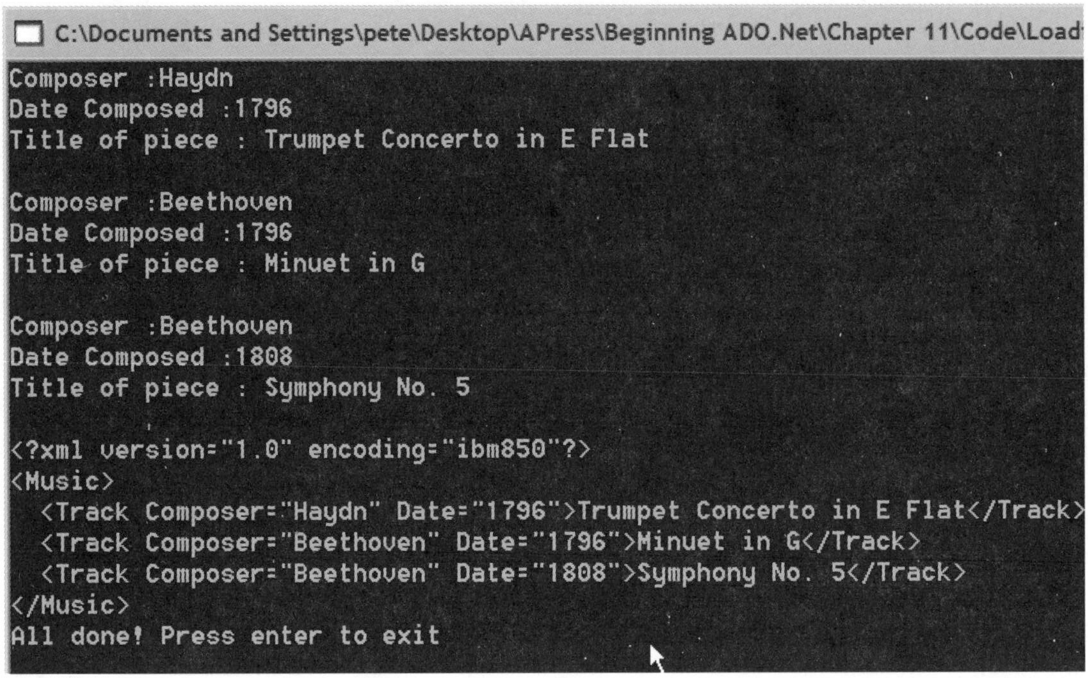

```
C:\Documents and Settings\pete\Desktop\APress\Beginning ADO.Net\Chapter 11\Code\Load
Composer :Haydn
Date Composed :1796
Title of piece : Trumpet Concerto in E Flat

Composer :Beethoven
Date Composed :1796
Title of piece : Minuet in G

Composer :Beethoven
Date Composed :1808
Title of piece : Symphony No. 5

<?xml version="1.0" encoding="ibm850"?>
<Music>
  <Track Composer="Haydn" Date="1796">Trumpet Concerto in E Flat</Track>
  <Track Composer="Beethoven" Date="1796">Minuet in G</Track>
  <Track Composer="Beethoven" Date="1808">Symphony No. 5</Track>
</Music>
All done! Press enter to exit
```

Figure 11-3. The Tracks XML document rendered manually and automatically

Streams

XmlDocument.LoadXml() works as long as the XML content you wish to work with exists in a string. This isn't as rare as you may think given that there are plenty of database servers out there that will quite happily store XML documents in a single column within a table. The majority of the time, you'll want to work with XML data in a file, regardless of whether that file is stored locally or on some remote server.

The overloaded XmlDocument.Load() method allows you to access these resources. You can pass in a string representing a URL:

```
MyXmlDocument.Load("http://some.web.server/xmldocument.xml")
```

or you can pass in a reference to an open file stream, a TextReader object, or XmlReader objects.

If you come from a C++ or Java background, then *streams* will be a familiar concept to you. They were a late addition to Visual Basic, though, and subsequently have been known to strike fear into some developers' hearts. They are really quite easy to use and represent a very powerful way of working with data.

The name "stream" was adopted to draw some analogy to babbling brooks in the real world. They are ever-flowing "streams" of data coming from somewhere and going to somewhere else. One end of the stream is usually your application, whereas the other end is some data source. This could be a file, or it could be the keyboard for an input stream, the console window for an output stream, or even some other program that is treating your output stream as its input stream. Since they all work the same way, streams provide developers with a way to hook up a flow of data between their application and some other source that can be changed with little, or no, impact on the code. You saw a hint of this in the last code example. The console has two built-in streams: One handles input from the keyboard, and the other handles output to the console window itself. You use the console's output stream, **System.Console.Out**, to write an entire XmlDocument's contents to the console window with just a single line of code. It would take very little effort to modify the application to use a stream that terminates in a file on your hard disk.

The .NET Framework supports a variety of stream types, all derived from the base abstract **System.IO.Stream** class. There are streams for working with files that allow seeking from one position to another instantly (**FileStream**), streams that can encrypt and decrypt data on the fly (**CryptoStream**), streams that work with chunks of memory inside your PC (**MemoryStream**), and streams that work with data from the network (**NetworkStream**). As if that wasn't enough choice, there are also Reader and Writer classes, highly specialized classes that make working with specific types of stream data easier. For example, the **XmlReader** and **XmlWriter** classes let you work with streams as a collection of nodes in an XML document, with methods to read and write on a node-by-node basis. Since all these classes derive from **System.IO.Stream**, you're free to use the stream that best fits your needs and use that as a parameter to the XmlDocument.Load() method.

Before you start, you'll need to create a simple XML file to work with. In Visual Studio, click the File menu and select New ? File. When the File Type dialog box appears, choose XML File. The editor will show a blank file now ready for you to start work. You'll look at some of the features of the XML Designer later in the chapter, but for now just key in content so that your XML file looks like this:

```xml
<?xml version="1.0" encoding="utf-8" ?>
<Music>
  <Track Composer='Haydn' Date='1796'>
    Trumpet Concerto in E Flat
  </Track>
  <Track Composer='Beethoven' Date='1796'>
    Minuet in G
  </Track>
  <Track Composer='Beethoven' Date='1808'>
    Symphony No.5
  </Track>
</Music>
```

When you're finished editing, name the file Music.xml and save it in your My Documents folder.

Next, start up a new VB .NET console project, and call it XMLFromFile. As always, the first order of business is to set up the Imports to make sure the namespaces you need are available. As you're working with both streams and XML, this means bringing in the System.IO and System.Xml namespaces.

```vb
Option Strict On
Imports System.Xml
Imports System.IO
```

Now you can start to add some code to the Main() function. The first order of business is to build up a string containing the full path to the Music.xml file you created. If you put this file into your My Documents folder, then it may be tempting to think that the full file name is "C:\My Documents\Music.xml". It isn't. My Documents is one of a number of special folders in the Windows operating system that really could live anywhere, even on a network, so you need to use .NET's Environment object to find out exactly where that folder is.

```vb
Module Module

    Sub Main()

        ' First find out where the file lives. If you put it
        ' in the My Documents folder,
        ' we can ask the system where that folder is.
        Dim fileName As String = _
            Environment.GetFolderPath( _
                Environment.SpecialFolder.Personal) + _
            "\Music.xml"
```

GetFolderPath() returns the full path to a folder specified in the
Environment.SpecialFolder enumeration. **SpecialFolder.Personal** returns
the path to your personal directory, the My Documents directory.

Once you have the full path to a file, opening a stream to read it is a snap:

```
Dim xmlStream As New FileStream(fileName, FileMode.Open)
```

The full file name and path is passed to the FileStream constructor along with
a FileMode. I'm sure you've already figured out that FileMode.Open "opens" a
stream for reading. Other common file modes (there are more than this) would be
FileMode.CreateNew, FileMode.Append, or FileMode.OpenOrCreate. The latter is
used to create and then open a file that didn't previously exist, as well as to just
open existing files. When you work with XML data and the FileStream object, the
most common modes you'll use are FileMode.Open and FileMode.CreateNew. The
former opens a file for reading; the latter ensures that the data you save always
ends up in a new file of its own.

To load the document into an XmlDocument object, all that remains to do is
to pass the open stream reference into XmlDocument.Load().

```
Dim musicDocument As New XmlDocument()
musicDocument.Load(xmlStream)
```

To prove that it worked, you can wrap the application up by saving to the
console's output stream once again.

```
musicDocument.Save(Console.Out)

Console.WriteLine()
Console.WriteLine("All done! Press Enter to exit")
Console.ReadLine()
End Sub
```

```
End Module
```

Run the application now and you should see your XML document output to
the console, just as in the earlier example. There is a chance that some exceptions
could occur. One would be an I/O exception if you didn't name the file Music.Xml
and put it in the My Documents folder. The other would be an XML exception if in
keying in the data you didn't close any open tags in the XML data itself. In either
case, check that the file is in the correct place and that its contents match the document shown earlier.

You've already seen how you can pass a stream into the XmlDocument.Save()
function. Saving to a file is an almost identical process to loading from one. Just
open a stream with a file mode of create or create new.

You can also build XmlDocuments using classes derived from XmlReader,
something you'll look at in a lot more detail in the next chapter when you explore
the XML features of ADO.NET.

Building a Document

Adding elements, text, and other nodes to a document is a two-stage process. You
first have to ask the document to create the node in question, and then you attach
the new node as a child of another node; this could be the root document node, or
some other node, depending, of course, on the format of your XML document. In
this section and the next, you'll work through building up the earlier DVD XML
document completely from code.

Fire up a new VB .NET console project in Visual Studio, and call it CreateDVDDoc.
As always, you'll start with the Import and the all-important Option Strict.

```
Option Strict On
Imports System.Xml
```

Next, you can go ahead and create an empty XmlDocument object, just as in
the previous examples.

```
Option Strict On
Imports System.Xml

Module Module1

    Sub Main()

        ' Create an empty XmlDocument and set its document node
        Dim DvdDocument As New XmlDocument()
```

This is a completely empty XmlDocument at this stage—it doesn't even have a
document element. You'll need to add one.

```
        DvdDocument.AppendChild(DvdDocument.CreateElement("dvd-collection"))
```

If you were to print out the document at this point, you'd have this:

```
<dvd-collection/>
```

In other words, you'd have an empty document, but a valid document none-theless. The XmlDocument class has a number of create methods that allow you to create the various kinds of nodes you'll need in the document. In this case, you're creating an element, a simple node that will contain other nodes. The string passed into the CreateElement method specifies the name of the node. The new node is then added to the document with a call to DvdDocument.AppendChild.

The XmlNode class, from which most of the System.Xml classes derive, brings the AppendChild() method to each of its subclasses. The XmlDocument class will only allow you to append a single child, and it's this element that becomes the XML document element. Most other types of XmlNodes support more than one child.

With a document node in place, you can now take a look at creating the rest of the child nodes. The next one is the DVD node, which describes an individual DVD title.

```
' Create a DVD node and add attributes to it to identify
   ' the movie in question. Finally, add the node as a child
   ' of the document node.
   Dim DvdTitle As XmlElement
   DvdTitle = DvdDocument.CreateElement("DVD")
```

Once again, your XmlDocument is used to create the new node, in this case an element called DVD. If you look back to the earlier example where you worked with this document as a file, you'll know that each DVD element contains two attributes: one holds the sound format of the DVD and the other attribute holds the Title of the DVD itself.

Attributes are very easy to add to a node; just call SetAttribute and pass in the name of the attribute and its value. If the attribute already exists, then its value is changed to the one specified in the call to SetAttribute. If, however, the attribute can't be found, a new one is created and attached to the node in question.

```
DvdTitle.SetAttribute("SoundFormat", "DTS")
   DvdTitle.SetAttribute("Title", "Mission Impossible")
```

Our DVD node is now complete, despite its lack of child nodes, so it can be added to the document node with another call to AppendChild().

```
DvdDocument.DocumentElement.AppendChild(DvdTitle)
```

Of course, this time the new element is appended as a child of the document element, and not of the XmlDocument object.

Creating the <Star> node for a DVD in the document follows pretty much the same pattern. Key in the rest of the code to complete the DVD element.

```
' Now create a new star for this dvd
DvdTitle.AppendChild(DvdDocument.CreateElement("Star"))

' Set up the actor and character nodes of the star
Dim actor As XmlElement = DvdDocument.CreateElement("Actor")
actor.AppendChild(DvdDocument.CreateTextNode("Tom Cruise"))
Dim character As XmlElement = _
        DvdDocument.CreateElement("Character")
character.AppendChild(DvdDocument.CreateTextNode("Ethan Hunt"))

' Add the actor and character nodes as children of
' the star node
DvdTitle.FirstChild.AppendChild(actor)
DvdTitle.FirstChild.AppendChild(character)
```

It looks messy, but it's really no different from the way the rest of the document has been built so far. The most important part to pay attention to is the addition of text nodes to the Actor and Character elements. As I explained in the overview of XML earlier, text contained within tags in an XML document is itself a node, a text node.

All you need to do to wrap the application up is prove that everything worked by printing the document to the console.

```
' Last but not least, write out the document to the console
DvdDocument.Save(Console.Out)
Console.WriteLine()
Console.WriteLine("All done! Press Enter to exit.")
Console.ReadLine()

End Sub

End Module
```

If you run the application you'll see most of the DVDs document that you worked with earlier. The code doesn't build the whole document since, as you can see, building an XML document by hand can be a pretty laborious process. In a live application you'd probably want to break out the creation of key nodes into reusable functions within appropriate classes. Better yet, the document can be created for you if you're working with ADO.NET, as you'll see in more detail in the next chapter.

Summary

I've not done System.Xml justice: Microsoft has added so much XML functionality in .NET that this is really a subject that deserves a book of its own. Nonetheless, you should now have a good grasp of just what facilities are available to you in System.Xml to create and manipulate an XML document at a high level. If this is an area that interests you, then there is much more to learn—in particular, XSLT and data transformations, the XPath query language, and the lower-level intricacies involved in really drilling down into the detail of an XML document.

In this chapter you covered

- A summary of the features of an XML document

- The System.Xml namespace and the classes it provides

- How to create and work with an XmlDocument

- How to load and save data to a stream

- How to build an XmlDocument from scratch in code

In the next chapter you'll put all this into context and see how tightly System.Xml integrates with ADO.NET.

CHAPTER 12

XML and ADO.NET

"The time-honored bread-sauce of the happy ending."

—Henry James, *Theatricals: Second Series*

IN THE PREVIOUS CHAPTER, I took you on a brief tour of the facilities available in the System.Xml namespace. Microsoft has been moving us toward XML for messaging, storage, and general formatting of sundry lumps of data for some years now, mainly through their MSXML COM libraries. With System.Xml they've taken a massive step beyond even this, not only implementing a fully DOM-compliant set of classes and methods in the System.Xml namespace, but also integrating XML itself with almost every aspect of application development using .NET.

One of the biggest and most important areas of XML use (aside from just using it for the fun of it, of course) is with ADO.NET. DataSets can persist themselves to XML. Typed DataSets are generated based on XML Schemas. XML documents and standard databases can be linked to really make access to and manipulation of data anywhere on any device a seamless possibility at long last.

In this, the final chapter, you'll explore just how to use these features and more. You'll learn what XSD schemas are, how to generate and work with them and, more important, why they are vital to ADO.NET. You'll visit typed DataSets once more, and you'll take a look into reading and writing XML documents through a DataSet. You'll also take a brief peek at SQL Server's current XML support and how to make use of it in your own applications.

Typed DataSets Revisited

I touched on **typed DataSets** back in Chapter 6. By dragging and dropping a DataAdapter and a Connection onto a form, it's quite easy to then ask Visual Studio .NET to generate a DataSet. The result is a typed DataSet that allows you to refer to tables and fields in those tables directly by name, instead of having to supply names as parameters to obscure fields and collections in a vanilla DataSet instance.

It's easy to fall under the impression that you can only generate typed DataSets when working with the GUI of an application. This is a common area of misunderstanding, and it throws up all sorts of questions about just how to implement a traditional n-tier architecture with .NET. Thankfully, the GUI is not the only place the typed DataSet can be used. In fact, it's actually easier to generate a typed DataSet in a class library or any other solution that doesn't have a nice GUI.

To demonstrate, let's build a console application that uses a typed DataSet. Start up a new VB .NET console solution and call it TypedDatasets. When Visual Studio .NET has finished working its magic and the project is ready for you to start work, right-click TypedDatasets in the Solution Explorer, choose Add from the pop-up menu, and then select Add New Item. The Add New Item dialog box shown in Figure 12-1 will appear.

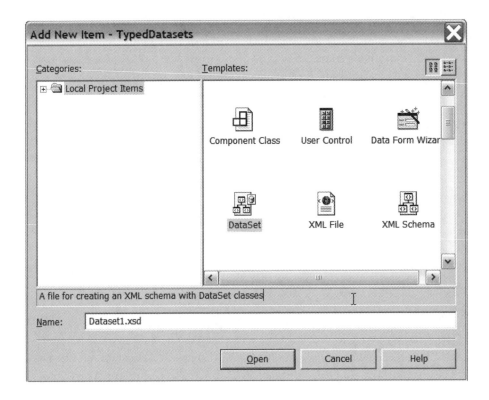

Figure 12-1. Building a typed DataSet in any tier is as easy as choosing it from the Add New Item dialog box.

Scroll down through the list of items that can be added to a project, and you'll find the DataSet item. I believe Microsoft goofed with this one; it should read "Typed DataSet," since selecting it inserts a shiny new typed DataSet into your project. So, select it, key in **NorthwindDS.xsd** as the name of the item, and then click Open.

If you take a look at the Solution Explorer now you'll see NorthwindDS.xsd at the bottom of the list of files. More dramatically, though, the main code editor/designer pane of Visual Studio .NET has taken on a yellow hue and looks much like an empty Web Form does when you first start an ASP.NET Web application.

XSD files are XML Schemas. They are a strange paradox actually, since an XSD file defines structure for an XML document, but an XSD file is itself an XML document. At the bottom left of the designer pane in Visual Studio .NET you'll see two tabs. One is labeled DataSet and the other is labeled XML. Click the XML tab (bottom left of the designer frame in Visual Studio .NET) and you'll see the XML inside the schema.

```xml
<?xml version="1.0" encoding="utf-8" ?>
<xs:schema id="NorthwindDS"
  targetNamespace="http://tempuri.org/NorthwindDS.xsd"
 elementFormDefault="qualified" attributeFormDefault="qualified"
      xmlns="http://tempuri.org/NorthwindDS.xsd"
      xmlns:mstns="http://tempuri.org/NorthwindDS.xsd"
      xmlns:xs="http://www.w3.org/2001/XMLSchema"
        xmlns:msdata="urn:schemas-microsoft-com:xml-msdata">
    <xs:element name="NorthwindDS" msdata:IsDataSet="true">
       <xs:complexType>
           <xs:choice maxOccurs="unbounded"></xs:choice>
       </xs:complexType>
    </xs:element>
</xs:schema>
```

It looks quite strange, I know, but it actually all makes perfect sense. You haven't added any content to the schema yet, so this is really a blank schema document that uses directives and tags to define the ground rules of the document.

The first tag shows that this is an XML version 1.0 document encoded with the UTF-8 character set (take a look at the online help if you're unfamiliar with what UTF-8 is). The next element uses the "xs" XML namespace to define a "schema" tag. This just tells you that this is indeed an XML Schema document. As you can see, it's called NorthwindDS, and it follows the XML Schema standard laid out at http://www.w3.org/XML/Schema. The "tempuri" is, as its name suggests, a temporary URI.

NOTE If you are new to the world of Internet-related technologies (which XML is), you may be wondering just what a URI is and how it differs from a URL. A URL is a *uniform resource locator* (for example, http://www.apress.com). It can change—it is not set in stone—but it is usually pretty accurate when it comes to finding a Web page. A URI, or *uniform resource identifier,* is much more concrete. This book's ISBN, for example, could be considered a URI—it will always refer to this book and no other. Obviously, when publishing schemas for XML documents to be used for corporations throughout the world, it's better to establish a URI than a URL. The use of URI is just a standard, though; there are no hard and fast rules preventing someone from moving a schema's URI.

If you were defining a schema here for XML data to be used worldwide, you should tell people where the document came from, effectively defining its global namespace. Since you are not developing a global standard help, a temporary URI is inserted (tempuri.org).

Switch back to the DataSet view and let's add some content to this schema. (If you like writing strange XML tags, you can define the schema in the XML view. I'll assume that you're human the same as the rest of us, though, and you want a slightly less painful way of doing things.)

Building the XSD is actually quite a painless affair. Simply drag and drop the tables from the Server Explorer onto the main page of the XSD Designer. Go ahead and drag the **Region**, **Territories**, **EmployeeTerritories**, and **Employees** tables from the Northwind database onto the XSD Designer, as shown in Figure 12-2.

Next, define relationships between Region and Territories (Region is the parent table, RegionID is the key), then between Territories and EmployeeTerritories (Territories is the parent, TerritoryID is the key), and finally between EmployeeTerritories and Employees (EmployeeTerritories is the parent, EmployeeID is the key).

NOTE Be careful when you define the relationship between EmployeeTerritories and Employees. Make sure you drag the relationship from the EmployeeTerritories complex type to the Employees complex type and not the other way around. In the database, EmployeeTerritories is naturally a child relationship to the Employees table; you would want to know which territories an employee services. In this example, though, you want to find territories within regions and then see which employee services the territory, so the relationship is inverted.

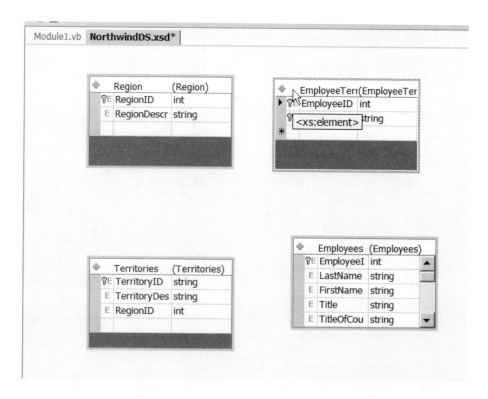

Figure 12-2. Dragging elements from the Server Explorer onto the XSD Designer is all you need to do to build your XSD content.

If you can't remember how to do this, just refer back to the walk-through in Chapter 6. When you're done, you should be looking at an XSD like the one shown in Figure 12-3.

XSD schemas are used not only for creating and defining the structure of a typed DataSet, but also for defining the structure of a standard DataSet. Using schemas allows you to control the output format of your DataSet when you serialize it to an XML document and checks that the data coming into the DataSet fits expected parameters. Let's take a look at what each component actually is. You'll stay in the diagram view for this, but I'll reference the underlying XML as well. According to the official XML Schema Definition (XSD) language specification, there are a whole bunch of types and elements that can be added to a schema, far more than I can cover here. I'll focus on the elements used by Visual Studio.

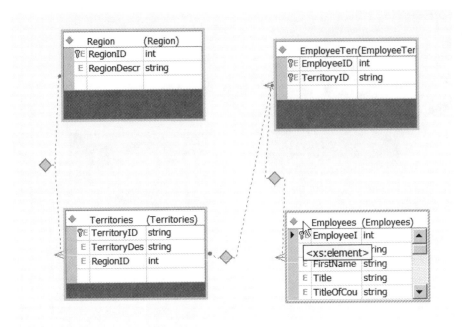

Figure 12-3. The finished schema for your typed DataSet

Each large box in the diagram is a **complex** element. In simple terms, a *complex element* is much like defining a structure in C or C++, or a type in Visual Basic 6.0. It defines a bunch of data that can be encapsulated into a single data type. So, your diagram holds complex types for Region, Territories, Employees, and EmployeeTerritories. In the underlying XSD, a complex type is defined like this:

```
<xs:element name="Region">
    <xs:complexType>
       :
       :
    </xs:complexType>
</xs:element>
```

The XSD standard allows you to specify optional elements inside the type as well as embed complex types in one another. None of these things make much sense from a database point of view, since you are never going to get a set of results from a database that occasionally has some fields and occasionally has others. Visual Studio .NET thus uses the **sequence** element next to define a sequence of elements that form the complex type.

```
<xs:element name="Region">
    <xs:complexType>
        <xs:sequence>
                    :
                    :
        </xs:sequence>
    </xs:complexType>
</xs:element>
```

Within the sequence, XSD elements are used to define the fields that make up the sequence and thus form the complex type. The Region type in all its glory looks like this:

```
<xs:element name="Region">
    <xs:complexType>
        <xs:sequence>
            <xs:element name="RegionID" type="xs:int" />
            <xs:element name="RegionDescription" type="xs:string" />
        </xs:sequence>
    </xs:complexType>
</xs:element>
```

Notice how the elements define not only the names of each field, but also the type. These types are again chosen using XML namespaces to select an entry from the <xs: namespace>.

If you take a look at the diagram once again, you'll notice that the RegionID field is flagged as a key field, but there isn't actually anything in the complex type that defines which fields may or may not be used as keys. Keys are defined separately in the XSD using the **<xs:unique>** tag. The Region's primary key is defined like this:

```
<xs:unique name="NorthwindDSKey3" msdata:PrimaryKey="true">
    <xs:selector xpath=".//mstns:Region" />
    <xs:field xpath="mstns:RegionID" />
</xs:unique>
```

<xs:selector> uses an XPath expression to select an element of the schema to relate the key to. In this case, the Region complex type is selected. The **<xs:field>** tag then uses another XPath expression to select a specific element inside the complex type to use for the key. If you have more than one field defining the primary key, then there will be more than one <xs:field> tag in the key definition.

The relationships drawn into the diagram are represented in a similar way. While the primary keys use the **<xs:unique>** tag to identify the fields that make a unique value within the type, the **<xs:key>** tag is used to identify specific fields to use as keys in relationships. A **<xs:keyref>** tag is then used to link a key to a separate field in a different type. For example, take a look at the Region and Territories complex types and their relationship to each other (see Figure 12-4).

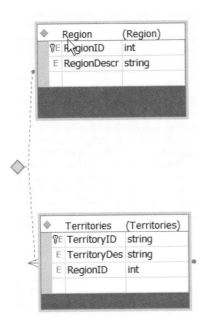

Figure 12-4. The relationship between the Region and Territories complex types

A key is defined on the RegionID field of Region. A key reference is then created to link the RegionID field of Territories to the key just defined on the Region type. Take a look:

```
<xs:key name="key1">
    <xs:selector xpath=".//mstns:Region" />
    <xs:field xpath="mstns:RegionID" />
</xs:key>
<xs:keyref name="RegionTerritories" refer="key1">
    <xs:selector xpath=".//mstns:Territories" />
    <xs:field xpath="mstns:RegionID" />
</xs:keyref>
```

Again, <xs:selector> is used to select the table to refer to in each case, and <xs:field> locates the field in question. When defining <xs:keyref>, the **refer** attribute is used to relate back to the original key to use to define the relationship in the keyref.

The relationship is named in the <xs:keyref> tag, and it's this name that gets used in the DataSet to refer to relationships by name. In a typed DataSet such as this one, the benefits are even greater: You can use the RegionRow member to refer to an instance of a row in the Region table, and then call GetRegionTerritories() on that row to get all territories linked through the relationship.

When you create your own schemas by hand, the XSD Designer can offer a great deal of help. If you click in a complex type, for example, you'll find that you can drop down a list from the first column in the type and choose the types of elements to add to the complex type itself. You can see this in action in Figure 12-5.

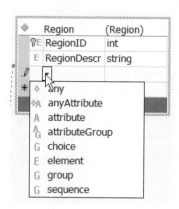

Figure 12-5. The first column of a complex type allows you to choose the types of embedded elements.

In addition, you can right-click in the XSD Designer to bring up a pop-up menu, and then choose Add to bring additional elements into the schema as a whole (see Figure 12-6).

As you can see, there is quite a lot to working with XSD schemas, and they play a valuable role when it comes to ADO.NET. If you wish to travel beyond the confines offered by the XSD Designer and implement your own custom schemas to add even more structure to your data, take a long, hard look at the online help—just search for "XML Schema Reference". You'll work with schemas some more as you explore the other XML-related features of ADO.NET throughout the rest of this chapter.

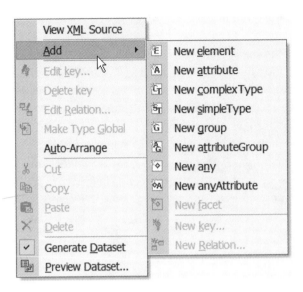

Figure 12-6. The right-click menu in the XSD Designer allows you to add more high-level elements to the schema quickly and easily.

For those of you wanting to wrap up this console-based typed DataSet example, go ahead and key this code into your application's module:

```
Option Strict On
Imports System.Data.SqlClient


Module Module1

    Sub Main()

        '-- First, load data into our typed dataset
        Dim northwindDataset As New NorthwindDS()
        northwindDataset.EnforceConstraints = False
        BuildDataset(northwindDataset._Region, _
            "SELECT * FROM Region")
        BuildDataset(northwindDataset.Territories, _
            "SELECT * FROM Territories")
        BuildDataset(northwindDataset.EmployeeTerritories, _
            "SELECT * FROM EmployeeTerritories")
        BuildDataset(northwindDataset.Employees, _
            "SELECT * FROM Employees")
```

```vb
'-- Start looping through the regions
Dim currentRegion As NorthwindDS._RegionRow
For Each currentRegion In northwindDataset._Region
    System.Console.WriteLine( _
        "Region : {0}", currentRegion.RegionDescription)

    '-- Now loop through each territory in each region
    Dim currentTerritory As NorthwindDS.TerritoriesRow
    For Each currentTerritory In _
      currentRegion.GetTerritoriesRows()
        System.Console.WriteLine( _
            "    Territory : {0}", _
            currentTerritory.TerritoryDescription)

        ' Resolve the link between employee and territory
        Dim currentEmployeeID As _
            NorthwindDS.EmployeeTerritoriesRow
        For Each currentEmployeeID In _
          currentTerritory.GetEmployeeTerritoriesRows()

            ' Print the employee that services this territory
            Dim currentEmployee As NorthwindDS.EmployeesRow
            For Each currentEmployee In _
              currentEmployeeID.GetEmployeesRows()
                System.Console.WriteLine( _
                    "        Employee : {0} {1}", _
                    currentEmployee.FirstName, _
                    currentEmployee.LastName)
            Next

        Next

    Next

Next

System.Console.ReadLine()

End Sub
Private Sub BuildDataset(ByVal tableToFill As DataTable, _
    ByVal selectCommand As String)
    Dim dataAdapter As New SqlDataAdapter( _
        New SqlCommand(selectCommand, GetConnection()))
    dataAdapter.Fill(tableToFill)
End Sub
```

```
Private Function GetConnection() As SqlConnection
    Dim connection As New SqlConnection( _
        "Data Source=localhost;" + _
        "Initial Catalog=Northwind;" + _
        "Integrated Security=SSPI")
    Return connection
End Function

End Module
```

The Dos and Don'ts of Typed DataSets

Typed DataSets bring a lot of benefits with them. Perhaps the most important benefit is *type-safety.* Since a typed DataSet is a class that exposes fields and tables as first-class members of the DataSet, the compiler can catch errors with those fields at compile time. Using a standard untyped DataSet, you have no way of knowing whether or not you specified the right table or field name in an operation until that operation runs. The results, if you get the name wrong, are invariably bugs that manifest themselves as either unhandled exceptions to the user or wasted nights debugging when you should be sleeping.

There are downsides to typed DataSets, though. In Visual Basic .NET, the generated code inside the typed DataSet is not particularly fast. The reason for this is that the typed DataSet does not make use of Option Strict On. This means that type checking and type conversion inside the typed DataSet occurs at runtime, not design time. You can try adding Option Strict On to the top of the typed DataSet class, but you will then find that the assumptions made by the generated code cause compile errors that you'll need to resolve.

NOTE I mention adding code to the typed DataSet here, but if you take a look at the Solution Explorer, there is no typed DataSet class, only an XSD file. This is because it's hiding. If you take a look at the Solution Explorer window, you'll see three icons at the top, underneath the window title. The second one of these, when clicked, shows all the hidden files in a solution, including your typed DataSets. You can then edit and browse the source for the typed DataSet itself, just like a normal source file. In general, though, making changes to this source is not a good idea—it is tightly integrated with the designers in Visual Studio .NET.

The other big issue with typed DataSets relates to the mapping of the generated members to the database itself. If you need to change the database schema for whatever reason, any typed DataSets that use the affected tables will no longer be in sync. Obviously, there are no such problems with untyped DataSets, other than the need for you to make changes to your code in places to cope with the changes. This may sound like case of damned if you do, damned if you don't, but it really isn't. You could, for example, change the name of a field in the database that's only used in the odd report or admin screen. The changes to your code necessary to accommodate this change with untyped DataSets is thus confined to those areas of the application. With a typed DataSet used throughout the application, the problems with the typed DataSet could manifest themselves throughout the entire application.

Again, this might not sound too serious, given that you only need to rebuild the typed DataSet once to make everything fine. However, what if your application is deployed and changes to the database are made? Your deployed application as a whole may now have problems, whereas when you use untyped DataSets you'll only see problems in the parts of the application that use the changed database information.

My feeling, though, is that typed DataSets rule, and they should be used. They simplify code (one of the major sources of bugs in the first place), and anything that simplifies your code and makes it easier to debug and maintain is a good thing. The risk of database changes can be negated by the use of stored procedures for all access to the database and a sturdy database design before application coding takes place.

As for the speed issues, these are easily worked around thanks to the language-agnostic nature of Visual Studio .NET. Just embed your typed DataSets in a separate assembly using C#, and then bring those compiled C# typed DataSets into your VB .NET application.

XML and the DataSet

You would think that getting a DataSet, an in-memory relational representation of data, to read from or write to an XML document, a hierarchical representation of data, would be a royal pain in the neck. It isn't. In fact, it's mind-numbingly simple. It's so simple, in fact, that the framework quite happily serializes DataSets to XML automatically when it needs to send a DataSet across a process or network boundary, making DataSets the staple food when it comes to working with Web services (though sending huge DataSets to Web services via a modem is never a good idea, thanks to the speed implications). You can read and write straight XML data, schemas, or even a mix of both.

Rendering XML from a DataSet

Getting a DataSet to render itself as XML can be achieved two ways. You can call **DataSet.GetXml()** to return the entire DataSet as a string, or you can call **DataSet.WriteXml()** to render direct to a stream or straight to a file. **WriteXml()** can even take a second parameter, one of the **XmlWriteMode** values: **XmlWriteMode.Diffgram**, **XmlWriteMode.IgnoreSchema**, or **XmlWriteMode.WriteSchema**. The values are quite easy to understand. Diffgram writes out an XML document highlighting the changes made within a DataSet. This is the format used for sending DataSet changes from one tier to another, and it can even be passed directly to SQL Server (with a patch to SQL Server in place). IgnoreSchema simply writes the DataSet as an XML document, and WriteSchema embeds XSD schema information in the document. Let's take a look at an example.

Start up a new VB .NET console application (call it DatasetToXML) and key this into the module:

```
Option Strict On
Imports System.Data.SqlClient


Module Module1

    Sub Main()


        Dim regionAdapter As New SqlDataAdapter( _
            "SELECT * FROM Region", _
            "Data Source=localhost; " + _
            "Initial Catalog=Northwind;" + _
            "Integrated Security=SSPI")
        Dim northwindDS As New DataSet("Northwind")
        regionAdapter.Fill(northwindDS, "Region")

        System.Console.WriteLine(northwindDS.GetXml())
        System.Console.ReadLine()

        System.Console.WriteLine(northwindDS.GetXmlSchema())
        System.Console.ReadLine()

        northwindDS.WriteXml(Console.Out, XmlWriteMode.WriteSchema)
        System.Console.ReadLine()

    End Sub


End Module
```

After creating a DataAdapter and filling a DataSet, the code writes out the XML returned with a call to GetXml(). Press Enter and the schema of the DataSet is written to the console, courtesy of a call to GetXmlSchema(). Press Enter again, and WriteXml() will output a single XML document containing both the XSD schema and data in one. You can see the application running in Figure 12-7.

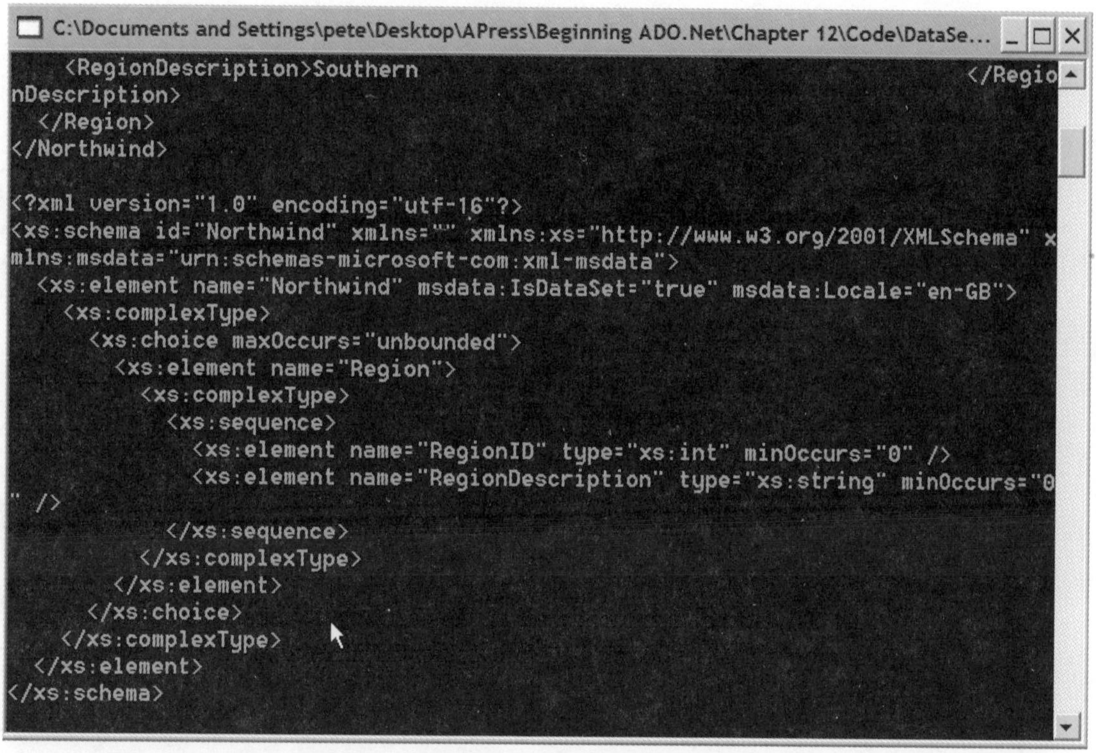

```
    <RegionDescription>Southern                                      </Regio
nDescription>
  </Region>
</Northwind>

<?xml version="1.0" encoding="utf-16"?>
<xs:schema id="Northwind" xmlns="" xmlns:xs="http://www.w3.org/2001/XMLSchema" x
mlns:msdata="urn:schemas-microsoft-com:xml-msdata">
  <xs:element name="Northwind" msdata:IsDataSet="true" msdata:Locale="en-GB">
    <xs:complexType>
      <xs:choice maxOccurs="unbounded">
        <xs:element name="Region">
          <xs:complexType>
            <xs:sequence>
              <xs:element name="RegionID" type="xs:int" minOccurs="0" />
              <xs:element name="RegionDescription" type="xs:string" minOccurs="0
" />
            </xs:sequence>
          </xs:complexType>
        </xs:element>
      </xs:choice>
    </xs:complexType>
  </xs:element>
</xs:schema>
```

Figure 12-7. The various modes of writing a DataSet as XML in action

Let's see how a DataSet with two related tables works. Start up a new VB .NET console project called ComplexXMLDataSets and key this code into the module:

```
Option Strict On
Imports System.Data.SqlClient


Module Module1

    Sub Main()
```

```
        Dim regionAdapter As New SqlDataAdapter( _
            "SELECT * FROM Region", _
            "Data Source=localhost;" + _
            "Initial Catalog=Northwind; " + _
            "Integrated Security=SSPI")
        Dim territoriesAdapter As New SqlDataAdapter( _
            "SELECT * FROM Territories", _
            "Data Source=localhost;" + _
            "Initial Catalog=Northwind;" + _
            "Integrated Security=SSPI")

        Dim northwindDS As New DataSet("Northwind")
        regionAdapter.Fill(northwindDS, "Region")
        territoriesAdapter.Fill(northwindDS, "Territories")

        northwindDS.Relations.Add("RegionTerritories", _
            northwindDS.Tables("Region").Columns("RegionID"), _
        northwindDS.Tables("Territories").Columns("RegionID"))

        northwindDS.WriteXml("regionterritories.xml", _
            XmlWriteMode.WriteSchema)

        Console.WriteLine("All done. Press Enter to exit")
        Console.ReadLine()

    End Sub

End Module
```

The code creates two DataAdapters, one to select the regions from the Northwind database, and the other to select Territories. As you know from the example at the start of this chapter, these two tables really should be related to each other. After using each Adapter to fill a DataSet, a new DataRelation is created, setting the parent column to the Region table's RegionID field and the child column to the Territories table's RegionID field. Once all that is done, the DataSet is rendered as XML.

If you run this project, it will output a file called regionterritories.xml to your project's bin directory. You can view this file by double-clicking it; this should display the file inside Internet Explorer.

NOTE In the previous Note, I mentioned the Show All Files button in the Solution Explorer. Clicking this button will show you not only the files in your solution, but also all the files in the directories your solution occupies. This includes the XML file just produced by the sample application. Just click the button to show all files, and then right-click the XML file and choose Open With to select Internet Explorer as the tool to view the XML.

In Figure 12-8, I've collapsed the file in Internet Explorer (IE) to only show the main elements of the DataSet.

```
<?xml version="1.0" standalone="yes" ?>
- <Northwind>
  + <xs:schema id="Northwind" xmlns="" xmlns:xs="http://
  + <Region>
  + <Region>
  + <Region>
  + <Region>
  + <Territories>
  + <Territories>
  + <Territories>
  + <Territories>
  + <Territories>
  + <Territories>
  + <Territories>
  + <Territories>
  + <Territories>
  + <Territories>
  + <Territories>
  + <Territories>
  + <Territories>
  - <Territories>
      <TerritoryID>10019</TerritoryID>
      <TerritoryDescription>New York</TerritoryDescription>
      <RegionID>1</RegionID>
    </Territories>
```

Figure 12-8. Clicking the red plus (+) or minus (–) sign to the left of an element in an XML file expands or collapses that element, respectively.

It's pretty easy in this collapsed view of things to see the structure of the XML document. It starts with a schema definition, then lists all the regions, and finally starts to list all the territories from the DataSet. If you take a "higher-level" view of the document in your mind's eye, though, there's a problem. In the DataSet, which is relational, the regions and territories are related to each other using a DataRelation object. In the XML document, you just have a flat list of the two tables with no indication that there's any relationship between the two.

If you expand the schema part of the XML document in IE, you'll see that the relationship is defined in the schema. That's no good, though, for someone who wants your application to output a truly hierarchical XML document.

This is how a DataSet renders to XML by default: It just lists the contents of all its tables one after the other. If there are DataRelations in the DataSet, then these will be rendered into the schema of the document to enable you to easily load the data back in, but the tables will still be listed sequentially.

To get the DataSet to render hierarchically, all you need to do is tell the DataRelations in the DataSet that they are "nested"—child rows of a relation will be rendered nested inside their parent rows.

Go ahead and add the line of code shown in bold into the application:

```
                :
                :
    northwindDS.Relations.Add("RegionTerritories", _
        northwindDS.Tables("Region").Columns("RegionID"), _
    northwindDS.Tables("Territories").Columns("RegionID"))

    northwindDS.Relations("RegionTerritories").Nested = True

    northwindDS.WriteXml("regionterritories.xml", _
        XmlWriteMode.WriteSchema)

End Sub
                :
                :
```

If you run the application now and take a look at the resulting XML, you'll see that territories are now nicely nested within their parent region (see Figure 12-9).

```
<?xml version="1.0" standalone="yes" ?>
- <Northwind>
  + <xs:schema id="Northwind" xmlns="" xmlns:xs="http://wv
  - <Region>
      <RegionID>1</RegionID>
      <RegionDescription>Eastern</RegionDescription>
    - <Territories>
        <TerritoryID>01581</TerritoryID>
        <TerritoryDescription>Westboro</TerritoryDescription>
        <RegionID>1</RegionID>
      </Territories>
    - <Territories>
        <TerritoryID>01730</TerritoryID>
        <TerritoryDescription>Bedford</TerritoryDescription>
        <RegionID>1</RegionID>
      </Territories>
    - <Territories>
        <TerritoryID>01833</TerritoryID>
        <TerritoryDescription>Georgetow</TerritoryDescription>
        <RegionID>1</RegionID>
      </Territories>
```

Figure 12-9. Setting Nested=true on a relation causes the output XML to be hierarchical.

Reading XML into a DataSet

On the surface, reading XML into a DataSet would seem to be just a question of calling **DataSet.ReadXml()**. There's actually a lot of flexibility built into such an innocuous method.

Just like DataSet.WriteXml(), ReadXml() can read from a string, a stream, or a file. It can also read from an XmlReader. You can also call ReadXmlSchema() to just load in a schema. This is actually quite important, especially if you are using SQL Server 2000.

SQL Server 2000 (and MSDE) will allow you to actually select schema information from a database, as well as select data in XML format. The ReadXml() method can also reject and discard data that doesn't match a schema. So, if you want to load data into a DataSet and ensure that it meets the database's schema requirements, you could first load up the schema from SQL Server, and then load in only the compliant parts of an XML file with a call to ReadXml. Let's take a look at these things in action.

Start up a new VB .NET console application (call it SqlServerXML), and key this code into the module:

```
Option Strict On
Imports System.Data.SqlClient

Module Module1

    Sub Main()

        Dim regionSchemaCommand As New SqlCommand( _
            "SELECT * FROM Region FOR XML AUTO,XMLDATA", _
            New SqlConnection( _
            "Data Source=localhost;" + _
            "Initial Catalog=Northwind;" + _
            "Integrated Security=SSPI"))
        regionSchemaCommand.Connection.Open()

        Dim schemaReader As Xml.XmlReader = _
            regionSchemaCommand.ExecuteXmlReader()

        Dim northwindDS As New DataSet("Northwind")
        northwindDS.ReadXmlSchema(schemaReader)

        regionSchemaCommand.Connection.Close()
        northwindDS.WriteXmlSchema(Console.Out)
        Console.ReadLine()

        northwindDS.ReadXml("regionterritories.xml", _
            XmlReadMode.IgnoreSchema)
        Console.WriteLine(northwindDS.GetXml())
        Console.ReadLine()

    End Sub

End Module
```

To run this application, you will need to build it first (Ctrl-Shift-B) and then copy the regionterritories.xml file produced in the last example into this solution's bin directory.

The first thing the code does is set up a command to fire at SQL Server. The command is this:

```
SELECT * FROM Region FOR XML AUTO,XMLDATA
```

The XMLDATA part of the Select statement tells SQL Server that you want schema, not data (it's a misleading name, I know). Alternatively, you could leave that part of the command out to get the data returned as attributes, or you could specify ELEMENTS to return the data as a standard XML document with regions containing elements representing each of the fields. Take a look at T-SQL's help in SQL Server for more information on this type of select.

ExecuteXmlReader() is then called on the command to run the select and return the results through an XmlReader object. The DataSet's ReadXml() and ReadXmlSchema() methods can both accept an XmlReader. Since you are only getting schema information, ReadXmlSchema() is used with the XmlReader to load up the schema of the DataSet. The schema then gets written to the console.

Up next is the fun bit. ReadXml() is used to load up the XML document produced in the last example. Notice the second parameter to the call

```
northwindDS.ReadXml("regionterritories.xml", _
    XmlReadMode.IgnoreSchema)
```

This is a powerful parameter to pass in. **XmlReadMode.IgnoreSchema** indicates that if the document you're loading contains embedded schema information (it does), then ignore it. In addition, if there's data in the document that doesn't match the schema already loaded into the DataSet, ignore that too. The result is that even though your XML file includes both regions and territories, only the regions get loaded. ReadXml() with IgnoreSchema will only load in data matching the DataSets schema, making it very useful for ignoring large chunks of useless data. Since you can do this on a file, stream, string or XmlReader, it also works in filtering out unwanted information when XML is passed to your code through a method call.

Run the application and you'll see it work its magic (see Figure 12-10).

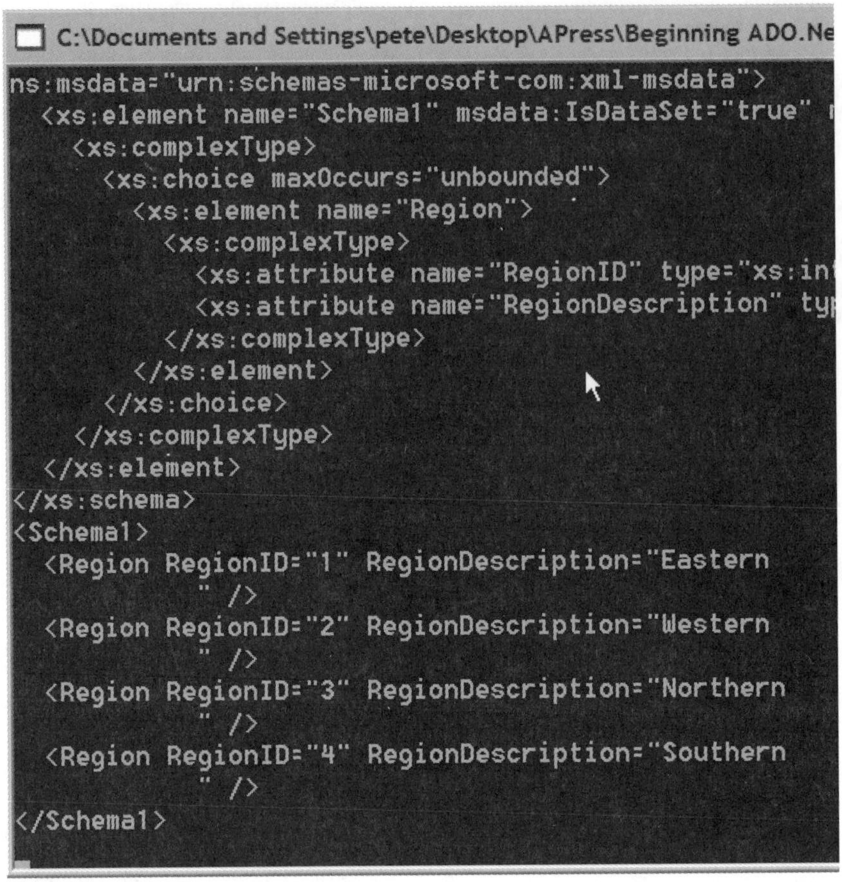

```
  C:\Documents and Settings\pete\Desktop\APress\Beginning ADO.Ne
ns:msdata="urn:schemas-microsoft-com:xml-msdata">
  <xs:element name="Schema1" msdata:IsDataSet="true"
    <xs:complexType>
      <xs:choice maxOccurs="unbounded">
        <xs:element name="Region">
          <xs:complexType>
            <xs:attribute name="RegionID" type="xs:in
            <xs:attribute name="RegionDescription" ty
          </xs:complexType>
        </xs:element>
      </xs:choice>
    </xs:complexType>
  </xs:element>
</xs:schema>
<Schema1>
  <Region RegionID="1" RegionDescription="Eastern
            " />
  <Region RegionID="2" RegionDescription="Western
            " />
  <Region RegionID="3" RegionDescription="Northern
            " />
  <Region RegionID="4" RegionDescription="Southern
            " />
</Schema1>
```

Figure 12-10. Loading a schema from a database and data selectively from a file

There are various values that you can use for the second parameter to XmlRead(). **XmlReadMode.Auto** is perhaps the most common, since it automatically selects the most appropriate read mode based on the data. Alternatively, **XmlReadMode.ReadSchema()** loads both the data and schema from a file, and **XmlReadMode.InferSchema()** makes an informed guess as to what the schema should be.

Now, there are some things to watch out for with ReadXml(). First of all, it will, by default, add any data it finds into the DataSet. If you load the Region table from the database and then ReadXml() a file with the regions in, you'll end up with duplicate data in your DataSet. Similarly, if you call ReadXml() and use XmlReadMode.InferSchema(), then the schema of your DataSet will be extended with whatever schema is found in the XML data being loaded.

The only exception is if **XmlReadMode.Diffgram** is used. Providing the data being read is in Diffgram format (i.e., it was written out from a DataSet as a Diffgram), the data will be merged into your DataSet. If you need to merge any other kind of XML data with existing data in a DataSet, the only way to do this is to create two DataSets and then call DataSet.Merge().

Synchronized DataSets

The final area you need to look at is the synchronized DataSet. Figuring out a use for these wondrous things is probably the trickiest aspect of them. However, when you do find you need one, you'll marvel at the power of ADO.NET once again.

A *synchronized DataSet* is quite simply the combination of an XmlDataDocument object and a DataSet, where both are talking to the same data. This provides you with the means to use ADO.NET to work with an XML document as if it were relational data. Similarly, it opens up all sorts of possibilities for working with relational data just as if it were an XML document (using XSLT, for example, to dynamically build a Web page based on a DataSet, extracting items from the DataSet using XQuery or XPath, and so on).

Using these things is quite simple. You have a DataSet with schema (you must have schema applied to accurately map between relational and hierarchical data), and then you "link" it with an XmlDataDocument. If your DataSet also has data in it when you do this, the XmlDataDocument will be able to work with that data. Similarly, if you have a schema-only DataSet (an empty data with just schema, which was demonstrated in the previous example), but an XmlDataDocument with data in it, you'll be able to access that data through the DataSet.

The schema part scares some people off—it shouldn't. A typed DataSet before it's filled with data is a DataSet with schema, and you've already seen how easy they are to create.

To create an XmlDataDocument synchronized with a DataSet, just pass the DataSet to the XmlDataDocument constructor. For example:

```
Dim myXmlDocument as New XmlDataDocument( myDataSet )
```

Alternatively, to get at the data inside an XmlDocument as a DataSet, just grab the XmlDataDocument's DataSet property.

```
Dim myDataset As DataSet = myXmlDocument.DataSet
```

XmlDataDocument descends from the XmlDocument object you examined in the last chapter and so works in much the same way. Take a look at the online help for more information.

Summary

So, there you have it. Your journey through ADO.NET is complete. There are areas that you've touched on only in minor detail, but if you read the book cover to cover you should now have a thorough grasp of every concept ADO.NET embodies and a great foundation to start exploring on your own. Microsoft seems to extend ADO.NET daily with other external technologies (SQLXML), additional providers, and additional support for integration with other members of the .NET family. With the knowledge you now have, these technologies lie within your grasp.

In this chapter, you explored the marriage between ADO.NET and XML. In particular, you focused on

- Typed DataSets and how to create them in any tier

- How to write XML data and schemas

- How to read XML data and schemas

- How to synchronize a DataSet with an XmlDocument

Good luck in your database travels.

Index

Symbols

">" button, adding columns to your Web Form with, 228–229

@ symbol, using to specify where a parameter lives, 64–65

@Description parameter, of InsertCommand property, 133

@ID parameter, of InsertCommand property, 133

+ (plus) operator, joining strings together with, 86

< and > (angle brackets), as part of XML tags, 293

<? and ?>, function of tags that begin and end with, 295

<%# %> tags, indicating code in templates with, 253

A

AcceptChanges() method

changing a rows status with, 98

deleting rows from tables with, 94–95

making sure only valid records are passed in by, 213–214

provided by the DataRow class, 95–103

AcceptRejectRule property, for DataSet constraints, 128–129

ACID properties

Consistency goal of, 262

Isolation in transactions, 262–263

Action property

of DataRowChangedEventArgs object, 108

for the RowChanging event, 210

values it can take, 108

ActiveX Data Objects 2.7 Library reference, selecting in Add Reference dialog box, 287

Add() method

adding parameters to the Parameters collection with, 62

calling to pass an array of objects into a table, 87

Add New Item dialog box, building a new typed DataSet from, 314–315

Add Reference dialog box

finding COM servers installed on your system in, 287

opening, 286

ADO

vs. ADO.NET, 2–3

mixing in with ADO.NET, 288–289

ADO code, using with ADO.NET, 286

ADO data provider vs. OLE DB data provider, 282–283

ADOInDotNet console application

creating and using, 286–288

writing ADO code in, 287–288

ADO.NET

in 5 minutes or less, 3–4

vs. ADO, 2–3

creating a SQLCommand object in, 38–45

the DataSets place in, 78–80

deleting rows from tables in, 94–95

fundamental code, 27–51

getting deeper into with Windows Forms, 187–216

manually adding parameters to the Parameters collection in, 61

F

FieldCount property, using to get number of columns in current row, 72–73

file modes, for working with streams, 307

FileStream, for working with files that allow seeking, 305

Fill() method

    calling to build your DataSet, 49

    calling to populate a DataSet, 119

    using to mix ADO with ADO.NET, 288–289

FirstChild property, implementation of by the XmlNode class, 300

For-Each loop

    iterating records by running over a SqlDataReader, 71–72

    iterating through a bunch of child elements with, 300

ForeignKeyConstraint

    code illustrating it in action, 125–128

    "gotchas" to be aware of, 126–128

ForeignKeyConstraint objects

    in ADO.NET, 121

    using in ADO.NET, 124–125

ForeignKeys console project, code for creating, 125–126

Form_Load event handler

    code for building the DataSet for the Navigation project, 179

    coding for the Windows Forms project, 204

    setting up to display employees from the Northwind database, 208

FrontPage server extensions, adding to your new virtual Web site, 223

functions, adding to your database, 25–26

G

garbage collection system, built into .NET Framework, 35

Generate DataSet dialog box

    opening from the Data menu of the Visual Studio IDE, 157–158

    setting the data set name in, 173–174

Generate Insert, Update and Delete statements option, in the Query Builder page Advanced tab, 154

Get...() methods, using to get data in a row, 74–75

GetChanges console project, for DataSets, 134–135

GetChanges() method, of DataSet class, 133–135

GetChildRows() method, of DataRow object, 115

GetConnection() function, code for, 241

GetDataset() function, code for, 240

GetElementByTagName() method, using to work through tracks in your XML document, 300

GetFolderPath(), getting the path to folder with, 307

GetParentRows() method, of DataRow object, 115

GetSchemaTable() method, function of, 74–75

GetSqlxxx methods, provided by every DataProvider, 45

GetValue method, calling on a DataReader, 45

GetXXX methods, provided by DataReader, 45

grid and data object events, creating a Windows Forms project for, 208–216

grid styles editor, accessing, 166